The Pedagogy of God's Image

THE COLLEGE THEOLOGY SOCIETY

ANNUAL PUBLICATIONS

1981
The Pedagogy of God's Image

Edited by
Robert Masson

ROBERT MASSON

THE PEDAGOGY OF GOD'S IMAGE

ESSAYS ON SYMBOL AND THE RELIGIOUS
IMAGINATION

The Annual Publication of the
College Theology Society
1981

Scholars Press
Chico, California

Published by
Scholars Press

THE PEDAGOGY OF GOD'S IMAGE

ESSAYS ON SYMBOL AND THE RELIGIOUS IMAGINATION

The Annual Publication of the College Theology Society

© 1982
The College Theology Society

Library of Congress Cataloging in Publication Data
Main entry under title:
   The Pedagogy of God's image.

   (The Annual publication of the College Theology
Society, ISSN 0276-2064 ; 1981)
   Includes bibliographical references.
   1. Image of God—Addresses, essays, lectures.
2. Symbolism—Addresses, essays, lectures.
3. Imagination—Religious aspects—Addresses, essays,
lectures. I. Masson, Robert. II. Series.
BL205.P43 1982   291.3'7   82-16812
ISBN 0-89130-598-X

Printed in the United States of America

TABLE OF CONTENTS

INTRODUCTION

THE PEDAGOGY OF GOD'S IMAGE

This modest volume bears a rather ponderous, perhaps even
pretentious, title. It requires some explanation. Although the
essays gathered here are all concerned with symbol and religious
imagination, they do not advance a single theory of symbol or
share a common understanding of the religious imagination. The
authors do not address each other directly. Nor do they address
a common set of questions about the volume's theme. The reader
could, and I expect some will, profitably read these essays selectively and in a different order. But the essays can also be read
as a coherent whole. The purpose of the title, and of this brief
introduction, is to suggest one way of doing so.

I believe we can speak legitimately, though somewhat poetically, about the "pedagogy of God's image," because the images
one uses to think and speak about God play a role analogous to
that of the slave in ancient Greece who led the student from home
to school and back again. The pedagogy of God's image, however,
though analogous, is not quite as easily described. God's image
cannot be enslaved. The idolater may try, but in the process
God's image is distorted and lost. Even when the divine pedagogy
is accorded its proper freedom, God's image remains elusive. We
can never be certain where our projections end and God's reflection begins. Nor is the pedagogy of God's image a simple leading
by the hand. The divine hand is not always so palpably present;
sometimes it seems absent altogether. The leading, when perceived,
often seems more a pushing and shoving, a tugging or even a letting
go. It simply is not clear how the image gets us from here to God
and back again. Indeed, for many of our contemporaries, it is not
clear that we can ever be led from here to God.

This ambiguity was certainly an implicit, if not explicit,
reason motivating the choice of *symbol and the religious imagination* as the theme for the 1981 Convention of the College Theology
Society, and for this, its annual volume. How could a society
devoted to the teaching of theology and religious studies, as well
as scholarly reflection, help but wonder about the pedagogy of
God's image? Consequently, I think it is legitimate for us to
bring this question to each of these essays, even though their
authors may not all have envisioned their problematic in exactly
this way. Furthermore, I think the reader, in light of this

1

question, will find that the volume can be read as a coherent
whole. If we ask, where is God's image to be found?, we will not
hear one answer, nor will we find a single response to the question, how does the image get us from here to God and back? But we
will find responses to both questions, and we will find, I believe,
that these responses are complementary. Those who share the pedagogical concerns of the CTS will also find much here about the
sort of symbols and imagination required for one to lead others
from here to God and back, although, this again, is not the explicit concern of any of the papers.

The order and division of these essays is somewhat arbitrary,
but not entirely without logic. The more theoretical ones in the
first part focus on some aspect or other of the religious imagination itself. Each of the essays in PART II focuses on a specific
symbol or cluster of symbols.

In the first essay, "The Historical Imagination and the New
Hermeneutic," John Hogan demonstrates that Wolfhart Pannenberg's
understanding of critical historical methodology is indebted to
Collingwood's *The Idea of History*. In Hogan's judgment, Pannenberg's retrieval of Collingwood's work, particularly of the notion
of a priori historical imagination, is an invaluable contribution
to Christian theology. Hogan also concludes, however, that
Pannenberg's selective use of Collingwood expects too much from
the historical method and historical imagination. The essay emphasizes and clarifies the role of imagination in the reconstruction of the historical past and in the interpretation of that past
in the present. Although the paper questions Pannenberg's emphasis, Hogan also demonstrates the significance of imagination for
the theologian's task, and by implication, underlines the significance of imagination for any pedagogy that would lead humanity
from its history to God.

Aquin O'Neill's essay, "The Anthropology of Amgibuity and the
Image of God," deals explicitly with the relationship of imagination to the *imagio Dei* in Paul Ricoeur's philosophical anthropology
and in his developing philosophy of imagination. She argues that
Ricoeur's conceptions of the mytho-poetic imagination and ambiguity
provide a clue for understanding the interaction in his anthropology between the image of God and the image of man. Her argument,
if I have understood it correctly, moves beyond the conclusion that
our images of God and humanity are bound together. She contends
that "Revelation, in the final analysis, is addressed to the human
imagination," and she implies, I think, that imagination, as

productive and creative, is itself an image of God, and so an
essential moment within the divine pedagogy.

Walter Ong's essay, "The Psychodynamics of Oral Memory and
Narrative," contends that memory and narrative function quite
differently in oral cultures than in cultures such as our own,
where writing and print so significantly influence the patterns of
our thinking. His illustration of this difference makes it clear
that the paradigms for narrative commonly presupposed in our print
culture are not adequate models for understanding the narratives
of oral cultures or for understanding the narratives of Scripture
where residual orality interacts with literacy. He concludes with
the suggestion that biblical studies should pay closer attention
to the psychodynamics of oral narrative operative in the formation
of the text. It does not seem too great a leap to argue, although
Ong does not do so here, that an understanding of religious imagination and of what I have called the pedagogy of God's image also
requires closer attention to the dynamics of oral thought.

William Shea seeks to clarify the nature of religious experience by examining the three terms designated in his essay's title,
"Feeling, Religious Symbol and Action." Taking his clues primarily from the American Naturalists and indirectly from Lonergan's
cognitional theory, Shea contends that religious experience can be
understood as a process of unification intimately related to the
human subject's cognitive and volitional intention of the transcendent. From this perspective, if I have understood him correctly, religious symbols can be described as images, rooted in human
self-transcendence, which link the subject with what Rahner calls
"Holy Mystery" or what Ernest Hocking calls the "intention of the
whole." If Shea is right, then even the naturalist's account of
religious experience has significance for the theist's understanding of the pedagogy of God's image. At least as appropriated by
Shea, this perspective offers a language for seeing that pedagogy
as a process of unification, grounded in the dynamism of the human
subject beyond self towards God, mediated by symbols and directed
towards concrete action.

In "Religious Imagination and Interreligious Dialogue," Paul
Knitter argues that religious dialogue can no longer be considered
a luxury. He maintains that for both epistemological and political
reasons, "Christian religious imagination, in our present age, not
only can but *must* be expanded and cross-fertilized through dialogue
with other faiths." This expansion of religious imagination, as he
sees it, is not only an *end* of interreligious dialogue, but also an

essential *means* for such dialogue. Although his principal aim is
to underscore the role of imagination in interreligious dialogue,
he also calls attention, I think, to the function which duch dialogue itself ought to play in the pedagogy of God's image.

In the final essay of PART I, "Liberation and Method,"
Roberto Goizueta presents an overview of Enrique Dussel's analec-
tical method. Goizueta's exposition seeks to respond to those who
charge that liberation theology is based on an uncritical assimilation of Marxism and so in the end is more "witness" than genuinely critical reflection. The first part of the essay examines
Dussel's admittedly dense discussion of the dialectical method in
European philosophy. Goizueta's aim, there, is to show that
Dussel's appropriation of the tradition is anything but uncritical.
The second part of the essay presents Dussel's alternative to dialectics, namely, the analectical method. As Goizueta sees it, the
analectical method stresses that the totalizing concepts, which
the dialectical method imposes on reality, must give way to the
symbolic imagination in a historical commitment to listen for, and
serve, the Other. Thus "Dussel's method moves toward symbol and
away from concept as the central hermeneutical cipher." This is
the point where the essay touches on the volume's theme. Goizueta's analysis brings to the surface, at least implicitly, a crucial
question about the appropriateness of any theological method for
adequately attending to the pedagogy of God's image.

In the first essay of PART II, "Self-Transcendence in the
Spiritual Life: Thérèse of Lisieux," Joann and Walter Conn contend
that the authentic Christian, and even human, understanding of
"self-fulfillment" and "self-sacrifice" must be distinguished from
the common and popular understandings of these notions. Their in-
sightful analysis of the concepts of self-transcendence and conversion, and of the example of self-transcendence and conversion
in Thérèse's life, argues on the one hand, that the self is realized only in its active movement beyond itself, ultimately towards
God, and on the other hand, that self-sacrifice is not a denial of
the self's authentic realization, but a discovery of self in the
other, and ultimately in God. Earlier essays emphasized the role
of transcendence and of attention to the other. This essay both
suggests an image of authentic spiritual life which clarifies how
the divine pedagogy concretely leads one from here to God, and
stresses the role of religious conversion in that process.

In "The Significance for Theology of the Doctor of the Church:
Teresa of Avila," Keith Egan uncovers and explores a rich resource

for understanding the pedagogy of God's image as it has been concretely incarnated in the cult and teaching of the Catholic Church.
His careful historical analysis leads him to conclude that the
evolution of the Church's practice of naming doctors of the church
is rooted in the search for authorities, in the biblical doctrine
of the Body of Christ and its charisms, and in the traditions of
lex orandi, *lex credendi*. In naming a person doctor, the Church
designates the individual's writings as classics to be studied and
celebrated. Egan suggests that in designating Teresa, in particular, as a doctor, the Church has broken new ground both for understanding the relationship between the charismatic teaching role
and the hierarchical teaching office, and for reclaiming the mystical classics' significance for theological reflection.

John Borelli's essay, although concerned with a rather specific symbol, "The Tree of Life in Hindu and Christian Theology,"
nevertheless, illustrates the pedagogy of God's image by showing
how that specific symbol, in both traditions, focuses the religious
imagination towards God as the source of life, and as humanity's
true abode. Borelli's thesis is supported by textual analysis of
the Vedanta tradition of Hinduism and of Bonaventure's *The Soul's
Journey into God* and *The Tree of Life*.

In the final essay, "Cosmos and Conscience in the History of
Religious Imagination," Robert Kress focuses on what he contends
are three paradigmatic moments in the history of humanity's understanding of the relationship between itself, the world and God.
He maintains that in the first of these moments, represented by
Oedipus Rex, human life is so significantly controlled by cosmic
fate that the individual's responsibility for his or her own life
is ultimately denied. "Conscience" in that context is not a reflection of human freedom, but an expression of a blind cosmic
order. In the second moment, represented by Sartre and Kerouac,
the human conscience is made the measure of all things, so that
the reality of a cosmos outside the self is denied. The sacramental
paradigm represented by St. Thomas and Dante, however, allows for
the reality of both human conscience and a world not simply reduc-
ible to human will, because, if I have understood Kress' point,
neither conscience nor the cosmos are subsumed in the other.
Rather, the emergence of the human and personal (i.e. conscience)
within the material and impersonal cosmos is seen as the finite
symbol of a reality, namely, God, that transcends and gives meaning
to both. From this perspective, the secret of the divine pedagogy

is not simply anthropology, as Feuerbach asserted, but rather
anthropology as the image, symbol and sacrament of God.

Marquette University   Robert Masson
May 1, 1982

PART I

THE HISTORICAL IMAGINATION AND THE NEW HERMENEUTIC: COLLINGWOOD AND PANNENBERG

John P. Hogan

In a volume focussed on religious imagination and symbol, it seems fitting, in light of the ongoing discussion about the relationship or lack thereof between critical historical method and hermeneutics,[1] that space be allotted to the role of imagination in the reconstruction of the historical past and the interpretation of that past in the present. The principal theoretician for singling out that role is R. G. Collingwood, the British philosopher and historian. Collingwood's achievements in both philosophy and history uniquely equipped him to establish an intelligible relation between hermeneutical consciousness and historical consciousness. Central to that relationship is what Collingwood called the a priori historical imagination. An exposition of the constructive role of imagination in the formation of the past is made even more pertinent to the current theological situation because of, on one hand, the discussion generated by Küng's dependence on the critical historical method for getting to the "real" Christ, and, on the other hand, Tracy's questioning of the importance of the historical Jesus for keeping alive the "dangerous memory" of him as a "disclosive-transformative word and manifestation of Jesus Christ now...."[2]

Collingwood's idea of history involves a hermeneutic in which understanding, interpretation, translation, and even explanation come together. Like the central axioms of contemporary hermeneutical theory, his understanding of historical knowledge is dialectical, centered on imagination and oriented toward the present. Although it does not emphasize the linguisticality of understanding to the extent Gadamer does, such presuppositions or "prejudices" are focal. History is an inquiry into the meaning of past human actions. It is constructed, or better, reconstructed, by interpreting evidence found in the present, and it is undertaken for human self-knowledge. History is hermeneutical in its object which is thought, in its method which is interpretation of evidence, and in its value which is human self-knowledge.

> Historical knowledge is the knowledge of what mind has done in the past, and at the same time it is the re-doing of this, the perpetuation of past acts in the present. Its object is therefore not a mere object, something outside the mind which knows it; it is an activity of

9

thought, which can be known only in so far as the knowing
mind reenacts it and knows itself as so doing. To the
historian, the activities whose history he is studying
are not spectacles to be watched, but experiences to be
lived through in his own mind; they are objective, or
known to him, only because they are also subjective, or
activities of his own.[3]

This quote indicates in a summary fashion the significance of
Collingwood for contemporary hermeneutics. His approach to history links rather than separates critical historical method and
hermeneutics. He admits of no "hard" historical facts isolated
from interpretation. History studies "facts" but only as they are
made known in human action. The meaning of such action is grasped
through the prism of human understanding. What the historian
seeks is the "inside" of an event--thought. Historical method
consists in the reconstruction by re-enactment of past thoughts
which are woven together by interpolation, inference and imaginative reconstruction. Human actions, the externalization of
thoughts, are the processive unfolding of mind. History is the
tracing of that continuous process. The past is significant because it remains integral to the present and "incapsulated" in it.[4]

Many of these ideas have found their way into the hermeneutical musings of contemporary thinkers, including Bultmann, Gadamer,
Lonergan, and Pannenberg.[5] While touching on a number of issues
and thinkers, this article will concentrate on what Collingwood
calls the a priori historical imagination and the use made of that
notion by Wolfhart Pannenberg. His approach to history, revelation
and theology is strongly influenced by the historical imagination
and by Collingwood's overall historical method.

After establishing Collingwood's role for imagination in historical reconstruction, we shall examine Pannenberg's appropriation of some of his insights. Our treatment of Pannenberg's use
of Collingwood will take place in the following three steps:
first, an examination of his use of the historical method and especially the notion of the historical imagination as a pre-
projection of a totality--a universal history; second, a discussion
of his treatment of the Resurrection; and finally, some conclusions
and criticisms.

I. The Historical Imagination

That there is an historical past, somehow still available in
the present, forms an absolute and transhistorical presupposition
for all historical knowing. Collingwood's understanding of history as the re-enactment of past thought incapsulated in the

present gains its dynamism from the constructive capacity of the
historical imagination. The notion of history, as an innate
a priori idea, forms an absolute presupposition for historical
thinking.[6] Such a strong role for imagination is usually reserved
for the formation of the future. Nonetheless, by the a priori
historical imagination, Collingwood is attempting to spell out
that the structure of mind itself, as a product of the past, contains an innate picture of that past or at least the innate capacity to reconstruct that past. The historical imagination represents the very capacity of the mind to construct, and in a sense
necessarily construct, a past for a particular present.

The idea of history is innate. Both self-knowledge and our
experience of the world are historical. When the mind knows something present, its past is implied and can be regained by interpreting the present. However, the criterion for historical truth
is not present evidence but rather the mind's imaginative capacity
for reconstruction, the historical imagination.

> That criterion is the idea of history itself: the idea of
> an imaginary picture of the past. That idea is, in
> Cartesian language, innate; in Kantian language, *a priori*.
> It is not a chance product of psychological causes; it is
> an idea which every man possesses as part of the furniture
> of his mind, and discovers himself to possess in so far
> as he becomes conscious of what it is to have a mind.[7]

Collingwood's theory of historical knowledge is as much, or more,
a philosophy of mind as it is a philosophy of history in the traditional sense. The structures of mind give form to the historian's picture of the past. Historical knowledge should be viewed
as an instance of the whole knowing process.[8]

Historical imagination indicates the mind's imaginative capacity for knowing the past, but it also indicates the "central act"
which the historian performs. It is by means of the imagination
that the historian puts himself back into the past, makes judgments
about alternative responses to a situation and re-enacts the
thoughts of the actor in the past. Memory and authority are not
the makings of history. Rather the historian selects from his
sources, interpolates into them what they leave out, and when
necessary, critiques them.[9]

Collingwood's inaugural lecture as Waynefleet Professor at
Oxford was the occasion for his programmatic essay, *The Historical
Imagination*, which called for an "inquiry into the nature of historical thinking."[10] History as the science of mind here came to
the fore. A clarion call was issued for critical, scientific
history as an imaginative constructive process which interpolates

"between the statements borrowed from our authorities, other
statements implied by them."[11] In this essay the historical past
is made more dependent on imagination and less on "fixed points
supplied from without."[12] Collingwood by no means wishes to do
away with hard data. He does demand however that all data, whether
text or tombstone, be treated as evidence to be interrogated and
imaginatively interpreted.

Both the use of evidence and its place in imaginative reconstruction of the past can be illustrated by taking a look at
Collingwood, the practicing historian. It is precisely a tombstone which provides the example. Goldstein relates that the last
chapter of *Roman Britain* depicts the gradual disappearance of the
Romanization of Britain. The island became Celto-Roman and lost
its Roman culture. In recounting this process, Collingwood states:

> This backwash of Celticism over the romanized regions...
> is traceable by archeological evidence. At Silchester
> a tombstone was found...written in the Irish, as distinct
> from the British, form of Celtic. An Irishman who died
> in Silchester and left friends able to make him an epi-
> taph in his own language must have been a member of an
> Irish colony in the town...the Silchester inscription
> shows a state of things in which parties of Scots are
> settling down peacefully in the lowland zone, and re-
> taining their own language and customs.[13]

This is an illustration of the working of the historical imagination. No texts tell Collingwood of an Irish colony. However, by
searching out all the evidence available about the time and place,
he can get behind the tombstone to its wider implications for
history. According to Goldstein, the whole question and answer
complex which history is involves conjecture. The Irish colony,
although it cannot be logically inferred, is "postulated," on the
evidence of the tombstone. The historical event of an Irish
colony, imaginatively reconstituted, is what best explains the
available evidence. Data and evidence, meticulously interpreted
in the present, play a large role in Collingwood's historical
method. However, rather than raw data being the criterion for the
truth or falsity of a historical event, it is the historical event
which, imaginatively reconstituted, explains the data.[14]

With both the facts of history and the narrative thrown back
on the constructive powers of the historian, Collingwood raises
the question of the criterion for historical truth. The justification of sources used, archeological ruin or text, no matter how
well accepted by authorities, is always open to question. The instrument for criticism is the a priori historical imagination.

The discipline of history is a continuous dialogue where the picture of the past is confirmed by present evidence and present
evidence is confirmed by the picture of the past. Any piece of
evidence must be critically appropriated as fitting in with a
picture which makes sense. That picture is neither a fanciful nor
intuitive grasp of the past. It is, however, an imaginary picture.
The historical past is the coherent, continuous, and holistic picture which is necessarily projected when the imagination is brought
face to face with historical evidence.[15]

Before turning to Pannenberg, it may be of some value to look
briefly at the use of this theory by other hermeneutical thinkers.
With the a priori imagination, Collingwood further exposes the
structure of understanding as historical. The a priori historical
imagination is the motor that drives the historically effective
consciousness. Imagination is that capacity within us to sense
the possibilities and alternatives present in the givenness of the
past, the immediacy of the present, and the openness of the future.
It involves intellect and will, as well as feeling and appetite.
The imagination, operating historically, is a further specification
of imagination, i.e. imagination with the capacity to flesh out
the givenness of the past. It is our capacity to project, one
might even say, to construct necessarily or automatically a context out of a text or an artifact which confronts us as a question.
That imaginative reconstruction is not done however in a mechanical fashion according to "rules" of interpretation; rather, it is
built up while interpreting the text or evidence and any allied
data.

What is important for theological hermeneutics is how the
past is integrated into the present. For Collingwood, of course,
the re-enactment theory is the key. However, re-enactment is
fundamentally possibly only because of the a priori capacity to
know the past and grasp it as coherent and continuous with our
present understanding and future hopes. Imaginative participation,
the excitement caused by evidence, an aliveness of the understanding subject, all are ingredients in the contemporary theological
hermeneutics discussion. That discussion is grounded in experience
and imagination as the gateway to understanding. Echoing Collingwood's position that the condition for the past being known is that
events "vibrate in the historian's mind," Bultmann remarks,

> ...genuine historical knowledge demands a very personal
> aliveness of the understanding subject, the very rich
> unfolding of his individuality. Only the historian who
> is excited by his participation in history (and that

means - who is open for the historical phenomena through
his sense of responsibility for the future), only he will
be able to understand history. In this sense the most
subjective interpretation of history is at the same time
the most objective. Only the historian who is excited
by his own historical existence will be able to hear the
claim of history.[16]

Perhaps the most concrete endorsement of the historical
imagination in theological hermeneutics may be found in Lonergan.
In his effort to relate historical reconstruction and historical
understanding to hermeneutics, he employs Collingwood's ideas
about the historical imagination. The past for Lonergan is not
known when a "string of credible testimonies" has been re-edited.
The historical past is truly understood only when the present
thinker is able to grasp imaginatively "what was going forward,"
which most likely was unknown or only vaguely known to past historical agents.[17] Grasping "what was going forward" is the result
of the historian's efforts at selection, criticism and construction. For the analysis of these tasks, Lonergan is clearly in
Collingwood's debt. He refers to the essays on imagination and
evidence as "brilliant and convincing."[18]

However, for the most thorough application of Collingwood's
historical methodology and the historical imagination, we now turn
to Pannenberg.

II. Pannenberg: History and Imagination

While accepting much of Gadamer's hermeneutical theory,
Pannenberg insists much more strongly on the reconstructive task
of the historical consciousness. History and hermeneutics, reconstruction or, as Pannenberg often calls it, "reproduction," and
understanding cannot be isolated from one another.[19]

In developing his own position, which involves a fullblown
theology of history, Pannenberg makes ample use of modern scientific historiography. Both his theology of history and scientific
historical method are woven together into a universal history made
possible by belief in God the creator who mediates all understanding of reality through the historical process. Revelation takes
place in the historical acts of God and is only understood at the
end of "revealing history." We are, however, afforded a glimpse
of that end in the fate of Jesus, since his fate is the anticipation of all that is human.[20]

A number of points here link Pannenberg with Collingwood. In
spite of Collingwood's criticism of medieval historiography[21] with

its heavy and direct reliance on God and providence, his understanding of God as an absolute presupposition for history, freedom
and the future[22] appears to be compatible with Pannenberg's understanding of God as the totality of all history. Also, as we shall
see below, Pannenberg uses Collingwood's doctrine of the historical imagination for his projection of the totality: a universal
history. Although Collingwood does not use the term often and
would not allow such a grandiose vision of history as a whole,
universal history is for him the "historian's conception of history as such."[23] This conception projects a grasp of history
which intertwines fact and interpretation, and shows the inter-
relationship of past, present and future. Collingwood's constant
plea that history be rewritten by every generation, as well as the
element of progress in the historical process itself, necessarily
include a future dimension. Re-enactment of past thought and the
incapsulation theory find close parallels in Pannenberg's history
as the transmission of traditions, which is "a hermeneutical process involving the ceaseless revision of the transmitted tradition
in the light of new experiences and new expectations of the
future."[24]

　　After these rather general comments, it is time to move on to
those elements of Pannenberg's theology of history which bear the
mark of the direct influence of Collingwood. Our contention here
is that Pannenberg's understanding of critical historical methodology is heavily indebted to Collingwood's *The Idea of History*.
While the ideas of the two men touch at many points, we will concentrate on two central issues: first, the image of totality in
universal history based on the historical imagination, and second,
the use of critical historical methodology in New Testament study.
Both issues are highlighted in Pannenberg's treatment of the
Resurrection.

　　Pannenberg contributes an important insight to the discussion
of historicity and the scriptures. Drawing on Collingwood's criticism of nineteenth century historiography as a collection of
isolated facts separated from interpretation, he maintains that
before the New Testament can be demythologized, it must be "de-
positivized."[25] Revelation cannot depend on some authority "which
suppresses critical questioning and individual judgement." Rather,
for Pannenberg, certain assumptions must first be put forth to establish the holistic nature of history. He bases these assumptions
on the biblical view of history.

> The universal-historical theme of modern philosophy of
> history was inherited from Jewish Apocalyptic and Chris-
> tian theology of history. The difficulty of speaking of
> a goal of history as a whole makes it questionable
> whether universal history can be understood as a unity
> without the biblical ideas of God.[26]

The Bible provides the opportunity to understand history as a
whole, with its beginning, middle and end. In this sense biblical
theology is a hermeneutic of all of human life. This is a key
notion for Pannenberg. For this reason the historical roots of
the universality of theology must be retrieved.

In discussing Israel's role in the origins of history,
Pannenberg relies on Collingwood, with whom he has some disagreement. He states: "According to Collingwood, it was not Israel but
the Greek Herodotus who discovered history."[27] But according to
Pannenberg, Collingwood here means by history the "methodical determination of past events--not *Geschichte* but precisely *Historie*."
The complaint here is that Herodotus, with the Greek substantialist
approach to history, was concerned with constructing monuments to
the bygone past, but was not concerned with historical change as
such, and therefore did not really contribute to a new understanding of reality. It was Israel rather which "finally drew the
whole of creation into history."[28] Collingwood's own position in
The Idea of History, in spite of some confusion, is in agreement.
The Greeks were responsible for history as a form of research, yet
history as universal and apocalyptic is most certainly the product
of the Judeo-Christian tradition, especially the doctrine of
creation.[29]

It is this image of history as a totality based on God the
creator which Pannenberg places into a wider historical methodology
by drawing on Collingwood's doctrine of the historical imagination.
He begins his historical hermeneutic of the Bible with an imaginative projection supported by Collingwood's teaching about absolute
presuppositions and the use of evidence. The evidence, under examination, may alter or even eliminate the projection. "The point
of departure for historical work is constituted by a spontaneous
pre-projection of nexuses of meaning which then are tested against
observation of all the available individual details, and confirmed
or modified in accord with each of these."[30] Not only is a notion
of universal history necessary for understanding historical events,
but also the historian's imaginative projected picture influences
his interpretation and judgment of historical events.

Pannenberg's pre-projection of a "totality" is neither funda-
mentalistic nor naive. He does not claim that the Bible contains

no mythology or that the historian can somehow bring back the past
as it actually was. The starting point for historical research is
the historical imagination's conception of a unity, a unity which
allows for contingency, yet, at least in retrospect, provides for
continuity. Research into historical particulars presupposes an
outline of history as a totality. Pannenberg cites Collingwood's
analogy for history as criminal investigation. Details provide
the detective with information for or against his conjecture of
the crime. Likewise, "documents accessible to the modern historian are indicators for or against the historian's spontaneously
projected model of the event."[31]

   The importance of the historical imagination's ability to
grasp the universal-historical horizon cannot be overestimated in
Pannenberg's theology. The historical imagination is the answer
to what he refers to as the central question for the debate between history and theology: "how is the conception of a unity of
history possible?"[32] The imaginative projection provides the means
of bringing together fact and interpretation, as well as the framework for the "cognitive value of the historical projection," a
point which Pannenberg thinks Collingwood overlooked. Familiarity
with a wider segment of Collingwood's writings on incapsulation,
rethinking and evidence would have indicated that this point was
indeed of great importance for Collingwood. On the other hand,
Pannenberg's emphasis on the poetic value of his projection indicates a deviation from Collingwood and from the scientific historical method. Pannenberg's emphasis is clear.

> To be sure, the historian with his own historical location
> belongs together with the effects of the event he is in-
> vestigating. But despite this "subjective conditioning"
> of his viewpoint he cannot change his picture of the
> course of history in any way he pleases without thereby
> surrendering the cognitive value of historical projection.
> If the historian does not want to lose sight of his own
> involvement in the event he describes, but on the other
> hand also does not want to surrender the cognitive claim
> of his historical projection, then he can only interpret
> this projection as a spontaneous reproduction of a pre-
> viously given unity of history, which, to be sure, only
> becomes conscious of itself in this reproductive act.[33]

The above clearly entails much more "poetically" than Collingwood
intended for the picture produced by the historical imagination.
Pannenberg's projection is too controlling. For Collingwood, the
historical imagination was more flexible, and not simply a projection of universal hypotheses to be corroborated by evidence.

   Following up on the idea of history as imaginative reconstruction, Pannenberg applies Collingwood's method. He avoids the traps

of applying the approach in its extremes, as on the one hand, the
collection of evidence and on the other, a form of intuition.
Thinking oneself, with one's own horizon, into the horizon of a
past context is a process which is the result of carefully collecting and interpreting evidence and thinking through the events
(processes) which they presuppose. Collingwood, according to
Pannenberg,

> avoids the problematical assumption that intuition is an
> independent source of historical knowledge alongside his-
> torical observation of the particulars. By referring the
> imagination to verification by detailed investigation, he
> avoids the danger of a dualism between the two, such as
> is expressed in theology in the dualism between the
> revelatory-historical and historical-critical formulations
> of the question.[34]

Collingwood's approach to history turns out to be exactly the
methodological tool Pannenberg needs to shore up the foundation
for his historicizing exegesis. The approach allows for both contingency and individuality, and yet does not deny continuity. Such
fundamental characteristics of the historical are focal for grasping the meaning of biblical events. The understanding of reality
as contingent yet continuous only gains clarity in the events of
Jesus' life, which disclose an understanding of the world as an
historical-redemptive process.

Pannenberg's view of this process is obviously different from
the usual understanding of redemption-history thinking in that, in
principle at least, his approach calls for historical verification.
However, such verification by no means implies verification in any
positivistic sense of apodicticity. He rather employs Collingwood's understanding of history as the imaginative reconstruction
of the past event inductively built up from evidence and testimony
found in the present. Verification here is the ongoing mutual
confirmation process carried out by the interaction between the
picture produced by the historical imagination and the available
evidence. Pannenberg, like Collingwood, is concerned with historical detail and inference. The event and its meaning is a projected construction, in principle at least, always open to further
findings.

It may be mentioned here that, although this qualifier is always included by Pannenberg, an obvious difficulty is that the
projected image is too controlling and at times appears impervious
to evidence. Concerning historical verification and revelatory
history, Pannenberg makes it clear that he is not claiming that
redemptive-historical thinking could be read directly from

historical evidence. Indeed using Collingwood's approach, such a
reading could not be gleaned from any historical projection. A
theological understanding of history could never meet a strictly
positivistic requirement that the continuity between faith and
history be derived from the simple observation of particulars. If
such a conception were the only available approach to history,
Pannenberg states, theology would be forced to retreat to a "supra
or primal history." He hastens to add, however, that

> this situation has been fundamentally changed by Colling-
> wood's proof that this positivistic demand is inappropri-
> ate to the historical object as such. A verification
> through subsequent testing by observation of the particu-
> lars may unreservedly be expected of a theological pro-
> jection of history. Its ability to take into account all
> known historical details would be the positive criterion
> of its truth; the proof that without its specific asser-
> tions the accessible information would not be at all or
> would be only incompletely explicable, can be used as a
> negative criterion.[35]

Christian faith, if it is to take the incarnation seriously
and radically, must seek not a proof but "intellectual confirmation" in history. Theology must absorb what is true in the "immanent" understanding of events. "It may not supplant historical
investigation by supernaturalistic hypotheses."[36] Pannenberg
finds that confirmation in Collingwood's method. He writes: "The
theological fruitfulness of Collingwood's historical epistemology
is easy to see."[37]

III. Historical Method and the Resurrection

In obvious contrast to Bultmann, Pannenberg applies Collingwood's historical methodology to the resurrection. He places
enormous weight on the historicity of the resurrection, and, at
least in his earlier writings, makes it determinative of his whole
theology.[38] Rather than faith being the basis of the resurrection,
resurrection understood as an historical event is the basis for
faith. This, according to Pannenberg, is Paul's position in
1 Corinthians 15. He does not hesitate to use the word "proof."
"The proof Paul gave us was for his time a historical proof, a
firsthand proof beyond doubt."[39] Of course, such a proof cannot
be tested in the present, but secondhand proofs can be validated
by means of the critical historical method.

Pannenberg's approach begins with the assumption that resurrection cannot be ruled out beforehand. Again a controlling factor
seems operative here. The possibility of resurrection is a by-
product of Pannenberg's anthropology. Humans cannot understand

themselves without a conception of resurrection. "That man has to
seek for his final destination beyond death is based on the specifically human structure of existence, on the so-called openness
to the world."[40] However, if the contingencies of history are
overruled by theories of historical explanation which render certain occurrences impossible, then understanding the resurrection
as historical is impossible. He opposes historians "who begin
dogmatically with a concept of reality according to which 'dead
men do not rise.'"[41] Pannenberg is not speaking of a resuscitated
body or just a "random miracle." He readily admits that the expression "resurrection" has a "metaphysical character." He relates it to the daily experience of rising from sleep.[42] What is
essential for an historical investigation of the narratives is the
projected image, the possibility of resurrection. The historical
investigation begins with a detailed and careful examination of
the traditions of the appearances and the empty tomb.[43]

Along with the detailed interpretation of the texts, the
historian-theologian must also think himself into the apocalyptic
context of the time. St. Paul's understanding of the resurrection
as a radical transformation was not simply the product of impres-
sions made on him by his experiencing of Jesus as risen. "Even
the understanding of the qualitative differences between the resurrection life as imperishable and the present life as perishable
has Jewish parallels.[44] In short, rather than unexpected, the
resurrection was expected and longed for.[45] Thinking back into
that context and examining the texts disallow the existential interpretation that the resurrection stories are merely the faith
products of the Christian community. Historical research forces
us to acknowledge an historical event which the historian may
validly, if metaphorically, reconstruct as resurrection. The resurrection is an historical event in the sense that it best explains the available evidence concerning the origins of Christianity.

> If the emergence of primitive Christianity, which apart
> from other traditions, is also traced back by Paul to
> appearances of the resurrected Jesus, can be understood
> in spite of all critical examination of the tradition
> only if one examines it in the light of the eschatologi-
> cal hope for a resurrection from the dead, then that
> which is so designated is a historical event, even if
> we do not know anything more particular about it.[46]

Although Pannenberg does not mention Collingwood directly in
connection with his treatment of the resurrection accounts, the
resurrection is for him the *locus classicus* for applying the

outside-inside theory of history. As Galloway indicates, "The
inside of an event or fact is the meaning it has within its total
context for those whose experience it touches."[47] He proceeds to
point out that for Pannenberg, as for Collingwood, meaning must be
for somebody and can be extracted from events because it does not
inhere as some ghostly existence but precisely as interpretation,
motives or thoughts. The "outside" of the event or fact lives on
in texts and evidence. The "inside" continues on as part of a
living tradition.

> The natural events that are involved in the history of a
> people have no meaning apart from the connection with the
> traditions and expectations in which men live. The events
> of history speak their own language, the language of
> facts; however, this language is understandable only in
> the context of the traditions and expectations in which
> the given events occur.[48]

Pannenberg's refusal, even in such a controversial instance as the
resurrection of Jesus to separate fact from interpretation, is
symbolic of his view of historicity. He weaves a pattern of hap-
pening out of the evidence and, based on his version of the whole,
unearths the meaning inherent in the event. Meaning is given in
the nexus of events. The historian-theologian gets to that meaning by imaginatively thinking back into that nexus and "reproduc-
ing" it. Of course, as we have seen, the specific meaning of the
resurrection is not totally alien according to Pannenberg, because
of his view of man and because it has been kept alive in the tradition flowing from the Jewish scriptures.

By a careful reading of the appearance narratives and the
stories of the empty tomb, bolstered by an anthropology which
hopes for and, practically speaking, demands life beyond the
grave, and an apocalyptic background for such a hope, Pannenberg
posits an historical resurrection which best explains the available evidence. Even from this brief sketch, it is apparent that
Pannenberg has almost equated his own "history of transmission of
tradition," complete with its eschatological emphasis, with critical historical method. The resurrection is an historical reality
because it fulfills the prerequisites for sound historical method.
First, it is a "reproduced" event which provides the "best explanation" for the available evidence. Second, it is part of a passed-
on living tradition, stretching backward to Jewish apocalyptic
hope and forward to modern man's "openness to the world." Third,
it is guaranteed by a philosophical analysis of human existence
which relates resurrection to present experience. And fourth, it
is given a covering metaphorical expression understandable to both

past and present. The resurrection of Jesus as the "prolepsis" of
human destiny which has occurred within history functions like a
key to history. The same method may be applied to all historical
events.[49]

Pannenberg has done an invaluable service for Christian theology in forcing it to reexamine its historical roots and pay attention to the obvious, the linkage between Christian faith and
history. However, it seems fairly apparent that his emphasis on
objectification is overstated. This is indicated by developments
in his more recent writings. His use of the historical method has
evoked much criticism. He has been accused of justification by
historical method, substituting history for the Holy Spirit, and
quite simply of maintaining too high a trust level in his acceptance of modern historical method. Since Pannenberg has already
responded to many of these criticisms, they will not be taken up
here.[50]

A brief comment may be inserted about Pannenberg's argument
for the historicity of the resurrection. Herbert Burhenn has
convincingly argued that, while Pannenberg's treatment of the appearance narratives and the empty tomb is not without historical
cogency, his defense of the historicity of the resurrection clearly goes beyond historical method. First, Burhenn questions whether
the evidence does point to an historical event of resurrection or
whether the historian is not compelled to admit an insufficiency
of evidence. In the background of Pannenberg's approach is the
position that the historian is almost compelled to account for the
origins of Christianity. While this remains an important and
necessarily somewhat open question for the historian, Burhenn
maintains that, based only on historical method, Pannenberg must
admit that another account beside an historical resurrection might
be a better explanation of the evidence. Secondly, he points out,
as should be apparent from the above discussion, that Pannenberg's
argument is more philosophical and theological than it is historical. Although his arguments are real historical arguments, and
this is Pannenberg's contribution, his conclusions "are no longer
simply historical."[51] The outcome of his argument is pre-
controlled by his view of divine action in history. In spite of
his disclaimers, he ends up resorting to some form of meta-
history.

Some Conclusions and Criticisms

At this point some concluding remarks are in order concerning Pannenberg's use of Collingwood. On the positive side, it can be said that, more than any other theologian, Pannenberg has exploited the methodological side of Collingwood's philosophy of history. Three factors stand out. First, he has clearly understood the implications of Collingwood's critique of historical positivism.[52] This allows him to integrate fact and interpretation, which amounts to realizing the subjective element in historical reconstruction without severing ties to the historical event. Second, and most importantly for our discussion, he has creatively appropriated Collingwood's notion of historical imagination as a pre-projection around which history is constructed. Third, he accepts the notion and its implications that the text is a piece of evidence which, when interrogated and interpreted, allows and even calls for the reconstruction of an event. In theory, at least, he claims to be willing to let the evidence lead where it will.[53]

On the negative side, points two and three above clearly indicate the misunderstandings in Pannenberg's application of Collingwood. While sensing the profound importance of the imagination for the reconstruction of a past continuous with the present, Pannenberg has trespassed the legitimate parameters even in the most creative interpretation of Collingwood's doctrine. Historical imagination explains history in its quality as an innate and a priori capacity of the mind and calls for interpolation. The projected picture and interpolations are always closely tied to evidence. The imaginative picture points to the possibility of history as such, not to a particular understanding of history as a whole, as Pannenberg conceives it. Collingwood's doctrine cannot be legitimately stretched to support the view that the historian has the ability to lay hold of a universal historical horizon. Although Collingwood places great importance on God as an absolute presupposition for history, he does not accept a notion of universal history understood as a vision of history as a whole. As a matter of fact, he would consider such a position an outlandish departure from scientific historical method. This would seem to be behind his criticisms of such sweeping views of history as Augustine's, Spengler's and Toynbee's.

In sum, it can be argued that Pannenberg stretches historical imagination beyond recognition and justifies far more than Collingwood allows. Concerning evidence, Pannenberg sets out to use it in

a scientific manner and, to a great extent, achieves his intent.
However, although he qualifies the history that rests on that
evidence as a provisional reproduction, his approach appears to be
overly guided by a pre-projected image and controlled by philosophical and theological assumptions. Certainly Pannenberg seeks to
take seriously the notion of text as evidence for event, yet, his
conclusions, couched perhaps in too objectifying terms, appear to
end up as spontaneous reproductions based on a faith position.
This is perhaps as it should be. Pannenberg himself would claim
that the historical method necessarily includes more than history,[54]
a contention for which he might also call on Collingwood for support. However, by allowing the projection to exercise such control,
he fails to see the importance of his own philosophical and faith
assumptions. The resurrection might well be the key to history,
but it is not clear from the historical method alone that it should
also be called an historical event.

Contrary to Bultmann, who earlier read Collingwood in support
of his own existential approach to history and paid little attention to his historical method,[55] Pannenberg employs Collingwood
methodologically without fully understanding his notion of history
as such, namely, human actions done in the past and understood in
the present by reconstructing thoughts, motives and purposes. In
Pannenberg's view of revelation and theology as history, history
is *theonomous*, rather than *autonomous*, which is the way Collingwood understood it.

Despite its strengths, Pannenberg's methodological use of
Collingwood is weakened by its excessive reliance on a "critical"
model of history. Although at various points he comes close to
the model Collingwood refers to as "scientific," Pannenberg never
fully moves into it. His use of it is also made somewhat ambiguous, because he comes dangerously close to grasping the method as
an attempt at historical explanation.[56] In contrast, as we have
seen, the primary concern of the imaginative reconstruction by rethinking is not explanation but understanding and interpreting.

In conclusion, Pannenberg makes selective use of Collingwood,
and ends up expecting too much from the historical method and historical imagination. It is obvious that his contribution is striking and somewhat unique in that he has shown the intertwining of
understanding and reconstruction in grasping the meaning of biblical history. It must also be said that he has to a great extent
applied the historical method correctly. However, it is only in
his later writings that he seems to realize the importance of his

own "tacit assumptions" which control the outcome of his
theological-historical endeavors. In *Theology and the Philosophy
of Science*, he does not reject his earlier stance, but he edges
away from an excessive dependence on an overly objective view of
history and historical method. There resurrection as history does
not play a role. Historical method is placed within a much wider
context of scientific method as articulated by Karl Popper. This
later book, worked out in dialogue with Popper, Dilthey and Gadamer,
does a great deal to explain much of what is left unsaid in the
earlier Pannenberg.[57] His working out of the relationship between
history and hermeneutic in his theological method is still
unfolding.

While the theological use of Collingwood has been fairly wide,
it has not always been deep. Theologians have selectively chosen
those aspects of his thought which support their own theological
positions. For the most part, they have failed to grasp the distinction as well as the interrelation between what may be called
the objective aspect of historical understanding (the method and
its subject) and the subjective aspect (the theoretical a priori
of history itself). Pannenberg, with his use of the historical
imagination as the means for reconstructing the event, has made
the most serious theological attempt to employ Collingwood methodologically. However, he fails to take full account of history as
past human actions. Just as Bultmann read the Oxford idealist
"subjectively" to free the New Testament from the demands of history, so Pannenberg read him "objectively" as a means of radically
historizing biblical events. In doing this, however, he seems to
objectify New Testament history to a point beyond the reach of
historical method.

Relating the "subjective," "present" and hermeneutical with
the "objective," "past" and historical is emerging as a focal task
for Christian theologians. Increasingly, imagination appears essential to that task.[58] Precisely because Collingwood conceived
of historical reconstruction of the past as a present, imaginative
and interpretive endeavor, Pannenberg's reading of him is fruitful
for New Testament hermeneutics. However, a more complete and
balanced reading could prove even more fruitful in overcoming the
sharp dichotomies that have grown up in biblical theology between
past and present, text and context, and the normative and the interpretive. In Collingwood's description of the historical imagination, historical consciousness and hermeneutical consciousness
overlap.

NOTES

[1]For an excellent overview see Anthony C. Thiselton, *The Two Horizons: New Testament Hermeneutics and Philosophical Description* (Grand Rapids: Eerdmans, 1980). For an excellent analysis of this study which raises pertinent issues for our discussion, see the review of Louis Brodie in *Thomist* 45 (1981) 480-86.

[2]David Tracy, *The Analogical Imagination: Christian Theology and the Culture of Pluralism* (New York: Crossroads, 1981) 334 n. 15. For an evaluation of Küng, see Peter Chirico, "Hans Küng's Christology: An Evaluation of its Presuppositions," *Theological Studies* 40 (1979) 256-72.

[3]R. G. Collingwood, *The Idea of History* (ed. T. M. Knox; Oxford: Clarendon, 1946) 218 (hereafter *IH*).

[4]Introductions to Collingwood's theory of history are provided by Errol E. Harris, "Collingwood's Theory of History," *Philosophical Quarterly* 6 (1957) 35-49, and G. Bachdahl, "Logic and History: An Assessment of R. G. Collingwood's Idea of History," *Australasian Journal of Philosophy* 26 (1948) 94-113.

[5]See John P. Hogan, "The Contribution of R. G. Collingwood to the Development of Hermeneutics" (Ph.D. dissertation, Catholic University of America, 1979).

[6]*IH*, 227.

[7]*IH*, 248. See also Lionel Rubinoff, *Collingwood and the Reform of Metaphysics: A Study in the Philosophy of Mind* (Toronto: University of Toronto, 1970) 287.

[8]Bernard J.F. Lonergan, *Method in Theology* (New York: Herder and Herder, 1972) 175, says the same and cites Collingwood for support.

[9]*IH*, 235. See also Joseph B. Tyson, *A Study of Early Christianity* (New York: Macmillan, 1973) 8-13.

[10]*IH*, 240.

[11]Ibid.

[12]Ibid., 245.

[13]Quoted in Leon J. Goldstein, "Collingwood on the Constitution of the Historical Past," p. 262 in *Critical Essays on the Philosophy of R. G. Collingwood* (ed. Michael Krausz; Oxford: Clarendon, 1972). See R. G. Collingwood, *Roman Britain* (Oxford: Clarendon, 1934) 282. In this quote "Scots" indicates inhabitants of Ireland.

[14]Goldstein, "Constitution of Historical Past," 264-65.

[15]*IH*, 245.

[16]Rudolf Bultmann, *History and Eschatology: The Presence of Eternity* (New York: Harper Torchbooks, 1957) 122.

[17]Lonergan, *Method in Theology*, 186.

[18]Ibid., 188 n. 9. For a summary of Lonergan's position on historical evidence and reconstruction, see pp. 205-6. His position is very dependent on Collingwood.

[19]Wolfhart Pannenberg, *Basic Questions in Theology* I (trans. George H. Kehm; Philadelphia: Fortress, 1970) 123-28, and Pannenberg, *Theology and the Philosophy of Science* (Philadelphia: Westminster, 1976) 169. See also Geoffrey Turner, "Wolfhart Pannenberg and the Hermeneutical Problem," *Irish Theological Quarterly* 39 (1972) 117.

[20]For a summary of Pannenberg's views on revelation, see his "Dogmatic Theses on the Doctrine of Revelation" in *Revelation as History* (ed. Wolfhart Pannenberg, Rolf Rendtorff, Trutz Rendtorff and Ulrich Wilkens; trans. David Granskow; London: Macmillan, 1968) 125-28.

[21]*IH*, 54.

[22]See R. G. Collingwood, *Essay on Metaphysics* (Oxford: Clarendon, 1940) 185-90, 290-95; *IH*, 315-20.

[23]*IH*, 104.

[24]Pannenberg, "Foreword" to *Basic Questions* I, xviii. He points out that the "history of the transmission of tradition" alters his earlier position of history as "event suspended between promise and fulfillment." See also E. Frank Tupper, *The Theology of Wolfhart Pannenberg* (Philadelphia: Westminster, 1973) 102-7. Here Tupper presents a summary of the "history of the transmission of traditions." Although Collingwood would have difficulties with Pannenberg's universal history, his notion of the rethinking process and incapsulation as presented in R. G. Collingwood (*Autobiography* [London: Oxford University, 1939]) might prove supportive of "transmission of traditions," and the unity of the future as creative of present and past. See Wolfhart Pannenberg, *Theology and the Kingdom of God* (Philadelphia: Westminster, 1969) 61. Unfortunately Pannenberg seems only to be conversant with *IH*.

[25]Wolfhart Pannenberg, "Response to the Discussion," pp. 228-29 in *New Frontiers in Theology*, Vol. 3: *Theology as History* (ed. James M. Robinson and John B. Cobb, Jr.; New York: Harper and Row, 1967); see also Turner, "Pannenberg and Hermeneutical Problem," 114.

[26]Pannenberg, *Basic Questions* I, 12.

[27]Ibid., 21.

[28]Ibid.

[29]*IH*, 49-52. It is Collingwood's position that history as the "historical understanding of reality" arose out of the biblical experience. See W. Taylor Stevenson, *History as Myth: The Import for Theology* (New York: Seabury, 1969) 33.

[30]Pannenberg, *Basic Questions* I, 199; see Tupper, *Theology of Pannenberg*, 97-98.

[31]Pannenberg, *Basic Questions* I, 70.

[32]Ibid., 68.

[33]Ibid., 71-72.

[34]Ibid., 70 n. 138.

[35]Ibid., 78.

[36]Ibid., 79.

[37]Ibid., 72.

[38]The numerous problems and critique of Pannenberg's treatment cannot be adequately covered here. Principal sources are:
Wolfhart Pannenberg, *Jesus-God and Man* (trans. Lewis L. Wilkins
and Duane A. Priebe; Philadelphia: Westminster, 1968) 88-106;
idem, "Did Jesus Really Rise from the Dead," *Dialog* 4 (1965) 128-
35. Helpful commentaries include: Herbert Burhenn, "Pannenberg's
Argument for the Historicity of the Resurrection," *Journal of the
American Academy of Religion* 40 (1972) 368-79; Daniel P. Fuller,
"The Resurrection of Jesus and the Historical Method," *Journal of
Bible and Religion* 34 (1966) 18-24; Ted Peters, "The Use of Analogy in Historical Method," *Catholic Biblical Quarterly* 35 (1973)
475-82; Robert North, "Pannenberg's Historicizing Exegesis," *The
Heythrop Journal* 12 (1971) 377-400; Carl E. Braaten, *New Directions in Theology Today*, Vol. 2: *History and Hermeneutics* (Philadelphia: Westminster, 1966) 91-102. Since our concern in this
study is methodological we will not examine in detail Pannenberg's
exegesis; however, his position will be briefly summarized.

[39]Pannenberg, "Did Jesus Really Rise," 128-31.

[40]Ibid., 131; see also Wolfhart Pannenberg, *What is Man?*
(trans. Duane A. Priebe; Philadelphia: Fortress, 1972).

[41]Pannenberg, *Jesus-God and Man*, 109, and *Theology and Philosophy of Science*, 145-47. Pannenberg appears to be defending
miracles at the expense of the historical method; his position,
however, is more complicated and sensitive to that method. For
example, he claims to accept the principle of historical analogy
but adds his own criticism about its limits. He is critical of
positivist historians' use of analogy and their failure to realize
its limits. He wants to protect the contingency of individual
events and leave room for the new and unexpected. With the intention of making historical space for the resurrection, he replies
to his critics: "My criticism is not directed against the critical
use of the principle of analogy, which is basic to the critical
historical method. This use is merely restricted. The instrument
of analogy gains precision, if judgements about the historicity or
nonhistoricity of events asserted in the tradition are based only
on positive analogies between the tradition which is being studied
and situations known elsewhere, but not on the lack of such analogies." Pannenberg, "Response to the Discussion," 264-65 n. 75.
See also Fuller, "Resurrection of Jesus and Historical Method,"
21-24, and Peters, "Use of Analogy in Historical Method," 475-82.

[42]Pannenberg, *Jesus-God and Man*, 74, and "Did Jesus Really
Rise," 129.

[43]Pannenberg, *Jesus-God and Man*, 105-6. Analyzing Pannenberg's
treatment of the biblical texts would take us far beyond our immediate task. Burhenn ("Historicity of Resurrection," 370) handily
summarizes his historical treatment in two theses: "(1) no coherent
or plausible naturalistic account can be given of the transition
from Jesus' death to the activity and message of the primitive
church; (2) the best explanation of this transition is one which

refers to 'real' appearances (i.e. with extra-subjective basis) of
the resurrected Lord and to a 'really' empty grave."

[44]Pannenberg, *Jesus-God and Man*, 81.

[45]Pannenberg qualifies this, indicating that the hoped-for
resurrection was of a general nature and not necessarily individual. See his "Did Jesus Really Rise?," 130-31.

[46]Pannenberg, *Jesus-God and Man*, 98.

[47]Allan D. Galloway, *Wolfhart Pannenberg* (London: Allen and
Unwin, 1973) 39.

[48]Pannenberg, "Doctrine of Revelation," *Revelation as History*,
152-53. See also Galloway, *Pannenberg*, 39.

[49]Niels Tjalve, "Collingwood og Theologerne: Historie og for-
staelse," *Dansk Theologisk Tidsskrift* 35 (1975) 7. Overall, Tjalve
rejects the interpretation of Collingwood offered by Pannenberg,
Sykes and Van Buren. He believes Bultmann has best understood and
applied Collingwood.

[50]Pannenberg, "Response to Discussion," 221-76.

[51]Burhenn, "Historicity of Resurrection," 378. See also
North, "Historicizing Exegesis," 396-400.

[52]Pannenberg accepts the critique but the question can be
raised as to whether he has moved far enough on the basis of that
critique. His understanding of revelatory history seems to fit
into Collingwood's category of "critical" history. He consistently uses the term "critical-historical method." Collingwood calls
his own approach "scientific history" and considers "critical" history as not too far removed from "scissors and paste" history (*IH*,
258-60 and 274-82). In critical history documents are viewed as
sources containing statements. Such statements may be used to
support historical hypothesis. Scientific history, on the other
hand, contains no ready-made statements. All statements are
treated as evidence which evokes meaning. Pannenberg's position
remains somewhat ambiguous since he uses both approaches. However,
his constant use of the term "critical" may betray something of
his overly objective approach to revelation and history and indicates a subtle dependence on Dilthey, who never really left the
positivist model of history. See *New Catholic Encyclopedia*, A,
1967 ed., s.v. "Dilthey, Wilhelm," by P. L. Hug. Pannenberg's
ambiguity in this and his movement at times closer to Collingwood's
model is indicated in the next note.

[53]Wolfhart Pannenberg, *Faith and Reality* (trans. John Maxwell;
Philadelphia: Westminster, 1977) 71. In this small book, Pannenberg again endorses the historical method and indicates his agreement with Collingwood's analogy of historical research to criminal
investigation. He also indicates an openendedness to history.
"The conclusions of such historical research are never completely
incontestable. They are always more or less probable and can be
changed by new discoveries and new approaches to the problem.
Nevertheless, historically-assured certainty is the greatest certainty we can ever have of past events. If Christian faith presupposes information about events of a distant past, it can gain
the greatest possible certainty about those events only by
historical research."

[54]See Ted Peters, "Truth is History: Gadamer's Hermeneutics and Pannenberg's Apologetic Method," *Journal of Religion* 55 (1975) 52-53 n. 66, where he refers to Burhenn's "Historicity of Resurrection" as "the only convincing critique of Pannenberg's proof...." Burhenn claims that the arguments Pannenberg offers are not specifically historical. Peters adds, "Pannenberg recognizes this fact and claims that the presuppositions of historical-critical method preclude a genuine evaluation of the evidence regarding Jesus' resurrection."

[55]Bultmann, *History and Eschatology*, 123-48.

[56]In this Pannenberg appears to follow a line similar to Alan Richardson, *History Sacred and Profane* (Philadelphia: Westminster, 1964) 197-211. See also Anthon Hanson, "Alan Richardson and his Critics in the Area of Hermeneutics," pp. 39-40 in *Theology and Change: Essays in Memory of Alan Richardson* (ed. Ronald H. Preston; London: SCM, 1975).

[57]See Pannenberg, *Theology and Philosophy of Science*. For an excellent analysis and evaluation of this work, see Edmund J. Dobbin, "Seminar on Foundations: Pannenberg on Theological Method," Catholic Theological Society of America, *Proceedings of the Thirty-Second Annual Convention* 32 (1977) 202-20. "Scientific method as it emerges from Pannenberg's dialogue with Popper then is: the systematic elaboration and critical corroboration of hypotheses in the light of the available evidence. This method, while recognizing the need for presuppositions in all interpretation, presupposes that there are no dogmatic or self-evident truths unassailable in principle by critical examination" (p. 205). History is a critical science in this sense. Dilthey is indicated as Pannenberg's source for "the central idea of his own thought, i.e. Dilthey's contextual definition of meaning. For Dilthey meaning is always a relationship between a whole and its parts. As experienced by human beings, meaning is the very structure of life. Human life is a system of interrelated experiences, open to itself, essentially historical, and forming a whole which at any given moment is not yet given" (p. 207). Dobbin concludes this section of his paper with a dialogue with Gadamer. "In contrast with Gadamer, then, Pannenberg presents the hermeneutical event of interpretation as a methodical event of construction, consciously controlled to a high degree by the interpreter. Pannenberg of course recognizes tacit factors involved in this process" (pp. 210-11). With hindsight afforded by *Theology and the Philosophy of Science*, it can be seen that Pannenberg's use of Collingwood's method is strongly affected by a contextualist definition of meaning and a critical rationalist view of science as the testing of hypothesis against data.

[58]See Sandra M. Schneiders, "Faith, Hermeneutics, and the Literal Sense of Scripture," *Theological Studies* 39 (1978) 719-36, and idem, "The Paschal Imagination: Objectivity and Subjectivity in New Testament Interpretation," *Theological Studies* 43 (1982) 52-68.

THE ANTHROPOLOGY OF AMBIGUITY AND
THE IMAGE OF GOD

Mary Aquin O'Neill, RSM

Paul Ricoeur's contribution to contemporary understanding of
the function of symbols and myths in religious language has made
him a central figure in any discussion of the imagination and its
role in religious thought. So familiar have some of his terms
like "second naivete" become, they appear without comment in the
writings of others and form part of the common vocabulary of those
who deal in the interpretation of mythopoetic texts.

Significant as his contribution has been at the level of
method, there is another dimension of Ricoeur's work that deserves
equal attention. It is the connection between his philosophical
anthropology and the developing philosophy of imagination. As one
way of approaching that connection, I will take a panoramic view
of his work to date in order to trace in this paper (1) the influence of Ricoeur's belief in the myths of innocence and the endtime on what he calls his anthropology of ambiguity; (2) the connection between this notion of ambiguity and Ricoeur's philosophical project; and (3) the resultant interaction in his anthropology
between the image of God and the image of humanity.

I. Imagining Ambiguity

Nothing could be clearer from a close reading of Ricoeur's
many articles and books than his conviction that human existence
is marked by a profound ambiguity. He has applied the term to
human history,[1] to human institutions (the Church and the State
are favorite examples),[2] to the fundamental human quests (possession, power and self-esteem),[3] to law, sexuality, language, even
to death itself.[4] What does Ricoeur mean by this ambiguity that
characterizes all human endeavors, all human experiences, humanity
itself? In the broadest sense, he means that human existence is
open to several interpretations, to multiple and conflicting
readings.[5]

In the first instance, Ricoeur sees in humanity a combination
of greatness and guilt, goodness and evil, being destined for the
good and inclined toward the evil that accounts for an initial and
problematic kind of ambiguity. Because of it, human beings are
always in danger of mistaking the contingent for the essential and

31

the historical experience of conflict and division for the last
word on the human adventure.

Though historical humanity is such that one cannot say of
anything human, "here is the primordial man, there is the evil
result of his contingent history,"[6] there is nevertheless a way
to distinguish between what is essential and what is accidental
with respect to human existence. That way is provided initially
by the myths that depict the "beginning" and the "end" of time.

Innocence

The myths of the beginning constitute pre-philosophical
resources for reflection on the nature of humanity. In Ricoeur's
case, the myth of preference is the Adamic myth in which the portrayal of an innocence "before" and a guilt "after" the fall provides a heuristic for imagining the relationship between good and
evil. The key contribution of this myth to anthropology, Ricoeur
notes, is "the *contingency* of that radical evil which the penitent
is always on the point of calling his evil nature."[7] Thus the
myth protects anthropology from the first and fatal error of identifying human nature with nothingness, human freedom with the
fault. The dimension of the myth that defends the essential goodness of human nature, according to Ricoeur's reading, is the affirmation of the human being as *imago Dei*. He writes:

> ...there we have both our being-created and our innocence;
> for the "goodness" of the creation is no other than its
> status as "creature." All creation is good, and the
> goodness that belongs to man is his being the image of
> God. Seen retrospectively, from the point of view of sin,
> as a "prior" state in mythical language, the likeness
> appears as an absence of guilt, as innocence; but his
> goodness is altogether positive; it is sin that is the
> nothingness of vanity.[8]

The goodness of being-created and the nothingness and vanity of
sin: this is the first meaning of the ambiguity that pervades human existence. Everything human is marked by the superimposed
brands of essential goodness and existential guilt, of destination
for the good and inclination toward the evil. Only the myths of
innocence, however, preserve a conviction of the radical anteri-
ority of the good, making it possible to think of the good creation as more fundamental than the distortions wrought by sin.

Recreation

The myths of the endtime constitute pre-philosophical resources for the effort to reconcile in thought what has been

broken apart by existence. What they offer to philosophy is a
source of hope for an ultimate unity beyond the divisions that
characterize experience, an ultimate triumph of the good creation
over the powers of nothingness and vanity. In this way, the myths
of the endtime promise a restoration of lost integrity, a "new
creation" of a new humanity, a new heaven and a new earth.

If the myths of the beginning provide an anthropological key
through the depiction of lost innocence "behind" us, the myths of
the endtime sustain anthropology by the vision of a recovery that
is "ahead" of us. Between them, says Ricoeur, there is a "sub-
terranean affinity" linking Genesis and Apocalypse--remembrance of
time past with anticipation of time to come. Not, however, that
Genesis begets Apocalypse; quite the reverse is true: "freedom
remembers its integrity to the extent to which it expects a complete deliverance." For this reason he can say, "there is a Genesis only in the light of an Apocalypse."[9]

To understand this is to grasp another meaning of the *imago*
Dei of Genesis: humanity can remember its status as created in the
image and likeness of God to the extent that it can experience and
act out of the hope for deliverance, restoration, recreation. The
image of God in humanity is not something lost with innocence to
be restored at the end of time in the new creation; it is something continually at work in history in "the striking power of
human creativity."[10] This second notion of the *imago Dei*, derived
from the reading which the early Fathers of the Church gave to the
Genesis account, provides Ricoeur with another anthropological
clue of enormous importance in the shift from the phenomenology of
the personal body to the phenomenology of culture: the vision of
historical creation. If the first understanding of the *imago Dei*
protected anthropology from identifying evil and human nature (and
in this sense undergirds the entire project of *Freedom and Nature*),
this later discovery protects anthropology from identifying evil
with history (and so undergirds his defense of culture). The ambiguity that characterizes human nature must be extended to human
history in such a way that the categories of creation and of history are superimposed. In this manner, Ricoeur notes, creation is
imagined not as something closed and finished before human history
began, but as continuing "in the midst of evil" and "by means of
grace."[11] The philosophical equivalent of this "grace" that continues creation is, for Ricoeur, the mythopoetic imagination.

There is a second way in which the eschatological myths, especially the myth of the "last day," function to protect anthropology

by preserving the ambiguity of history. The expectation of a
"last day" keeps history *open*, preventing thought from declaring
ultimate what is still penultimate.[12] As the myths of innocence
guard against declaring division, strife, conflict, greed, tyran-
ny, vanity, venality to be the first word on humanity, the myth of
the "last day" keeps open the possibility that it will not be the
last word either. No one can say with certainty how the drama
that is human existence will turn out. But thanks to the eschatological myths, philosophical anthropology--which must always
admit that the worst is still possible--need not bow to the conviction that the worst is inevitable.

Fault

The tension between an anthropology of ambiguity and an ontology of reconciliation ultimately effects a double-reading of
the fault itself. In the first place, the fault can be judged as
both a loss and a gain; in the second place it can be located as
originating within and without human freedom.

In the rich and dense narration of the fall given in Genesis,
Ricoeur discerns a twofold attitude to the incursion of evil. On
the one hand it is definitely portrayed as a "loss"--of innocence,
of the easy and graceful coexistence with nature and with God,
loss of harmony and unity. In this way, innocence is exalted over
experience and primordial time over the time of history. Yet, on
the other hand, the advent of the fault represents a gain for humanity, a "certain advance in self-consciousness." Seen from this
angle, history is taken seriously and experience appreciated for
its power to bring to consciousness a realization of the *imago Dei*
which innocence hides from view.[13] If innocence depicts our being-
created, the fault ratifies our being-created-free. For this reason, he notes, the Gnostics could not embarrass a Church Father
like Irenaeus with the problem of evil, for he could interpret the
fault as part of the "divine pedagogy" by which God draws humanity
toward its maturity.

In that same Genesis narration, the source of the fault is
depicted as both "inside" and "outside" the human will. The
Adamic myth, read from one direction, concentrates all its power
on the disobedience of Adam blaming freedom for the division that
cuts across all things because of evil. At the same time, however,
the virulence of this accusation is mitigated by the inclusion of
other figures in the drama. In Eve, and most clearly in the ser-
pent, the other side of evil is represented in the myth--the evil

that is always there "before" freedom's choice, luring and seducing
the will through its many powers of attraction.

The pursuit of this line of thought accounts for Ricoeur's in-
sistence on the ambiguous status of ethics and the ethical view
of the world. There is, he insists, both a grandeur and a limitation to the view that would interpret evil by freedom and freedom
by evil. For that reason it is both the narrow gate by which one
enters on the question of freedom and the vista that must be
transcended precisely because the human being--both in myth and
in history--is no less victim than guilty, and as such is deserv-
ing of pity as well as wrath.

The double-reading of the fault, then, protects ethics from
the mistake of exalting the Pharisee over the sinner. The sinner
is closer to the saint than the "just man," Ricoeur insists, with
characteristic irony. To understand that, it is necessary to understand the "participation à rebours," the reverse participation,
that makes the admission of guilt a moment of freedom and the experience of fault an encounter with the holy "in reverse."[14]

Such an understanding of the sinner calls for a radically
paradoxical ethics, one built on what Ricoeur has called the
"logic of extravagance." A paradoxical ethics depends also on
the mythopoetic imagination and its powers to conjure up a relationship between freedom and its source that goes beyond the categories of law and command, obedience and disobedience.[15]

II. Reconciling Thought

Ricoeur's appreciation of the ambiguity that marks all things
human enables him to recognize the ambiguity of the history of
philosophy and to undertake his work in an attitude of hope that
differences can be reconciled. "I hope I am within the bounds of
Truth," he says.[16] The "openness" of history, its unfinished character, founds the "openness" of this philosopher to all other philosophers.

> I hope that all great philosophers are within the same
> truth, that they have the same pre-ontological understand-
> ing of their relationship to being. I think, then, that
> the function of this hope lies in always keeping the
> dialogue open and in introducing a fraternal intention
> into the most bitter of debates. In this sense, hope is
> the vital milieu of communication, the "light" of all
> our debates. History remains polemic but illuminated;
> as it were, by this ἔσχατον/eschaton/ which unifies and
> eternalizes history without being able to be coordinate
> to history. I maintain that the unity of truth is a
> timeless task only because it is at first an eschatologi-
> cal hope.[17]

Anthropology and ontology are ultimately linked by this single theme of ambiguity, as Ricoeur writes:

> This *ambiguous* status of the history of philosophy is that of communication which modulates on the Same and the Other, on the One and the Many. It is ultimately the ambiguous status of *mankind*, for the history of philosophy, in the last analysis, is one of the privileged roads on which mankind struggles for its unity and its perenniality.[18]

A "communication which modulates on the Same and the Other, on the One and the Many" is a perfect description of the work of the imagination, for it is the function of the imagination to hold together the one and the many, the same and the different. It is the imagination and its works that preserve ambiguity. A mediating function, as I will show in what follows, the imagination gives access to the "both and" that marks all things human.

Imaginative Variation

Without a preliminary understanding of Ricoeur's anthropology of ambiguity it is difficult to understand the structure and the method of his philosophy of the will. The commitment to the myths of innocence and the myths of the endtime, from which he derived a notion of the ambiguity of historical existence, forms the backdrop for the project of identifying the essential structures of the will (the eidetic analysis), the conditions of possibility for the fault (the transcendental analysis), the meaning of the experience of fault (the hermeneutical stage), and the meaning of the experience of transcendence (the poetic stage). As Ricoeur says in his introduction to *Freedom and Nature*:

> ...the psychological genesis of an overall work shares something of its total scope, and...the methodological order according to which it will be presented does not coincide with the psychological succession of ideas. Though man moves beyond the fault through a myth of innocence, though man receives himself through remorse at the center of his freedom, we shall nonetheless attempt to *understand* the articulation of the voluntary and the involuntary by bracketing at the same time both the mythical consideration of innocence and the empirical consideration of the fault.[19]

Thus the philosophy of the will, conceived by a back-questioning from fault to fallibility to essential structures, must begin by both presupposing and putting out of play the ambiguity I have been describing. It will do so in the interest of bringing to light the fundamental *reciprocity* of the voluntary and the involuntary and the essential *mediation* of the infinite and the finite.

The very attempt to do this, to reach the level of the essential with respect to human willing, represents for Ricoeur an act
of hope thoroughly dependent on the imagination and its powers.[20]
Ricoeur observes:

> ...we must also add that inspection of the fundamental
> possibilities of man in fact depends on the concrete myth
> of innocence. This is what gives us the desire to know
> man apart from his fault and puts a stop to an obsessive
> and exclusive representation of the world of passions and
> of the law. Subjectively, the myth of innocence reveals a
> a fundamental nature which, however, is constituted solely
> by force of the concepts introduced. It is the *courage*
> of the possible. At the same time it provides that *imagi-
> nary* experience of which we have spoken above in Husser-
> lian terms and which serves as the springboard for the
> knowledge of human structures. Imagination, particularly,
> by recounting stories of primitive innocence, enchants
> and conjures up that diffuse sense of bodily mystery con-
> joined with our very essence as being free, without which
> pure description would be swallowed up in paradox. The
> myth of innocence is the desire, the courage, and the
> imaginary experience which sustains eidetic description
> of the voluntary and the involuntary.[21]

I do not mean to imply that the depth of understanding of
myths--particularly the cycle of the myths of evil--manifest in
the exegesis of *The Symbolism of Evil* was already Ricoeur's before
he began *Freedom and Nature*. I do maintain, however, that a certain pre-understanding of the Adamic myth and of the myths of the
endtime is evidenced in the text of *Freedom and Nature* and, above
all, makes possible the novel application of the Husserlian technique of the *epoche*. Were he not committed to the contingency of
evil, Ricoeur could not abstract the fault and Transcendence and
still hope to reach the essence of human freedom. It is in this
sense that the mythopoetic imagination is the key to his imaginative variation.

The same can be said of *Fallible Man*. Having committed himself in that volume to a transcendental deduction of the conditions
of possibility for the fault, Ricoeur nevertheless stands in need
of the mythopoetic imagination when he tries to unearth from the
faulted (read ambiguous) forms of the threefold human quest the
"underlying" and essential structures that make them at once fundamentally human quests and the place where human fragility is
most vividly displayed.

> It is *necessary* to proceed in this way: for although we
> only *know* these fundamental quests *empirically* through
> their hideous and disfigured visages, in the form of greed
> and the passions of power and vanity, we *understand* these
> passions *in their essence* only as a perversion of....[sic]
> No doubt the understanding of the primordial requires a
> kind of imagination, the imagination of innocence or a

"kingdom" wherein the quests for having, power and worth
would not be what they in fact are. But this imagination
is not a fanciful dream; it is an "imaginative variation,"
to use a Husserlian term, which manifests the essence by
breaking the prestige of the fact. In imagining another
state of affairs or another kingdom, I perceive the possible, and in the possible, the essential.[22]

In this seminal passage Ricoeur refers once again to the power of
the mythopoetic imagination to reach "behind" the empirical through
the depiction of "innocence" and "ahead" of the historical by the
portrayal of the eschatological, this time imaged as a "kingdom."

The goal of *Fallible Man*, then, the attainment of an understanding of human mediation even to the depths of affective fragility, can only be won by recourse to the mythopoetic imagination
and the technique of the imaginative variation. It is this power,
once again, that protects anthropology from error. Thus the quest
for possessions is not originally guilty such that "human communion
is possible only at the price of a deprivation of having."[23] Nor
does the evil attached to power make an innocent authority unimagi-
nable. Finally, the quest for self-esteem is not contaminated by
nothingness at its source, for it is possible to imagine a relationship of mutual esteem in which human beings build each other
up through love, transcend themselves through mutual devotion,
come to know themselves through belief in a word that is truth and
not mere opinion. It is imagination which brings to light the re-
sistance of an essence and prevents the too ready judgment that
having, power, and respect are intrinsically evil and must be
excised from human experience if humanity is to be free.

The mythopoetic imagination stands behind the philosophical
anthropology of *Fallible Man*, however, not only at its terminus,
but also at its source. By direct admission on Ricoeur's part, it
is the precomprehension of what he calls "the *pathétique* of misery"
that forms the backdrop for his hypothesis about disproportion as
an ontic characteristic of human being, and that "*pathétique*" is
conveyed in the progression from myth to rhetoric to philosophy.
"This progression," Ricoeur notes, "develops in the very interior
of images, figures and symbols, and it is through these that
pathos reaches mythos, which is already discourse."[24]

Once again, it is myth that preserves the ambiguity of human
existence, even of human feeling itself, and which provides philosophy with the matter of its reflection. In the myths of the
Symposium and the *Phaedrus*, Ricoeur finds the theme of "misery"
represented in an undifferentiated fashion; that is to say, in
these myths "misery" is indivisibly both primordial limitation and

original evil. This finding gives rise to another instance of
"double reading" whereby "we may read these great myths succes-
sively as a myth of finitude on the one hand, of guilt on the
other."[25] Practicing his particular brand of "discernment,"
Ricoeur seeks to distinguish the one from the other and to capture
the "misery" that belongs to the "melange" before it is complicated by the actual fall of freedom. Let me give the example of
his commentary on the myth of the *Phaedrus*:

> In point of fact, the *Phaedrus* links a myth of fragility
> to a myth of downfall; the fragility that precedes every
> fall is that of those teams of winged horses in the celes-
> tial procession which represent human souls. Prior to
> any fall, those souls are already composed, and their
> composition conceals a point of discord in the team it-
> self: "The charioteer of the human soul drives a team,
> and one of the horses is beautiful, good and formed of
> such elements, whereas the make-up of the other one is
> quite the opposite." Thus, before the fall into a ter-
> restrial body, there is a primordial incarnation: in
> this sense the gods themselves have a body, but the
> body of the nondivine souls contains an inherent principle
> of heaviness and obstinacy. And the myth of fallibility,
> in the chiaroscuro and ambiguity, turns into a myth of
> fall.[26]

It is precisely that moment of "chiaroscuro and ambiguity"
that Ricoeur seeks to capture in pure reflection, showing that
there is a structural ambiguity that accounts for the fault, that
makes fault a possible though not a necessary human experience.
The other dimension of the myth--captured in narrative when the
teams "mutually impede each other and founder in the eddies"--
points toward the historical ambiguity that results from a freedom
that is not only fallible but guilty.[27] This dimension of the
Platonic myth will be pursued when the reflective method yields
to a hermeneutical method in a full-fledged confrontation with
the symbolism of evil.

"The myth of fallibility," preeminent philosophical myth,
protects anthropology from other fatal errors: from identifying
finitude and guilt or identifying humanity and finitude. "Before"
the fall there is already a "composition" in the human being. From
this Ricoeur derives the notion that--even before the advent of
evil--there is what I have called a "structural ambiguity" to human existence: human being can be read alternately from the point
of view of the finite or the point of view of the infinite because
the finite and the infinite come together in the human being such
that the very essence of humanity is to be located in the fragile
mediation between them. The truth is that the human being is both
finite and infinite at once.

Long before Ricoeur coined the aphorism, the symbol was indeed giving rise to thought in his philosophy of the will. In a
curious way that characterizes his entire career, I think, the
practice of hermeneutics precedes reflection on it, just as the
capacity for "stereoscopic vision" or the apprehension of truth
within and by means of conflicting interpretations is evident long
before he can account for it in the theory of metaphoric truth.

Imaginative Interpretation

With *The Symbolism of Evil*, however, reflection on the mythopoetic imagination and its works reaches a new level. Now the
myths and symbols are no longer restricted to the function of
"guide" for philosophical method through imaginative variation or
source of reflection through prephilosophical comprehension. At
this stage the products of the mythopoetic imagination constitute
the material to be worked on directly. This change is also ex-
plicable through the anthropological clue originally given by the
Genesis myth of innocence. If the fault is contingent, that means
it is also an accident with respect to freedom and, as such, is
essentially absurd. The experience of the fault, Ricoeur hypo-
thesizes, cannot come to thought through direct concepts, but only
through the indirect language of symbol and myth. It is on this
premise that he bases his hermeneutical endeavor of *The Symbolism*
of Evil. Moreover, the experience of the fault cannot be raised
to the level of the global anthropology he seeks unless a multiplicity of symbols and myths are examined.

With the hermeneutical turn of *The Symbolism of Evil*, the
method of the imaginative variation is replaced by the technique
of "re-enactment," that is, "the sympathetic re-enactment in
imagination" of the confession of the religious consciousness.
Not that this re-enactment takes the place of philosophy, for it
does not; but it is the method by means of which the transition
from the experience of the fault to thought about the fault can be
made, just as the imaginative variation was the method by which
the transition from the empirical to the essential was made.

The decision to approach the fault through the language of
the mythopoetic imagination, however, is directly in keeping with
the precedent established in the first two stages of Ricoeur's
philosophy. *Freedom and Nature* attempted to preserve the rich
mystery of incarnate existence, yet raise the experience of an
only human freedom to the level of thought. *Fallible Man* sought
to preserve the fullness of the human pathos, while giving a

philosophical account of human fallibility. *The Symbolism of Evil*,
then, is Ricoeur's attempt to guard the fullness of mythopoetic
language--that is, of the myths and symbols of evil--yet bring the
experience of evil to the level of reflection. Once again, however, thought that would combine the depth of experience with the
clarity of philosophy demands a bracketing that will "break the
prestige of the fact." In *The Symbolism of Evil*, the *epoche* takes
the form of bracketing the etiological dimension of the myth in
order to set free the ontological dimension. In order to give
rise to thought, religious confession must be treated as the
double-intentioned language of symbol and not the univocal language of causal explanation, or literal description.

If the wager in *Freedom and Nature* was on a reciprocity between the voluntary and the involuntary in essential human freedom
and the wager in *Fallible Man* was on the hypothesis of the essential intermediacy of the human being, the wager in *The Symbolism
of Evil* is on the presupposition that mythopoetic language preserves and expresses the bond between human existence and the
sacred. The hermeneutics of mythopoetic language, then, like the
eidetics of incarnate freedom, has a restorative aim--to restore
through reflection post-scientific humanity's contact with the
sacred.

> The dissolution of the myth as explanation is the necessary
> way to the restoration of the myth as symbol. Thus, the
> time of restoration is not a different time from that of
> criticism; we are in every way children of criticism, and
> we seek to go beyond criticism by means of criticism, by
> a criticism that is no longer reductive but restorative.[28]

In Defense of the Imagination

The Symbolism of Evil culminates in the concept of the servile
will, even as *Freedom and Nature* climaxes in the notion of an "only
human freedom" and *Fallible Man* in the concept of affective fragility. At each stage, Ricoeur thinks to have identified a *truth*
about humanity and human possibilities. At each stage, the attainment of that truth is, as I have shown, dependent on the contribution of the mythopoetic imagination to philosophical reflection.
As he says at the end of *The Symbolism of Evil*, "it is as an index
of the situation of man at the heart of the being in which he
moves, exists, and wills, that the symbol speaks to us." For that
reason he can exclaim that "every symbol is finally a hierophany,
a manifestation of the bond between man and the sacred."[29] Only
one who has thoroughly grasped the extent to which Ricoeur's

eidetics and empirics of the will depends on the mythopoetic imagination can appreciate the crisis in his philosophy brought about
by a confrontation with those who would accuse the mythopoetic
imagination of hiding the truth from human beings too infantile
to face it.

In order to meet this challenge, Ricoeur must extend his notion of ambiguity even to the works of the mythopoetic imagination, giving to the function of the symbol a double reading, re-
gressive as well as progressive. In this way, the *"pathétique"*
of *Fallible Man* reappears in *Freud and Philosophy* as the *pathétique* of symbolic expression itself. If "man is language,"[30] then
the language created by human beings will reflect the disproportion of the human heart. For this reason Ricoeur comes to say of
the symbol what he had earlier said of the *thumos*: it is the fragile mediation between *bios* and *logos* in its structure, and in actuality gives rise to the birth of idols as well as to thought
about being, recovery of the bonds with the sacred. The encounter
with Freud gave new meaning to the demythologization practiced by
Ricoeur. From *Freud and Philosophy* on, "the critique of idols
remains the condition of the conquest of symbols."[31] The critique of idols represents the new dimension of discernment: the
external critique of religion mounted by the masters of suspicion
turns into an internal critique of the language of faith itself.

The recognition that religious language--that is the language
of symbol and myth--is fundamentally and existentially ambiguous
leads to a new hypothesis, another affirmation of unity where none
is apparent.

> I believe the goal (of generalized hermeneutics)--which
> I can only catch a glimpse of--is to attain a point where
> we will understand that there is a profound unity between
> *destroying* and *interpreting*. I think that any modern
> hermeneutics is a hermeneutics with a double edge and a
> double function. It is an effort to struggle against
> idols, and, consequently, it is destructive. It is a
> critique of ideologies in the sense of Marx; it is a
> critique of all flights and evasions into other worlds
> in the sense of Nietzsche; a struggle against childhood
> fables and against securing illusions in the sense of
> psychoanalysis....
>
> But we understand better that this task of destruction
> pertains also to the act of listening, which is finally
> the positive aspect of hermeneutics. What we wish to
> hear through this destruction is a more original and
> primal word, that is, to let speak a language which
> though addressed to us we no longer hear, which though
> spoken to us we can no longer speak.[32]

Metaphorical Imagination

Is there, then, no "innocent" language? Is all language
subject to the mixture of greatness and guilt that marks everything originating in the faulted human will? In the language of
the poet--"most innocent of languages"[33] according to Ricoeur--
the philosopher thinks to find a language free of fault, a language that emerges not from the will to power or the flight from
reality or the desire for consolation but from an openness to
being that is the fruit of an active receptivity, a receptive activity that transcends the will and so escapes its guilt. But the
condition for truly poetic activity is an *epoche* of natural reality that frees the poet's speech from the ordinary vision of the
world. The poet must leave off the attempt to control language
for any purpose other than that of creation. Then there is
poiesis, the introduction of the genuinely new by a metamorphosis
of what we take to be reality.

> By preserving color, sound, and the flavor of the word,
> the artist, without willing it explicitly, revives the
> most primitive truth of the world of our life which the
> scientist shrouds. By creating figures and myths, the
> artist interprets the world and establishes a permanent,
> ethical judgment on our existence, even if he does not
> moralize, and especially if he does not moralize.
> *Poetry is a criticism of life....*[34]

Recognizing the greatness of poetic language and understanding how it works are, of course, two different things. Taking the
metaphor as a "poem in miniature," an abridged poetic text,
Ricoeur sets the stage for his poetics of the will by examining
the operation of the metaphor. In it he discovers a power to
generate new meaning through an absurd predication that gives rise
to two different and mutually exclusive interpretations. The absurd predication, the conflict of interpretations, forces a search
for a unity of meaning despite the vivid display of difference.
This original meaning, often called "figurative," emerges in the
interplay of identity and difference. "Metaphor," maintains
Ricoeur, "is that place in discourse where this schematism is
visible, because the identity and the difference do not melt together but confront each other."[35]

The new ambiguity of "is/is not" differs radically from the
existential ambiguities with which I have dealt up to this point,
in that it does not concern the question of good and evil but of
being and not being. In that sense, Ricoeur has reached with the
study of metaphor the level of the pre-ethical and the hyper-
ethical. Poetry affects our way of acting in the world not

through the external relationship of law, but through the internal
transformation that is a change in our way of seeing the world.
If "one lives only that which one imagines,"[36] as Ricoeur said in
The Symbolism of Evil, metaphors change one's way of living by
changing images. But to understand this properly, it is necessary
to change the traditional way of seeing the imagination.

> Our conclusion should also "open up" some new vistas.
> On what? Maybe on the old problem of imagination....We
> are prepared to inquire into the power of imagination,
> no longer as the faculty of deriving "images" from sen-
> sory experiences, but as the capacity to let new worlds
> build our self-understanding. This power would not be
> conveyed by emerging images but by emerging meanings in
> our language. Imagination, then, should be treated as a
> dimension of language.[37]

In deciding to take as his field of investigation the practical phenomenon of human willing, Ricoeur had already broken with
the perceptualist bias of Husserl's phenomenology and with the
concept of the Transcendental Ego that was central to it. It was,
he indicates, the mystery of incarnate existence that led him to
depart from that obscure doctrine. Yet, at the time of *Freedom
and Nature*, Ricoeur's understanding of the imagination was still
governed by the perceptualist model, a fact that accounts for the
distrust of the imagination discernible in that work. In *Freedom
and Nature*, that is, the dominant understanding of the image is
that it is a "faded perception." For this reason, the images of
language are understood to be what I will call "a saying that
follows seeing." With *Fallible Man*, Ricoeur turns to another understanding of imagination, that of Kant. There, the imagination
is "transcendental" and, as such, is a mediation between seeing
and saying. The transcendental imagination unites perception and
meaning in such a way that, as Ricoeur says, "I say more than I
see when I signify."[38] With this step, Ricoeur's understanding of
the imagination began the shift from the perceptualist to the linguistic model, from the reproductive imagination to the productive.

The Symbolism of Evil and the phenomenological analysis of the
symbol as multi-valenced expression achieved an understanding of
"overdetermination" in language: "I say more than I say when I
speak." Symbolic language mediates between the conscious and the
unconscious, the cosmos and the sacred. As such, it has a verbal
and a non-verbal element, a semantic and a non-semantic "moment."
Only with metaphor does Ricoeur have the resource to capture the
"purely semantic" moment of language, language at the height of
creativity. Metaphorical imagination gives rise to a "seeing that

follows saying." Because it destroys our ordinary ways of perceiving reality, it gives rise to new perceptions by *redescribing*
reality and thus enables us to receive dimensions of reality hidden from view by our habits of organizing, categorizing, understanding the world. This redescription accomplishes what Ricoeur
considers to be a "metamorphosis" of reality as well as of language.

Far from being the "faded image of perception," then, imagination is a place of emergent meaning, the place where new worlds
emerge to open up new possibilities and rescue us from resignation
to what we take to be reality. It is in this way that the imagination is to Ricoeur a "grace," because it defends human freedom
and, especially through forms he calls the "social" imaginary,
gives rise to projects to change the world according to the models
provided by it.

Due to Ricoeur's discovery of the imagination as a dimension
of language, his notion of the "practical" imagination--that
imagination which mediates between need and willing, between freedom and nature--has taken a new form. The reciprocity of freedom
and nature originally glimpsed in the mystery of the personal body
has been sighted again in the objects of culture, most recently in
the essentially linguistic creations of ideology and utopia.

At the same time, Ricoeur's appreciation of the metaphorical
imagination has greatly enriched Biblical hermeneutics with an
interpretation of the metaphorical nature of the parables, and he
has made a foray into a more systematic realm of theology by proposing a different approach to the questions of revelation and in-
spiration, one which relies on his increasingly nuanced understanding of the imagination and its role in human life.

Throughout Ricoeur's work his own imagination has shown itself in the intuition of a unity where none had been perceived,
followed by a philosophical analysis to "justify" it. It is this
imagination that has enabled him to develop the "anthropology of
ambiguity," protecting reflection at every step from an under-
estimation or an overestimation of what it is to be human.

III. The Image of God and the Images of Humankind

The anthropology of ambiguity and the philosophy of the
imagination have unfolded together as Ricoeur has discovered
diverse ways to defend his belief in the human being as *imago Dei*--
not only created in the image of God, but continuing that creation

in history. This belief was expressed most clearly in a very
early essay on "Faith and Culture":

> God, in creating man, creates his creators; all creation,
> fundamentally, participated in this original gift of
> humanity to man. We do not believe that man had to steal
> his humanity from a jealous God or that man should be
> condemned to be stirred up in the fire in order to become
> man. This is the tragic God presupposed by the modern
> critics of Christianity, Marxists or existentialists,
> when they enclose all our culture in the alternative:
> either a God who is object, essence, value, who condemns
> man to sleep in ignorance and obedience, or else a man
> subject, transcendent, creating values, who begins his
> reign by the murder of a jealous God. Our God is a
> God-Act, a God-Gift, who makes man a creator in his turn
> in the measure in which he receives and is willing to
> receive the gift of being free.[39]

The roots of Ricoeur's anthropology of ambiguity plunge down
into a level of thought where the images of God and the images of
humanity are fundamentally bound together. His own images of humanity are fundamentally derived from the images of God preserved
in the Bible: belief in the creator God sustains throughout his
commitment to human creativity. But at the same time, Ricoeur the
philosopher knows that critical thought demands an answer to the
problems of human existence, challenging the received images of
God: belief in suffering humanity sustains Ricoeur's commitment
to a suffering God.

The medium of exchange between the image of God and the image
of humanity is the embodied word: the imaginative word of poetic
language, whose contexts are the genres developed out of religious
worship and out of practical life. In his corpus of philosophical
writings, Ricoeur has assembled the elements for an epigenesis of
human consciousness. He describes it as an epigenesis of the consciousness of guilt, but, because the experience of evil is a
"participation à rebours," the evolution of the consciousness of
guilt is also an evolution of the consciousness of God and of the
human being as *imago Dei*. From the pagan world (Babylonia and
Greece) to the Jewish world to the Christian world, Ricoeur traces
a development in consciousness intrinsically connected to a development in possibilities mediated by images of God and of human
beings.

The pagan consciousness, which I believe to characterize both
the theogonies and the tragedies, imagines a God who is inimical
to humankind--a "wicked God" who is capricious and seems to delight
in bringing humanity to its knees. It is the image of God operative in Freud and in Sartre, among other dialogue partners of

Ricoeur. The images of humanity created by such an image of God
bifurcate into what appears in theogonies and tragedies: suppli-
cant humanity, bowing before the all-powerful gods, or defiant
humanity, rising up to challenge the gods themselves. Either divinity or humanity: that seems to be the choice spawned by the
pagan images when they come up against the rising critical consciousness of autonomous humanity.

   While much of this pagan consciousness is taken up into the
religion of the Hebrews, it is not this image of God that characterizes the Jewish world. Instead, the Jewish consciousness
imagines a God who freely binds himself to humanity by a "covenant," and gives an "instruction" that spells out the mutual expectations arising from the covenant. Here is no capricious God,
but a God of righteousness and justice--a God who punishes the
evil and rewards the good. This image of God sustains an image of
humanity as capable of "respect" for one another's rights in the
formation of a people who are to be "holy" as their God is holy.
Ricoeur's enduring fascination with the story of Job can be accounted for--at least in part--because it is with Job that the
truth of the tragedies clashes headlong with the image of the
ethical God, generating out of the clash another image of God and
of human beings. Inasmuch as the moral God is one who can be
justified, this image of God is appealing to those who would have
reasons. Wherever in the history of philosophy reason has given
rise to theodicies, to the attempt to justify God, this image of
God is at work.

   Beyond the wicked God and cowering or defiant humanity,
beyond the just God and responsible humanity, there is the loving
God and desiring humanity. The consciousness of Christians certainly embraces both pagan and Jewish elements; but what characterizes the consciousness of Jesus is an imagination of God in and
through personal images that transcend the categories of the ethical vision as much as they transcend the categories of the magical
vision. Though Ricoeur cannot, as a philosopher, deal with Jesus
as any more than a "figure" like Job or Adam, he can "give an account of the enrichment that the fundamental images received from
their being remolded by Jesus in the Synoptic Gospels and from
their convergence in his own person."[40] In other words, he can
trace the development of the *images* and, with it, of humanity's
consciousness.

   The marvelous thing about Ricoeur's anthropology, in my estimation, is that it embraces the truth of all these stages of human

consciousness. Development is at once a purification and a "taking up" of the most primitive into the most highly developed; it
is also a reminder that these stages in humanity's history may
also be stages that each individual has to pass through on her or
his way to adulthood. The pedagogical implications of Ricoeur's
study of the epigenesis of guilt and of the consciousness of the
sacred are immense.

In this appreciation for the pagan and the Jewish, while being firmly committed to the Christian, Ricoeur is following in the
footsteps of the one whom he acknowledges as his Lord, even if he
cannot, as a philosopher, argue from faith in Him. In the Beatitudes, there is also this dynamic movement from the pagan to the
Jewish to the Christian. And it is a movement of consciousness
preserved by the structure itself. The first four beatitudes
bless the revelation to the pagans or, if you will, to anyone who
considers her or his own humanity. They apply to those who experience limitation, suffering, powerlessness and a deep desire to
do what is right. The next three I think of as the "Jewish beatitudes," because they come from the specifically Jewish experience
and are part of their legacy to the world: to be "holy" as God is
holy is to be merciful, to have a single transcendent loyalty, and
to be bent on making peace, not war, in the community. The eighth
beatitude is the beatitude of the suffering servant and is the
heart of the revelation of Jesus: "Blessed are those who are per-
secuted because of righteousness" (Matt 5:10). It is the revelation that goodness can call forth evil; it can so sting guilty
human hearts that they seek to extinguish the life of the righ-
teous one rather than experience the pain of conversion or the
shame of self-knowledge. Finally, there is the ninth beatitude,
the Christian beatitude: "Blessed are you when people insult you
and persecute you and falsely say all kinds of evil against you
because of me" (Matt 5:11). All these ways are blessed in the
vision of Jesus that comes to expression in the beatitudes; at the
same time, there is a progression that is at once a journey into
the imitatio Dei, the imago Dei, and the mystery of suffering.

At the same time, it is necessary to say that the poets of
all time have caught sight of the higher stages and so they have
functioned as prophets to humanity. Despite the limitations of
their image of God, Prometheus and Antigone love with a whole-
hearted passion that foreshadows the suffering servant.[41] Despite
the predominance of the ethical God, the literature of the Hebrew
scriptures preserves the vision of a covenant that is much, much

more than a contract--a covenant that binds hearts and not wills
with a love that is "strong as death" (Song of Songs 8:6). There
can be a communication among cultures because *poiesis* is always
an intuition of the world as created and sustained by love.

It is in imagining possibilities, then, that human beings
move forward. And as they progress, *bios* is taken up into *logos*
and *eros*. New images of humanity generate new human beings; new
images of God generate new images of humanity.[42] Revelation, in
the final analysis, is addressed to the human imagination. For
this reason, the mythopoetic imagination is key to a philosophical
or a theological anthropology.

> Therefore, the ultimate stake is what I have just called
> the mytho-poetic center of imagination and which is at
> the same time the point of origin of the word--of man as
> word. Feuerbach, the common master of all atheism, tells
> us: let us return to man what he has given to God, so that
> man reappropriates what he has poured into the sacred by
> emptying himself. But I think that our question--and we
> understand it better after Marx, Nietzsche, and Freud--
> is: what is man? Do we know man better than we know God?
> In the end, I do not know what man is. My confession to
> myself is that man is instituted by the word, that is,
> by a language which is less spoken *by* man than spoken *to*
> man.
>
> Finally, what constitutes our answer to the apology of
> Necessity and resignation is the faith that man is founded,
> at the heart of this mytho-poetic power, by a creative
> word. Is not The Good News the instigation of the possi-
> bility of man by a creative word?[43]

If images of God and images of human beings are inextricably
bound up together, then the revelation of possibility goes on in
and through the words of human culture--especially in the works of
the artists of language, of the word, who are the poets of humankind.

Conclusion

The *imago Dei* of the Genesis story is of crucial significance
for Ricoeur's vision of humanity. By preserving the essential
goodness of being created, the notion of the human being as the
image of God provides not only a counter weight to the historical
evidence of human inclination toward evil, but a structure for
thinking about the relationship between goodness and evil in the
human being. Ricoeur's conviction is that the depiction of the
human being as the image of God points to the contingency of evil
and gives reason to hope for an ultimate victory of good over evil
in the endtime.

The anthropology of ambiguity developed out of reflection on the myths has led Ricoeur to an ever greater appreication for the mythopoetic imagination as the mediating function that holds the disparate "readings" of the human together and as the human power that most steadfastly defends thought against considering the human being to be a necessary being, in the sense of being subject only to irrevocable necessities. Imagination preserves the power of the possible by its productive or creative powers, and in this power Ricoeur sees the good creation being continued in the midst of history.

One of the ways in which human beings are drawn forward in history is through the generation of anthropological images, images that shape traditions of self-understanding. In and through his study of the myths, Ricoeur has demonstrated that the images of humanity have developed in a dialectical relationship with images of the divine. From the metaphysical to the ethical to the affective, the epigenesis of meaning that Ricoeur traces moves toward locating the divine/human interaction in the most imatimate and fragile realm of the human heart.

NOTES

[1]See "Christianity and the Meaning of History" in *History and Truth* (trans. Charles Kelbley; Evanston, IL: Northwestern University, 1965). Note especially p. 92 where Ricoeur says that a Christian theology can only be propagated on the grounds of an ambiguous history. This volume hereafter cited as *History*.

[2]See "Truth and Falsehood" in *History*, pp. 165-91. Comments on the "ambiguity of the ecclesial reality" appear on p. 179. For the ambiguity of the State, see "State and Violence" in *History*, pp. 234-46.

[3]See "The Image of God and the Epic of Man" in *History*, pp. 113-28.

[4]See *The Symbolism of Evil* (trans. Emerson Buchanan; New York: Harper & Row, 1967) 246-47; hereafter cited as *Symbolism*. I understand the "caesura" of which Ricoeur writes to be an image for the ambiguity he finds in human existence, and I take the myth to be the source of revelation for it.

[5]"Ambiguity is a feature of discourse, that is to say, of the stretch of speech longer than or equal to the sentence. Ambiguity or equivocity means that for one string of words we have more than one way of interpreting it"; "Creativity in Language," *Philosophy Today* 17 (1973) 102.

[6]*Symbolism*, 247.

[7]Ibid., 251.

[8]Ibid.

[9]*Freedom and Nature: The Voluntary and the Involuntary* (trans. Erazim V. Kohak; Evanston, IL: Northwestern University, 1966) 29. Hereafter cited as *Freedom*.

[10]*History*, 111.

[11]Ibid., 112.

[12]I would note that the only break I have seen in Ricoeur's characteristically irenic attitude toward those with whom he disagrees occurs with C. Virgil Gheorghiu, author of *La Vingt-cinquième heure*, whose title he calls "blasphemous" and the epitime of "unhope"; *History*, 94.

[13]*Symbolism*, 253.

[14]Ricoeur takes the notion of "participation à rebours" from Jean Nabert. He says, "Nabert thereby detects in the consciousness of fault an obscure experience of non-being. He even goes so far as to make it a kind of reverse participation: any act whatsoever of the self, he says, 'does not create by itself alone all the non-being which is in fault: it determines it and makes it its own. The non-being of fault communicates with an essential non-being that passes through the actions of the individual self without lessening the gravity of them for consciousness.' It is this reverse participation which must be rediscovered, traversed and surpassed by a reflection which would break through to what Nabert

calls the 'primary affirmation.'" The "holy in reverse" is
Ricoeur's imaginative interpretation of this philosophical concept. *Fallible Man* (trans. Charles Kelbley; Chicago: Henry Regnery, 1965) xxviii; hereafter cited as *Fallible*.

[15]See "The Problem of the Foundation of Moral Philosophy,"
Philosophy Today 22 (1978) 175-96.

[16]*History*, 54.

[17]Ibid., 55.

[18]Ibid., 56.

[19]*Freedom*, 28.

[20]"Thus the intention of this book is to understand the mystery as reconciliation, that is, as restoration, even on the
clearest level of consciousness, of the original concord of vague
consciousness with its body and its world. In this sense the
theory of the voluntary and involuntary not only describes and
understands, but also restores"; *Freedom*, 18.

[21]Ibid., 28.

[22]*Fallible*, 170.

[23]Ibid., 175.

[24]Ibid., 12.

[25]Ibid., 16.

[26]Ibid., 19.

[27]Ibid.

[28]*Symbolism*, 350.

[29]Ibid., 356.

[30]Ibid., 340.

[31]*Freud and Philosophy: An Essay on Interpretation* (New
Haven: Yale University, 1970) 543.

[32]*The Philosophy of Paul Ricoeur: An Anthology of His Work*
(eds. Charles E. Reagan and David Stewart; Boston: Beacon, 1978)
234-35; hereafter cited as *The Philosophy*.

[33]*Political and Social Essays* (eds. David Stewart and J. Bien;
Athens: Ohio University, 1974) 94.

[34]*History*, 174.

[35]*The Rule of Metaphor* (trans. Robert Czerny; Toronto: University of Toronto, 1977) 199.

[36]*Symbolism*, 278.

[37]*The Philosophy*, 148.

[38]*Fallible*, 44.

[39] *Political and Social Essays*, 131.

[40] *Symbolism*, 269.

[41] I am indebted to Sister Augusta Reilly, RSM, for this insight. She has taught me over and over again--out of her knowledge and love for the classics of western world literature--not to exalt the Judaeo-Christian vision at the expense of the geniuses of all time, whatever be their religion.

[42] There is a new and important ambiguity buried in this sentence, but it goes beyond the scope of the present work. The question is whether change relates only to consciousness or to being--and it applies to God as well as to human beings.

[43] *The Philosophy*, 237-38.

THE PSYCHODYNAMICS OF ORAL MEMORY AND NARRATIVE
SOME IMPLICATIONS FOR BIBLICAL STUDIES ©

Walter J. Ong, S.J.

Of all verbal genres, narrative has the most evident and
straightforward relationship to memory. Narrative is fundamentally retrospective. Even a live radio broadcast of a football game
tells you what is just over with. A science-fiction story cast in
the future is normally written in the past tense.

The creative imagination as such has curious alliances with
memory. Wordsworth insisted that poetry "takes its origin from
emotion recollected in tranquility." I have heard a fiction
writer from the Midwest explain passionately to an audience how
in creating a story his entire imaginative activity is one of
memory. What he is making up--his plot and his characters--
present themselves to him as remembrances of what has been.
Creative activity is nostalgic. This is why the artist who deals
with the future, as perhaps artists now must, is under particularly heavy strain.

All narrative, moreover, is artificial, and the time it
creates out of memory is artificial, variously related to existential time. Reality never occurs in narrative form. The totality of what has happened to and in and around me since I got
up this morning is not organized as narrative and as a totality
cannot be expressed as narrative. To make a narrative, I have to
isolate certain elements out of the unbroken and seamless web of
history with a view to fitting them into a particular construct
which I have more or less consciously or unconsciously in mind.
Not everything in the web will fit a given design. There may be,
for example, no way to fit in the total series of indescribable
moods that I lived through in the few moments after I was shaving.
It is hard even to distinguish these clearly from everything else
that was going on in and around me. So, with almost everything
else, such matters are dropped in favor of more standard topoi.
Writers such as James Joyce or William Faulkner enlarge the number
of topoi--to the dismay of complacent readers--but the number
remains always limited. The totality of existence-saturated time
is simply too much to manage. "There are still many other things
that Jesus did, yet if they were written about in detail, I doubt
there would be room enough in the entire world to hold the books
to record them" (John 21:25).

Something other than the events themselves must determine which events the narrator cuts out of the incessant and dark flow of life through the density of time and frames in words. He or she must have a conscious or unconscious rationale for the selection and shaping. But what the rationale is in any given case is difficult and often impossible to state fully or even adequately. "Jesus performed many other signs as well--signs not recorded here--in the presence of his disciples. But these have been recorded to help you believe that Jesus is the Messiah, the Son of God, so that through this faith you may have life in his name" (John 20:30-31). Here a rationale is stated. It is what we call "salvation history": the author picks from Jesus' life what is particularly relevant to human beings' salvation. But such statement is exceptional. Few historians can put down so straightforwardly as the author of the Fourth Gospel the rationale they have settled on for their selection and structure of events. Even fewer fiction writers could adequately state their own rationale when they bring into being the artificial construct that we call narrative. There is no reason why they should have to. But neither is there any reason why we should not ask what rationale is.

The ways of articulating memory, of bringing to mind and representing the past are various. They differ from culture to culture and from age to age. In particular, as we have become increasingly aware, bringing to mind and representing the past is quite different in oral cultures from what it is in cultures such as our own, where writing and print, and now electronic processes, have been interiorized so deeply that without great learning, skill, and labor we cannot identify what in our thought processes depends on our appropriation of writing and the other technologies into our psyche and what does not. Often oral narrative processes strike us as divergent from what we consider "normal," whereas in fact many mental processes which seem "normal" to us have only recently been feasible at all.

Here I propose a few reflections concerning oral noetic processes centering on the way memory and narrative plot are related in some primary oral cultures as contrasted with the ways they are related in chirographic and typographic cultures and electronic cultures, the ones to which we ourselves are closer. I understand plot in the ordinary sense of the temporal and causal sequence in which events are presented in a narrative.

Some of these reflections do not have to do directly with the Bible as such but with oral narrative generally. However, they suggest ways we should think of and approach biblical narrative, as I shall try to indicate in my conclusion. The reflections are not comprehensive, although at times they may seem sweeping (with warrant, I hope), and they are not intended to be definitive but only suggestive. They come out of work in progress on a book, *Orality and Literacy*, to be published by Methuen in London and the United States.

I

Memory, in its initial role and in its transformations, is in one way or another a clue to nearly everything that went on as discourse moved out of the pristine oral world to literacy and beyond. Memory is still with us, but it is no longer with us in the way it used to be.

The retention and recall of knowledge in primary oral culture calls for noetic structures and procedures, largely formulaic, of a sort quite unfamiliar to us and often enough scorned by us. One of the places where oral noetic structures and procedures manifest themselves most spectacularly is in their effect on narrative plot, which in an oral culture is not quite what we take plot typically to be. Persons from today's literate and typographic cultures are likely to think of consciously contrived narrative as typically designed in a climactic linear plot often diagrammed as the well-known "Freytag's Pyramid": an ascending action builds tension, rising to a climactic point, which consists often of a recognition or other incident bringing about a *peripeteia* or reversal of action, and which is followed by a dénouement or untying--for this standard climactic linear plot has been likened to the tying and untying of a knot. This is the kind of plot Aristotle finds in the drama (*Poetics* 1451b-1452b)--a significant locale, for Greek drama, though orally performed, was composed as a written text and what the first verbal genre, and for centuries was the only verbal genre, to be controlled completely by writing.

Ancient Greek oral narrative, the epic, was nct plotted this way. In his *Ars Poetica*, Horace writes that the epic poet "hastens into the action and precipitates the hearer into the middle of things" (lines 148-49). Horace has chiefly in mind the epic poet's disregard for temporal sequence: the poet will report a situation and only much later explain, often in detail, how it came to be. He probably has also in mind Homer's conciseness and vigor:[1] Homer

wants to get immediately to "where the action is." But whatever
these further implications, literate poets eventually interpreted
Horace's *in medias res* as making *hysteron proteron* obligatory in
the epic. Thus John Milton explains in the "Argument" to Book I
of *Paradise Lost* that, after proposing "in brief the whole Subject" of the poem and touching upon "the prime cause" of Adam's
fall, "the Poem hastes into the midst of things."

Milton's words here show that he had from the start a control
of his subject and of the causes powering its action that no oral
poet could command. Milton had in mind a plot, with a beginning,
middle, and end (Aristotle, *Poetics* 1450b) in a sequence corre-
sponding temporally to that of the events he was reporting. This
plot he deliberately dismembered in order to reassemble its parts
in a consciously contrived anachronistic pattern.

Exegesis of oral epic has commonly seen oral epic poets as
doing this same thing, imputing to them conscious deviation from
an organization which was in fact unavailable without writing.
Such exegesis smacks of the same chirographic bias evident in the
term "oral literature"--which is to say, "oral writing." Radically unfamiliar with the psychodynamics of a given phenomenon, you
take a later or secondary phenomenon and describe the earlier or
primary phenomenon as the later or secondary phenomenon reorga-
nized. Oral performance is thought of as a variant of writing,
and the oral epic plot as a variant of the plot worked out in
writing for drama. Aristotle was already doing this sort of thing
in his *Poetics* (1447-1448a, 1451a, and elsewhere), which for obvious reasons shows a better understanding of the drama, written and
acted in his own chirographic culture, than of the epic, the product of an oral culture long vanished.

In fact, an oral culture has no experience of a lengthy, epic-
size or novel-size climactic linear plot, nor can it imagine such
organization of lengthy material. In fact, it cannot organize
even shorter narrative in the highly climactic way that readers of
literature for the past two hundred years have learned more and
more to expect. It hardly does justice to oral composition to describe it as varying from an organization it does not know, and
cannot conceive of. The "things" that the action is supposed to
start in the middle of have never, except for brief passages, in
anyone's experience been ranged in a chronological order to establish a "plot." There is no *res*, in the sense of linear plot, to
start in the middle of. The *res* is a construct of literacy. It
has to be made, fictionalized, and it cannot be made before writing.

You do not find climactic linear plots ready-formed in people's
lives, although real lives may provide material out of which such
a plot may be constructed. Any real Othello would have had thou-
sands of more incidents in his life than can be put into a play.
Introducing them all would destroy the plot. The full story of
Othello's whole life would be a bore.

Oral poets characteristically experience difficulty in getting a song under way: Hesiod's *Theogony*, on the borderline between
oral performance and written composition, makes three tries at the
same material to get going.[2] Oral poets commonly plunged the
reader *in medias res* not because of any grand design, but perforce.
They had no choice, no alternative. Having heard perhaps scores
of singers singing hundreds of songs of variable lengths about the
Trojan War, Homer had a huge repertoire of episodes to string together but, without writing, absolutely no way to organize them in
strict chronological order. There was no list of the episodes nor,
in the absence of writing, was there any possibility even of con-
ceiving of such a list. If he were to try to proceed in strict
chronological order, the oral poet would on any given occasion be
sure to leave out one or another episode at the point where it
should fit chronologically and would have to put it in later on.
If, on the next occasion, hypothetically smarting under the earlier disgrace, he remembered to put the episode in at the right time,
he would be sure to leave out other episodes or get them in the
wrong order. Neither he nor any other poet ever had the poem by
heart at all. Oral narrative poets do not memorize a poem word-
for-word, but only a potentially infinite number of recitations or
rhapsodies of formulas and themes in various configurations, de-
pending on the particular situation. (The Greek *rhapsoidein* means
to stitch together song.)

Moreover, the material in an epic is not the sort of thing
that would of itself yield a climactic linear plot in any event.
If the episodes in the *Iliad* or the *Odyssey* are rearranged in
strict chronological order, the whole has a progression but it
does not have the tight climactic structure of the typical drama.
It might be given that sort of structure, as might the real life
of a real person, by careful selection of certain incidents and
by-passing of others. But then most of the episodes would vanish.
An epic put in straight chronological order remains a loose con-
catenation of individual episodes, with only very weak climactic
progression. There is really no *res*, in the sense of linear plot,
in the epic, waiting to be revealed.

What made a good epic poet was not mastery of a climactic
linear plot which he manipulated by dint of a sophisticated trick
called plunging his hearer *in medias res*. What made a good epic
poet was, among other things of course, tacit acceptance of the
fact that episodic structure was the only way and the totally
natural way of handling lengthy narrative, and possession of supreme skill in managing flashbacks and other episodic techniques.
Starting in "the middle of things" is the original, natural way to
proceed for lengthy narrative (very short accounts are perhaps
another thing). Lengthy climactic linear plot, with a beginning,
a middle and an end is essentially artificial. Historically, the
classic dramatic plot is a literate transmutation of episodic pro-
cedure, not vice versa. If we take the climactic linear plot as
the paradigm of plot, the epic has no plot. Strict plot comes
with writing.

Why is it that climactic linear plot comes into being only
with writing, comes into being first in the drama, where there is
no narrator, and does not make its way into lengthy narrative until more than two thousand years later with the novels of the age
of Jane Austen? Earlier so-called "novels" were all more or less
episodic, although Mme. de La Fayette's *La Princesse de Clèves*
(1678) and a few others are less so than most. The climactic
linear plot reaches a kind of plenary form in the detective story--
relentlessly rising tension, exquisitely tidy discovery and reversal, perfectly resolved dénouement. The detective story is generally considered to have begun in 1841 with Edgar Allen Poe's *The
Murders in the Rue Morgue*. Why was all lengthy narrative before
the early 1800s more or less episodic, so far as we know, all over
the world (even Lady Murasaki Shikibu's otherwise precocious *The
Tale of Genji*)? Why had no one written a detective story before
1841? The answers to these questions must be sought in a deeper
understanding of the history of narrative than we have thus far
had, an understanding beginning from the fact that in lengthy oral
narrative climactic, plot is not really central to what the narrative is "about," to the aims of the narrator, or to the audience's
participation and enjoyment. Structuralist analysis by Claude
Lévi-Strauss and others has revealed some of the organizing principles of oral narrative as these can be described in terms of
binary themes and parts. But structuralism leaves out a lot of
what is going on. It is unfamiliar with much relevant scholarship,
largely American.

II

Some new insights into the relationship of memory and plot
have been opened in a recent lengthy work by Berkley Peabody, *The
Winged Word: A Study in the Technique of Ancient Greek Oral Composition through Hesiod's Works and Days* (1975). Peabody builds
on the work of American scholars now famous for their pioneering
work on oral epic, notably Milman Parry and Albert Lord and (less
obviously) Eric Havelock, as well as upon work of earlier Europeans such as Antoine Meillet, Theodor Bergk, Hermann Usener, and
Ulrich von Wilamowitz-Moellendorff, and upon some cybernetic and
structuralist literature. He situates the psychodynamics of Greek
epos in the Indo-European tradition, showing the intimate connection between Greek metrics and Avestan and Indian Vedic and other
Sanskrit metrics and the connections between the evolution of the
hexameter line and noetic processes. This larger ambience in
which Peabody situates his conclusions suggests still wider horizons beyond: very likely what he has to say about the place of
plot and about related matters in ancient Greek narrative song
will be found to apply in various ways to oral narrative in cultures around the entire world. And indeed Peabody in his abundant
notes makes reference from time to time to Native American Indian
and other non-Indo-European traditions and practices.

Partly explicitly and partly by implication, Peabody brings
out the negative correlation of linear plot (Freytag's Pyramid)
and memory, as earlier works were unable to do. He makes it clear
that the true "thought" or content of ancient Greek oral epos
dwells in the remembered traditional formulaic and stanzaic patterns rather than in the conscious intentions of the singer to
organize or "plot" the narrative a certain way.[3] "A singer effects, not a transfer of his own intentions, but a conventional
realization of traditional thought for his listeners, including
himself."[4] The singer is not conveying "information" in our ordinary sense of "a pipe-line transfer" of data from singer to listener. Basically, the singer is remembering in a curiously public
way--remembering not a memorized text, for there is no such thing,
nor any verbatim succession of words, but the themes and formulas
that he has heard other singers sing. He remembers these always
differently, as rhaposodized or stitched together in his own way
on this particular occasion for this particular audience. "Song
is the remembrance of songs sung."[5]

    Creative imagination, in the modern sense of this term, has
nothing to do with the oral epic (or, by hypothetical extension,
with other forms of oral narrative in other cultures). "Our own
pleasure in deliberately forming new concepts, abstractions, and
patterns of fancy must not be attributed to the traditional
singer."[6] The bard is always caught in a situation not entirely
under his control: these people on this occasion want him to sing.[7]
The song is the result of interaction between him, his audience,
and his memories of songs sung. Since no one has ever sung the
songs, for example, of the Trojan Wars in any chronological sequence, neither he nor any other bard can even think of singing
them that way. His objective is not framed in terms of an overall plot. In modern Zaire (then the Democratic Republic of the
Congo), Candi Rureke, when asked to narrate all the stories of the
Nyanga hero Mwindo, was astonished:[8] never, he protested, had anyone performed all the Mwindo episodes in sequence. We know how
this performance was elicited from Rureke: as he narrated, now in
prose, now in verse, with occasional choral accompaniment, before
a (somewhat fluid) audience for twelve days, three scribes, two
Nyanga and one Belgian, took down his words. For print, the text
of course had to be massively edited. How the entire *Iliad* and
Odyssey were elicited from a singer and doubtless edited to give
us our texts in the complete--though still episodic--forms in
which we have them, we do not quite know, but it was very likely
in some similar fashion.

    What the singer remembered in ancient Greece--and seemingly
also in modern Zaire--were themes and formulas, although the formulas are apparently more obtrusive in the Greek than in the Nyanga story because the Greek is all in verse, while the Nyanga is
a mixture of verse and prose narrative. For the simple reason
that the singer has never heard a linear plot in chronological
sequence from beginning to end of a lengthy narration, he does not
remember such a chronological sequence--though he may keep pretty
close to temporal sequence in shorter narrative of a few lines
generated out of a theme. He cannot create a linear plot out of
his ordinary resources, since he is a rememberer, not a creator--
in the sense of a creative narrator, though he is a creator in the
sense that he creates an interaction between this specific audience, himself at this particular period in his development, and
the memories he has. In this sense, a full linear plot of the
Iliad and the *Odyssey* in chronological sequence never existed in

anyone's imagination or plans, which is the only place it could
have existed before writing. These and other comparable oral per-
formances came into existence episodically, and in no other way.
Episodes is what they are, however masterfully strung together.

By contrast, the situation was utterly different with Milton
when he sat down to compose *Paradise Lost* aloud, for, even though
he was now blind and composing by dictating, he was doing essentially the same sort of thing he did when he learned to compose in
writing. His epic was designed primarily as a whole. Milton
could have his dictated lines read back to him and revise them, as
an oral narrator can never revise a line spoken or sung: Milton
was creating, not remembering. Though he of course used some
memory in his creating, it was not the communal memory of themes
and formulas that Homer had dwelt in. *Paradise Lost* is not the
"remembrance of songs sung" as the *Iliad* and the *Odyssey* and *The
Mwindo Epic* are.

Peabody's profound treatment of memory throws bright new
light on many of the characteristics of orally based thought and
expression, notably on its additive, aggregative character, its
conservatism, its redundancy or copia (which helps produce the
constant feedback that characterizes oral thought development and
gives it its often bombastic quality), and its participatory
economy.

Of course, narrative has to do with the temporal sequence of
events, and thus in all narrative there is some kind of story line.
As the result of a sequence of events, the situation at the end is
subsequent to what it was at the beginning. Nevertheless, memory,
as it guides the oral poet, often has little to do with strict
linear presentation of events in temporal sequence. The poet will
get caught up with the description of the hero's shield and lose
completely the narrative track. We find ourselves today, in our
typographic and electronic culture, delighted by exact correspon-
dence between the linear order of elements in discourse and the
referential order, the world to which the discourse refers. We
like the sequence in verbal reports to parallel exactly what we
experience or can arrange to experience. When narrative abandons
or distorts this parallelism, as in Robbe-Grillet's *Marienbad* or
Julio Cortazar's *Rayuela*, the effect is utterly self-conscious:
one is aware of the absence of the normally expected parallelism.

Oral narrative is not much concerned with exact sequential
parallelism, which becomes an objective of the mind possessed by
literacy. Parallelism between the sequence of events in a

narrative and its real-life referent was precociously exploited,
Peabody points out, by Sappho and gives her poems their curious
modernity as reports on temporally lived personal experience.[9]   By
Sappho's time (fl. c. 600 B.C.), writing was already structuring
the Greek psyche. But there is little of this parallelism at all
in epos--or, for that matter, in other discourse in oral cultures.[10]
Similarly, "narrative description in the epos is seldom the description of an Aristotelian causal chain."[11] Philosophical and
scientific analysis are entirely dependent on the interiorization
effected by writing.

Thought in oral cultures develops, but it develops with
glacial slowness, for individuals cannot move far from the tradition in which oral culture stores its knowledge without losing
both their auditors and themselves.[12]   "The amount of effort, in-
ventive imagination, and technical skill" needed for an oral per-
former to work up in recitation (his only resource for working out
thought) a story of new information discovered and organized by
himself is simply prohibitive, as Peabody points out. For an individual to work out with conscious intent truly original thought
on any appreciable scale, "some time-obviating mechanism like
writing is necessary to organize, formulate, and realize" the
thought. Instead of being analytically linear, oral thought is
highly redundant and echoic: this is the only way it can proceed,
by feedback loops out of and into itself.[13]

Further details of Peabody's creative extension and deepening
of recent scholarship on orality are too complex and, at times, too
involuted for full treatment here, especially since his most fecund
and wide-ranging discussions emerge from his primary concern with
the sources of the pentameter line as such--sources which are
treated not just metrically, however, but psychodynamically in full
social contexts. One can question or qualify certain features of
his argument, as Havelock has done in a lengthy article-review,[14]
but one must at the same time affirm, as Havelock forthrightly
does, the incontrovertible value of a work "so close to the realities of the oral situation"[15] and to the mentality that uses the
oral medium in what I have called a primary oral culture. Peabody's work shows how profoundly and suggestively our understanding of the shift from orality can be expanded and deepened.

III

With writing, and even more intensively with print and the
computer, the operation of human memory is drastically altered and

the noetic processes that mark oral cultures are transformed.
Writing, and later print and computer, enable knowledge to be
stored outside the mind--though of course only after a manner of
speaking, because there is no knowledge outside the mind. Unless
a human mind knows the code for interpreting writing, letters on a
page are no more knowledge than random scratchings would be. It
is what is in the mind that makes the letters signify. Writing
and its sequels do not, strictly speaking, store "knowledge" outside the mind but rather set up structures outside the mind which
enable the mind to engage in intellectual activity otherwise unavailable to it. This is why writing and its sequels become more
effective as the human mind "interiorizes" them more and more,
incorporates them into itself by adjusting itself to using them
without having to reflect on them, so that operations supported
by the technology of writing, and later of print and electronics,
seem to it as normal as its unsupported natural operations. Today, as we have seen, most literates are totally unaware that
their most characteristic kinds of thinking--those that organize
a school textbook or even a newspaper article, for example--are
unavailable to oral peoples, are not "natural" at all in the sense
that they cannot be carried on by a mind unaffected, directly or
indirectly, by writing. Chirographically conditioned or imple-
mented thought is technologically powered, although at the same
time it is of course "natural" in the sense that it is totally
natural to man to devise artificial technologies to improve his
own native prowess.

A helpful analog for the use of writing is performance on a
musical instrument. Musical instruments are tools, the products
of technology, totally outside the human being who plays them, as
a written or printed text is outside the reader. When Beethoven
composed, he was imagining sounds made with tools ("instruments"
is the more commendatory word, but it says the same thing), and he
was writing down exquisitely specific directions on how to manipu-
late the tools. *Fortissimo*: hit the keys very hard. *Legato*: do
not take your finger off one key until you have hit the next. An
orchestral performance is a demonstration of what human beings can
do with tools. Some music-making devices, such as a pipe organ,
are not just tools but huge, complex machines, with sources of
power separate from the player. Electric guitars and other elec-
trified instruments are machines, too. Modern instrumental music,
whether that of an electronic orchestra, a classical orchestra, or
a piano, or a flute is a technological triumph. Try to make a
musical instrument and see.

And yet, the violinist has interiorized his tool, the violin cradled in his arm, so deeply that its sound seems to come from the very depths of his soul. He has humanized the tool, interiorized it, so that to him and his audience it seems a part of himself. The organist similarly humanizes, interiorizes a huge machine whose mechanism he by no means fully understands. This is what human beings have also done with the technologies of writing, print, and computers. Writing can be compared to a violin or flute or trumpet, print to a piano (far more mechanical and dismayingly complex), the computer to the pipe organ or electronic organ.

Human memory does not naturally work like a written or printed text or like a computer. Natural, orally sustained verbal memory is redundant, essentially and not by default, echoic, nonlinear, and, unless supplemented by special intensive training, it is never verbatim for any very lengthy passage. Rather, it is thematic and formulaic, and it proceeds by "rhapsodizing," stitching together formulas and themes in various orders triggered by the specific occasion in which the rememberer is remembering. It works out of and with the unconscious as much as within consciousness. Peabody has made the point that the performance of the oral narrator or singer is very little determined by conscious intent: the formulas and themes--the tradition--control him more than he controls them. This is the ultimate difference between human memory and language on the one hand and, on the other, the retrieval and communication systems set up by writing and print and electronics. Human memory and language grow out of the unconscious into consciousness. Writing and print and electronic devices are produced by conscious planning--though of course their use, like all human activities, involves the unconscious as well as the conscious.

We have interiorized tools and machines so deeply that we are likely--unconsciously--to use them as models for human activity. We think of retrieval of material from the written or printed text or from the computer as the model of native human memory. It is not an adequate model. Human memory never recalls simply words. It recalls also their associations. Literate scholars of an earlier age, predisposed to take as the model of mnemonic activity the literate's verbatim memorization of texts, commonly supposed that since oral peoples clearly had prodigious memories, they had prodigiously accurate verbatim memories. This supposition is untrue. Literates can normally reproduce a lengthy narrative in

metrically regular verse only when they have memorized a pre-
existing text. Oral performers can reproduce a lengthy narrative
in metrically regular verse, as Lord has shown,[16] by quite different techniques--not by learning verbatim a string of words but by
expressing themselves with vast stores of metrically tailored formulas, accommodated to the narrative themes and forms they know.
Out of these formulas they construct metrical lines *ad libitum*
which tell the same story in perfect metrics but not at all word
for word. Memory here works not out of an actively conscious attempt to reconstitute perfectly a string of words, but rather out
of a passion for what Peabody styles the "flight of song."

This is not to say that oral cultures never ambition or
achieve verbatim repetition, particularly in ritualized recitation
learned by intensive drill.[17] But even ritual is not typically
altogether verbatim, either in oral cultures or in chirographic
cultures retaining a heavy oral residue. "Do this in memory of me"
(Luke 22:19), Jesus said at the Last Supper. Christians celebrate
the Eucharist because of Jesus' command. But the words of institution which he spoke before he gave this command and to which the
command refers, the words that Christians repeat in their liturgy
as Jesus' words ("This is my body...; this is the cup of my
blood...."), are not set down in exactly the same way in any two
passages of the New Testament that report them. The command to
remember does not call for verbatim memory. Even in a text here,
the still highly oral Christian Church remembered in the original,
resonant, pretextual way, rich in content and meaning--a way that
can frighten unreflective literate and computer people disposed
to associate recall with verbatim retrieval, which is to say with
itemization rather than with truth.

IV

What we have lately found out about oral noetic processes can
open the way to new understanding of the various books of the
Bible. The text of the Bible is obviously the product of writing,
but, as we have noted, the modes of expression and the mental processes the text registers are still strikingly oral. Residual
orality interacts with literacy in the biblical text in a variety
of ways, which we have not even begun to catalog. Let us consider
four examples briefly, not exhaustively, simply to suggest what
some of the ways can be.

The first we can find is the Book of Proverbs, a nonnarrative
work. Since this book consists basically of oral sayings, it would

appear to be simply an oral genre. However, this it cannot be,
not only because oral cultures cannot compile lists of anything
but also because compiling proverbs into a collection runs counter
to the oral experience of how proverbs function. When oral peoples encounter a number of proverbs together, it is quite commonly
in a polemic setting,[18] in which one person tops the proverb ut-
tered by another with a proverb more apropos or otherwise more
striking. Or it may be in litigation, where proverbs are used to
settle disputes.[19] In oral cultures, speech is regularly a high-
dominance activity, and proverbs, which are sayings or speech *par
excellence*, are commonly dominance devices even when they are
purveying long-treasured wisdom. An oral culture's experience of
proverbs in series is thus likely to be experience not of a list
but of a duel. Putting proverbs into written collections, quiet
and irenic in form, removes them from their natural habitat and
establishes them in a new genre which is basically literary, the
product of *literae*, letters, writing. Perhaps the emergence of a
new genre, the compilation, is one reason why the epilogue to
Quoheleth (Eccl 12:9-12) reflects so self-consciously on the process and value of assembling in writing "pleasing sayings" and
"true sayings."

     Our second example can be from Genesis. Unlike Proverbs,
Genesis is mostly narrative, organized in a fairly linear and
lengthy temporal sequence impossible without writing. Genesis
belongs to a literary, not an oral, genre, despite its heavy oral
residue. It converts anecdote and episode into continuous history,
if not quite the kind of history we commonly compose in writing
today. But the paratactic mode of utterance common in Genesis remains almost purely oral. Present-day translations have to adjust
to a sensibility conditioned by writing and print to hypotaxis,
subordination of one thought to another. They tend to do away
with the recurrent coordinative "and" in favor of varied subordinate constructions. The Douay translation for the residually oral
Jacobean English readers renders the opening of Genesis: "In the
beginning God created heaven and earth. *And* the earth was void
and empty, *and* darkness was upon the face of the deep; *and* the
spirit of God moved over the waters. *And* God said: Be light made.
And light was made" (Gen 1:1-3; italics added). The *New American
Bible* renders: "In the beginning, *when* God created the heavens and
the earth, the earth was a formless wasteland, and darkness covered
the abyss, *while* a mighty wind swept over the waters. *Then* God
said, 'Let there be light.' and there was light" (italics added).

We may still today use the basically oral paratactic mode in oral anecdote: "And then I said to him....And then he went and did it. And then he said to me...." But in formal discourse we no longer expect such style. It may sound delightfully antiquarian, but biblical scholars and theologians and pastors are often not very happy with a translation that fixes the word of God in past time and reduces the entire Bible, even that written in koine Greek, to a uniform antiquarian format. The paratactic style was not so antiquarian-sounding at the time when Genesis was composed in writing.

The present relevance of the biblical text to believers always challenges translators. How devise a present-day translation of Genesis that will have the effect on an audience today that the original had on an audience when it was first put into writing? Texts as texts relate differently to different cultures. For ancient Hebrews, a text was something to be read aloud to others or, for the few who could read, oneself. Outside liturgical services, present-day audiences are not used to having texts read aloud to them at all--except from teleprompters which, especially at political conventions, are deliberately concealed to give the impression that a carefully prefabricated text is spontaneous oral delivery.

The Gospels provide a third example. In the past, naively chirographic commentators have tended to interpret the Gospels as though their authors sat down to compose in writing biographies of Jesus. We know now that the highly oral milieu in which they wrote made biography, in the modern sense of this term, an unlikely objective, though there are of course biographical elements in the Gospels. Biographies as such do not exist in oral cultures. Anecdotes do. So do adages, in the Erasmian sense of wise sayings attributable to an identifiable person as a source--as against proverbs, which have no identifiable personal source. We have come a long way from the views of earlier naive commentators. Everyone today is aware that the Gospels are essentially narratives of the redeeming passion and death and resurrection of Jesus to which the evangelists have added large masses of his sayings woven into various more or less episodic events in his life.

In another way the Gospels can provide a fourth example of the persistence of oral habits of mind in a literary context. The organization of the Gospels is connected with the fact that Jesus was an itinerant, a traveler.[20] Lengthy oral narrative can handle episodic events conveniently in travel format: movement from one place to the next establishes some kind of continuity. A very high

percentage of oral narratives are strung on journeys undertaken by
heroes and heroines. Journeys provide structure which is not only
simple but also adjustable. When the narrator's sequence of
events shifts from one telling to another, as it commonly does in
oral narrative, the itinerary of the protagonist can be varied
accordingly, for its exact sequences are not that important any-
how; it is simply advantageous that there be some sequence or
other. Thus the four Gospels variously pattern Jesus' travels.
So long as lengthy narrative maintains an oral mindset, as it does
to a degree throughout the world until the age of Jane Austen,
heroes will tend to be itinerants--from the *Odyssey* through the
vast picaresque literature from *Lazarillo de Tormes* and *Gil Blas*
into and beyond *Tom Jones*. Only with the advent of the novel and
its complex, "round" characters, is the hero fully domesticated
so that Freytag's Pyramid takes shape in narrative for the first
time.

Readers will be able to provide other examples of orality-
literacy contrasts in biblical narrative and other biblical genres.
These few will, I hope, suggest some sorts of insights that knowledge of oral psychodynamics can open to us.

Conclusion

This paper ends more in exhortation than in conclusions. To
know that the text of the Bible has an oral background does not
help much if we unwittingly think of the oral materials as though
they were simply vocalized written texts. We still tend to think
of primary oral culture in privative rather than in positive,
circumstantially descriptive terms: it is a culture without writing. Those who people it are simply illiterate. We have to do
better than that to know what orality is. We need to remind ourselves that you cannot be illiterate until after writing is in-
vented. If a primary oral culture does not have writing, what
does it have that implements its narrative and other verbal powers?
What is oral memory like if it is not verbatim but formulary and
thematic, if it does not have the sense of narrative plot that
writing brings into being? To what degree and how is the pristine
oral noetic economy modified first by the knowledge of writing as
a special craft practiced by a few artisan-scribes and then by the
deeper and deeper interiorization of writing in the various books
of the Bible? This sort of question has been studied hardly at
all except by Werner Kelber in some of his recent pioneering work.[21]

I leave these thoughts with you to make of them what you can in discussion, with the firm conviction that unless we undertake seriously to come to terms with the Bible in terms of the transit from oral to literate mental processes as well as modes of expression, with close attention to the in-depth psychodynamics of oral narrative and other oral performance, we shall not understand the Bible as Christians and Jews and others need to understand it in order for the Bible to live its full life in the late twentieth century.

NOTES

[1]Charles Oscar Brink, *Horace on Poetry: The "Ars Poetica"* (Cambridge: Cambridge University, 1971) 221-22.

[2]Berkley Peabody, *The Winged Word: A Study in the Technique of Ancient Greek Oral Composition as Seen Principally through Hesiod's Works and Days* (Albany: State University of New York, 1975) 342-33.

[3]Ibid., 172-79.

[4]Ibid., 176.

[5]Ibid., 216.

[6]Ibid.

[7]Ibid., 174.

[8]Daniel Biebuyck and Kahombo C. Mateene (eds.), *The Mwindo Epic from the Bayanga* (Berkeley: University of California, 1969) 14.

[9]Peabody, *The Winged Word*, 221.

[10]Walter J. Ong, *The Presence of the Word* (New Haven/London: Yale University, 1967) 50-53, 258-59.

[11]Peabody, *The Winged Word*, 173-76.

[12]Ong, *The Presence*, 231-34.

[13]Peabody, *The Winged Word*, 173-76.

[14]Eric A. Havelock, "The Ancient Art of Oral Poetry," *Philosophy and Rhetoric* 12 (1979) 187-202--a review article treating *The Winged Word* by Berkley Peabody.

[15]Ibid., 189.

[16]Albert B. Lord, *The Singer of Tales* (Harvard Studies in Comparative Literature 24; Cambridge: Harvard University, 1960).

[17]Joel Sherzer, "Tellings, Retellings, and Tellings within Tellings: The Structuring and Organization of Narrative in Cuna Indian Discourse," paper presented at the Centro Internazionale de Semiotica e Linguistica, Urbino, Italy, July 1980, to be published in the Proceedings, pp. 2-3 of typescript, and n. 3; "The Interplay of Structure and Function in Kuna Narrative, or, How to Grab a Snake in the Darien," to appear in *Georgetown University Round Table on Languages and Linguistics 1981* (Washington, DC: Georgetown University, scheduled for 1981) n. 3.

[18]Ong, *The Presence*, 195-209; Roger D. Abrahams, "Introductory Remarks to a Rhetorical Theory of Folklore," *Journal of American Folklore* 81 (1968) 143-58; "The Training of the Man of Words in Talking Sweet," *Language in Society* 1 (1972) 15-29.

[19]Walter J. Ong, "Literacy and Orality in Our Times," *ADE Bulletin* 58 (Sept. 1978) 1-7, p. 5.

[20]Werner H. Kelber, "Markus und die Mündliche Tradition,"
Linguistica Biblica 45 (1979) 5-58; "Mark and Oral Tradition,"
Semeia 16 (1980) 7-55.

[21]Ibid.

FEELING, RELIGIOUS SYMBOL AND ACTION

William M. Shea

Were the theologian to tire of the apparently endless stream
of philosophical material on the existence of God, were one to
admit finally that one can make little or no sense in that context of "God exists" and "God does not exist" and to plead for
some rest and respectful silence, still what gives rise to belief
and argument will provoke at least curiosity and even absorbing
interest. By now it is clear that even if God is dead, religion,
theology and philosophy of God are not. The "problem of God" does
not disappear even where God's existence is denied. As long as
the issue of the meaning of existence remains and as long as religion remains, that is, as long as we remain, fundamental theology
and philosophy of religion remain. (This likelihood may even provide consolation and some hope in a bad academic job market.)
Religious experience, as a complex way in which we interact with
the natural and human environment, continues to call for the attention even of philosophical naturalists.

Religious experience, it is commonly pointed out, has to do
with unifications in several areas of human life. First, the subject's inner life is touched in its psychological, affectional,
imaginal, and decisional aspects so that there is overcome what
William James called the divided self: conversion and religious
experience are a unification of the self.[1] Second, the subject
finds a home in nature: there is a reconciliation of the subject
to the physical conditions of existence, death not least among
them. Third, time is unified by its falling into a single meaning
perspective: the subject's past, present and future are made one;
the person has not only a nature and a history but a story as well.
Finally, the subject finds a community of life and speech, meaning
and hope: there is social unification, and so the story is not the
person's alone.

While the modern masters of suspicion maintain that unification is often achieved in religion at the expense of truth,[2] and
although there is considerable risk involved in choosing any few
aspects of this complex process to discuss while appearing to
gloss over others, nonetheless I will discuss three facets of the
process in this brief essay. In limiting myself to them, I mean
neither to slight the masters whose suspicions are now unalterably

ours in common, nor to avoid the many further questions which the
subject elicits and my discussion will not touch.

The terms in which I am best able to make sense of religious
experience are these: it has its ground in feeling, its instrument
in symbol, and its outcome, indeed its goal, in liberated and unified acting. These three I wish to discuss against the background
of my conviction that the basic and authentic form of religious
experience and life is the human subject's cognitive and volitional intention of the transcendent.

I. Religion and Feeling

Ironically, modern philosophical atheism takes a theologian's
position that religion is grounded in feeling. Unlike Schleiermacher, however, modern atheism finds the religious interpretation
of feeling in images of God uncritical and the feelings uncriti-
cized. After Feuerbach, Marx, Freud, and Neitzsche, we cannot
assume that, because we feel dependent, therefore God is and is
worthy of our attention, nor can we inject the word "feeling" into
a discussion of religion without defining it critically.

On the other hand, each of these masters of suspicion recognized the enormous importance of the feeling and of the attempt to
explain it and its "true object." "Feeling and God" remained a
problem for them all, and each proposed a solution. John Dewey
maintained that without a "sense of the whole" we would go mad.[3]
But what is this whole and how is it sensed? In fact it is not
literally sensed at all, nor can it be perceived. Dewey (with the
others) took a Kantian track in his answer: the whole (for the
religious person, 'God') enters experience not as a datum of sense
but as an ideal, first in symbol and then in concept, so that the
whole is experienced reflectively but not unreflectively.[4] What
is experienced unreflectively is merely the symbolic carrier or
term; the meaning is a projection of imagination, an ideal construct, and only so a content of reflection. What is needed, according to Dewey and the others, is a critique and reinterpreta-
tion of the images, and perhaps a replacement of them, if the
unification achieved is to have its proper overflow in action in
and for this world.[5]

In the context of such a critique, if one claims that the
whole is in fact felt, even though it is neither sensed nor perceived, and that symbols, though they are "projections" and "con-
structs," mediate the content of feeling, and that authentic human
action is possible only on the condition that the whole is felt

and responded to (all of which propositions I think true), then
one had better address the question, "What do you mean by feeling?"

I do not mean by feeling "touched with the body," nor do I
mean that the whole is felt as one feels pleasure or pain; God is
not a pin-prick. Nor do I mean by feeling "emotion," a response
to an object that is situation-bound, such as hatred of one's
enemy or awe at the sight of the Grand Canyon. Nor do I mean even
the feelings that profoundly interpenetrate and guide one's entire
life, like love of liberty, of one's country, of one's spouse and
children, *nor even the love of God or "religious feelings."* Emotions come and go, reactions of psyche and organism to something
sensed or perceived. Feelings in the ordinary sense are directed
to quite specific entities within one's world of meaning and at-
tach to this or that value.[6]

At the same time, while feelings are not emotion, neither are
they thoughts. Feelings are direct, not inferential; they are the
evaluative tone accompanying all our intentional operations, including questioning, understanding, thinking, judging, and deciding. Feelings are not an operation of understanding and concep-
tualizing. They do not mediate intelligibility; they mediate
qualities and values. In ordinary usage, feelings include states
such as depression and tiredness which are caused but which have
no object other than themselves; they are not intentional. There
are as well feelings that are teleological, instinctive and impersonal, but which are not intentional in the sense that they
intend this or that object (sexual itch and hunger are examples).

Feelings ordinarily presuppose knowing; they presuppose a
world of actual and possible meaning, an intentionally constructed
world. They also accompany the intentional operations as an ap-
praising that is direct, immediate, intuitive, unwitting.

Now feeling, in the sense in which I wish to use the term, is
an unreflective yet conscious presence to things, to ourselves,
and to our operations, a *sensus aestimativus*, a "knowing feeling"
preceding and accompanying the overtly cognitional and volitional.
After our organic and biological placing in the world, it is the
prime placing of a human being whereby the world is valued, prized,
and so forth. In its profound reaches, feeling is our contact
with ourselves, our world and God, and it places us, it is our
place, in relation to all three. Feeling in the sense of presence
to self, world and God is what is touched by and touches art, what
gives shape and direction and tone to our dreams of night and day,
what gives endurance to the saint's chosen love for God and to the

ordinary person's love for family. Finally, feeling is what is
discovered and affirmed by human beings in such events as falling
in love and religious conversion. Feeling is mediated to direct
awareness in these events; in them one comes upon what Dewey called
the "sense of the whole." Feeling is always there, given, immediate, the first instance of connection with the world of sense immediacy; it is with us from the womb. Throughout life it is the
basis for the common sense appropriation of objects and the prag-
matic use of them for goals, before the refinement of aesthetic
taste and before the decisions by which we pick our way through
the maze of life's goods and evils. It settles us in relation to
all that is, long before theory does its critical job, and it
forces us to and supports our serious thinking.

Dewey's "sense of the whole" is common to human experience,
to all human thinking and acting. When Schleiermacher suggested
that we are characterized by a "feeling of absolute dependence" he
did not mean a good feeling or bad feeling about an object; he
meant the presence of an absence of our independence, something
quite different from devotion to a cause or even love of one's
neighbor.[7] When Karl Rahner writes of "Holy Mystery," he is not
throwing out another pseudo-symbol for the jaded Catholic theological imagination; he pins down the terms quite precisely as the objective correlate to an intention of Being that rides with our intending of any being in knowledge and love.[8] When the author of
the *Cloud of Unknowing* urges us on to beat against that cloud with
"loving desire" and to put all else beneath the cloud of forget-
ting, he is talking about allowing ourselves to intend explicitly
what is implicit in every other intention.[9] Finally, to step outside the theological tradition, here is what William Ernest Hocking, the American philosopher, had to say on the subject.

> ...knowledge keeps getting smaller and finer, more tangled,
> more systematic all the time: there are more threads and
> pins in the loom, more shuttles in the air. Such is the
> general aspect of the growth of knowledge--a mid-world
> growth as we have said. But with what does all this
> growth and weaving begin? In the beginning was at least
> *the Loom*; and always remains, the simple-total frame of
> things. Huge, inevitable, abiding Loom, loom-motion and
> loom-law: these, we may say, are *given*; stuff also to
> weave with, and withal the command to weave. Such total
> world-fact, always present in idea, contains the growth
> of knowledge--is not in its wholeness any mere final
> achievement thereof.
>   The whole, then, is knowable: is the one thing per-
> manently known. Any first idea of any dawning conscious-
> ness, whatever its stimulus-object, must be at the same
> time idea-of-the-whole, never to forsake that consciousness

while it remains such....The whole-idea, then, while ever
present, has its vicissitudes, its fortune to make and
ever remake, its frequent seeming life and death struggles.
It is no idle spectator of mental progress, but partaker
of all mind-growth, mind-revolution. And all this is
consistent with, nay implies, the truth that this same
infinite whole-idea is that with which every rational
existence begins.[10]

I might wish to replace Hocking's phrase "idea-of-the-whole"
with "intention of the whole" and, in doing so, correct his Idealist language, but the passage has its profound truth. The possibility of knowing is infinite; being shades off from consciousness
to infinity; questions tumble out far in advance of our answers;
for every mystery solved, ten more press themselves on our poor
minds. Yet all is already present, not, I would say, in idea but
in anticipatory intention. We feel the whole in every question we
raise and in every answer we find, we love the whole in our every
act of loving, we prize it in every value we espouse--even when we
do not know that we do.

We intend with our every cognitive intention all that is; an
absolute horizon is the Looming-background and accompaniment of
our intending any and every object. The whole is immediately
present to the human subject in anticipation, as its final cause,
its lure; experienced but unknown, conscious but not attended to
or articulated, felt but not yet thought. The whole is in this
sense present in every part, the transcendent immanent in every
object; and this is why any object, absolutely any object, can
direct us past itself to the whole. The very terms whole and
transcendent are meant to specify the correlative objective of
our intending.[11]

The whole, then, is felt before it is symbolized, named, or
in any way mediated, felt before a judgment declares it real or
ideal, felt before it is known and loved. Religious practice
makes explicit what is felt immediately, and aims at a return to
what, in its pristine form, is immediate. But the return is now
to an immediacy articulated and appropriated, to an attentive
immediacy.[12]

The self, world, and God are felt; they are immediately present to human intentional operations, but *heuristically* in the sense
that all three are anticipated but unknown. The presence, although
obscure for focal consciousness, is what makes the various symbols
and concepts of self, world, and God possible. The symbols are not
only transcendental or regulative ideals of reason; they offer explicit, though necessarily inadequate, indication of what is

immediately present to consciousness. Nor are they generalizations
of this or that aspect of or object in existence, although they are
uses of objects and aspects. Rather, they are terms which mean a
presence, present in fact but unknown in full, present as desired
but absent because unpossessed.[13]

The work of religion is to allow the subject to recognize the
given whole and to live in its presence, and thus to break the
terrifying and destructive hold of the parts and reconstitute them
as mediations of the whole.[14] The event called religious conversion is this sort of a unification of the subject. Dewey described
unification as an adjustment of the person to the totality of the
conditions of existence. In conversion, the primal presence of the
self to the self, world and God, on the one hand, and the feelings
and knowledge of and actions toward objects and events, on the
other, are reconciled; the disorienting pluralism of objects and
values is smoothed by a single overriding intention which quite
readily becomes a "vision" in which all other intendings, desir-
ings, feelings and knowings are discovered to be part of a whole.
Conversion renders explicit what has been implicit and obscure;
at its heart it is a moment of attention to what does not appear
but which is felt.

The various religious traditions and various forms of life in
religions traditions, while distinct in their symbolic and concep-
tual renderings of the meaning of God and world for self, are
nonetheless attempts to explicate the one basic human desire for
God. Whether one traces the intention of the ascetic, the mystic,
the theologian, the priest, the prophet, celibate or dionysiac,
and no matter how critical one can be of them all, one finds that
they are following the clue of feeling and the same desire for
unity. Even for the dionysiac, drinking and orgy are not merely a
matter of getting drunk and fornicating; they are a mediated return to immediacy for the sake of unity with the god. (One can
fornicate in the ditch or haystack; having intercourse in the
sacred grove under the influence of the god's vine, this is another
matter.)

There are many sensations, perceptions, motions and emotions,
feelings, thoughts and decisions, and many symbols, signs, objects,
dogmas, and rites, yet there is one feeling among many, a *Grund-
gefühl*, that underlies, accompanies and sets the goal for all.
Religion is an attentive intention to live with the whole anticipated in feeling, a negation of restriction of feeling to objects
and consequent narrowing of vision, an appropriation in image,

concept and act of the immediacy of horizon to consciousness.
Religion's point is consummation, bringing the self to the self,
to the world and to God in feeling and imaginative vision. This
is splendidly articulated in Dante's *Paradiso:*

> In that abyss I saw how love held bound
>   Into one volume all the leaves whose flight
>   Is scattered through the universe around.
>
> How substance, accident, and mode unite
>   Fused, so to speak, together in such wise
>   That this I tell of is one single light.
>
> Yes, of this complex I believe mine eyes
>   Behold the universal form--in me,
>   Even as I speak, I feel such joy arise.
>   ***
> For everything the will has ever sought
>   Is gathered there, and there is every quest
>   Made perfect, which apart from it fall short.[15]

No matter how dim and distant for any of us, this is the vision
without which, as Dewey said, we would go mad. But we must be
careful here. The vision is, no doubt, a consummation, but the
archetypal religious person, the mystic, does not remain consumed
and silent in union. Consummation is followed, as it was preceded, by speech and action.

II. Religion and the Symbol

Something over a decade ago, in a classroom discussion of
religion in the ancient near east, a Christian student at Columbia
University remarked on the idolatrous behavior of the Egyptian
worshipping the crocodile. Theodor Gaster, who looked on ancient
peoples with more respect than he was inclined to pay some of his
students, asked the young man (who happened to be a Catholic)
whether the young man would prefer the shavings of Gaster's toe-
nails or those of St. Peter; he further suggested that, had these
been the middle ages and had he, Gaster, sauntered up the isle of
St. Patrick's Cathedral and expectorated on the main altar, he
would have been burned at the stake. Why St. Peter's toe nails
rather than his own? What is it about the altar that is worth a
life? Why rub the Virgin's marble foot and genuflect before the
tabernacle? Gaster was not interested in exposing the curiosities
of Catholic behavior to ridicule; he was quite interested in convincing the young man that Egyptians were no more stupid and no
more idolatrous than the Catholics. The Egyptian knew that the
crocodile is not the god, just as the Catholic knows that neither

the altar nor the bread is the god. Yet *both* know that to fall
down before the animal and the bread is to worship the god.

Religious people know how to use symbols. Granted that religious people sometimes misuse them and more often misunderstand
their meaning when they get around to thinking about them, by and
large the Ka'aba and the eucharistic elements are not misused or
misunderstood. But the question arises: What do we do with religious symbols? We use them in the process of self-transcendence.[16]

To sense is not the same as to perceive; to perceive is to
direct attention to a content of sensing.[17] Questioning is not
the same as perceiving; questioning asks for a meaning of what is
sensed and perceived. Understanding is not the same as perceiving
or questioning; it is an answer to a question about what is perceived among the contents sensed. Thinking is not the same as
understanding; thinking is unfolding the implications of the understanding and checking whether one has understood correctly.
Judgment puts one's understanding on the line as the correct understanding. Deciding plunges one into action, into establishing
new relations with what has been sensed, perceived, questioned,
and understood. All these distinct operations are intentional;
each, and the entire set in dynamic unity, has an object, and none
is without an object. Each promotes the subject to a new stage
in self-transcendence, the culminating context of which is value,
decision, and action.

In each operation the data of sense and the data of imagination play a crucial role. What is grasped in understanding is the
intelligibility immanent in the data of sense or imagination. What
is judged true is judged with reference to the data of sense and
imagination. Concepts are not without their associated images.
Even values and ideals are "carried" in images. From dreaming to
deciding, from praying to playing or thinking, the human world of
meaning is a world constituted by self-transcendence and carried
and expressed in images.

Bernard Lonergan defines a symbol as "an image of a real or
imaginary object that evokes a feeling or is evoked by a feeling."[18]
Symbolic imagination mediates between feelings and the self-
transcending operations of the human subject, between the organic
and biological structure of the subject and the subject's intentional operations. Symbols are images used to mean. They carry
no intrinsic meaning, no more than do the black marks on the white
surface without a mind meaning by them. Symbols "carry" meaning
in a tradition by convention, even when tradition canonizes the

convention. Surely some images are more suitable as symbols than others, but suitability is always relative. A range of images may be used to mean a nation's common good; the range of images that have been used to mean the divine is broad indeed, from the croco- dile to the crucifix. Symbols are images used as "connectives," a term used to great effect by John Herman Randall in his theory of signs and symbols.

> ...Connectives are operations functioning in Substance or the Situation to connect or conjoin other factors, to in- stitute relations between other operations and ways of operating. Connectives thus lead us from one operation to another, they 'organize' or 'order' operations, they 'unify' them. They serve in general as instruments of relating....The power, or the instrument of relating, I am taking as the Connective proper.[19]

They are the tools of meaning which in history and community loom large and exercise huge power in the unification of heart and mind for action. Although images *can* mean anything as symbols, yet they are determinate in use in traditions and communities. While the bread is only bread in the bakery and *can* mean anything in the world of sign and symbol, yet in the Christian world of meaning and on the sanctuary table, it means something quite spe- cific. There it means what John 6 means, and nothing else.

In the religious world the symbol is the image by which the transcendent is meant. What is sought in it is not its immanent intelligibility or its this-worldly significance; what counts is its usefulness in meaning transcendent intelligibility and value. Its immanent intelligibility and its this-worldly value is taken up in the intention of the transcendent: transubstantiation means that the bread, although it is eaten, is no longer bread for the secular table.

The religious symbol mediates to focal consciousness, to at- tention and understanding and valuing, what cannot be an object *within* the field of consciousness since it is the horizon or boun- dary within which all objects are. The symbol stands in the place of something else, but in this one case it stands in for what can- not stand for itself, what cannot appear.

The fact that an object, an image, can be used to mean the horizon is accounted for in the metaphysical ruminations of theo- logians from Plato and Plotinus to Rahner and Tillich. One works out a theory of the use in an analogy of being or analogy of faith or even an intentionality analysis. Ricoeur was correct when he said that the symbol is "food for thought,"[20] thought on function as well as thought on content. But first it is an instrument of

use, to mean what cannot otherwise present itself or be understood. While it is true that we cannot *know* the boundary or the
whole, that we can only know what falls within it and against it
as a backdrop, yet what falls within can be used to mean what
cannot itself become an object of knowledge.[21]

Because it links intention and boundary, life and its limits,
the religious symbol evokes feelings of great power and significance and is itself invested with "power." My father is my pro-
genitor, and that is simply a matter of biological fact; but the
word means all he means to me and all I mean when I use the word
of him--and what "father" means cannot be adequately or fully spoken without the symbol(s). The word serves me well; it is a
symbol. Think, then, of the complication of meaning when I say
"I believe in God, the Father almighty..." and the theoretic com-
plications when I subsequently ask (and try to answer) the question of what it means to say "God is my Father." Watch the connections made in thought and feeling when one prays, "*Our* Father...
give *us* today tomorrow's bread."[22] The word serves us well. It
is a religious symbol.

The symbol in its religious use is joined by the storytelling
that goes on between myself, my fellows, and the mysterious boundary of existence; it is followed by beliefs that answer questions
about the story and the symbol, and then by doctrine and dogma,
and by the thinking that goes on in religion on the proper ways to
use the symbols, and finally by the thinking in religious studies
on how symbols work, how they are used, and the conditions and
criteria for their truthful use.[23] It could be objected that doctrines are rationalizations of primary symbols and myths and, as
such, are a mistake and a danger. But the doctrines can be and
often are a legitimate, proper, perhaps unavoidable and sometimes
even necessary clarification of the meaning of the symbols and
stories by those who tell them. For religion is not only attention to, valuation of, and decision for the transcendent; it is
as well understanding, reflection, judging and speaking truly, if
inadequately, about it.

James Leuba, in his otherwise seriously flawed study of the
Catholic mystics, noted the connection between mystical union (he
equated this with trance) and action.

> Whatever the mystics may say that seems to subordinate
> unselfish activity to the passive enjoyment of God is
> belied by specific passages..., by the general trend of
> their writings, and still more convincingly by their
> lives; all of them, so soon as unity was established in

their consciousness, have spent themselves without stint
in the service of their fellowmen. The delight of the
ecstatic trance is for them, in the final instance, God's
way of encouraging them to greater efforts towards
saintliness, of clarifying their moral vision, and of
making them more useful instruments of divine action.[24]

Granted that the locus of the symbolic function is the inner life,
the meeting point of heart and mind, the active intention of the
horizon of experience, that its ground is the sense of presence,
and that one of its proper communal forms is beliefs, what is the
relationship between its meaning and action, especially action in
the life of the political community? We have spoken of feeling,
transcendence, and symbol. But there is the final moment of self-
transcendence yet to consider: action. Unification has its point
for life in this world.

III. Religion and Acting

The most penetrating and most valuable American philosophical
criticism of traditional religions is on religion's frequent failure to appreciate and proclaim the values necessary for progressive action and democratic life.[25] It is an old criticism; the
Americans inherit it from the Enlightenment. On its philosophical
point, their discussion has to do with the relation between theory
and practice, and it makes reflection on religion and action imperative. Since I am concerned here chiefly with the unification
promoted in religious life, I will address only two aspects of the
far broader topic of theory and practice: first, the unification
of the plurality of action in the intention of the transcendent;
second, an illustration of my understanding of the relationship
between the intention of the transcendent and action by means of
three theses on the relation between religion and political life.

John Dewey made it clear early in this century that action is
the primary form of the relationship between the human being, the
community and the environment, and that theory is secondary. The
designations of Dewey's theory of method as "instrumentalism,"
"pragmatism," and "experimentalism" all bespeak his conviction that
theory is the servant of action.[26] Reason in any abstract sense,
as for example in "rationalism," is not the criterion of action or
truth. George Santayana had no doubt that all elements of human
life and civilization must be understood in relation to action, to
the life well lived, to desires and their negotiation in the ideal
and in their fulfillment in practice.[27] Frederick Woodbridge,
Dewey's colleague and fellow naturalist, although he was critical

of some aspects of Dewey's pragmatism, nonetheless situated the
pursuit of knowledge in the context of the pursuit of happiness,
and allowed that the latter had exigencies that the former could
not meet or deny.[28] John Randall's history of ideas embodies a
theory of the relation between ideas and action in which philosophy
itself is interpreted as an intellectual politics of criticism for
the sake of better use of ideas.[29] For Randall, and for them all,
the world of action is primary and the world of knowledge secondary. They assert that the power of the ideal over the actual
unifies the subject for action and unites subjects in common action. All action requires the ideal, that is, the imaginative and
intelligent projection of goals.[30] There is no human action without the ideal and without thought.

Now action is plural and goals are many. But implicit in
every action is the intention of the whole. For action is constructive meaning; action presses on toward a fully constructed
world of meaning. And action is relational meaning, for it in-
variably takes place in a context which, when analyzed, turns out
to be the whole. Every action is a part of the whole in which the
whole is anticipated and heuristically present. Even sin, the attempt to negate the whole, supposes the whole. The intention of
being is not restricted to knowing, for it fructifies in acting.
Every decision implicitly regards not just this or that value but
value itself, a unity, a whole of values.

Human action rests on the ability of human beings to project
in imagination an ideal for the sake of which the present can be
understood and transformed. The ideal promotes a unification of
feeling and understanding which in turn becomes a unification of
action. Every action requires an ideal, every action requires
some minimal unification of heart and mind. The task of religion
is to bring to focal consciousness the "what for," the whole of
all action. Religious vision mediates the implicit, transcendent
goal of every action and form of life. In religious vision actions
are unified, their point rendered symbolically explicit.

Human life is not an irremediably scattered collocation of
unrelated or competing desires, ideals, and acts. Actions can be
unified in broad worldly ideals and, unfortunately, even in narrow
worldly ideals. But even the broadest worldly ideal is in need of
criticism and of the unification provided by an otherworldly love.
Frederick Woodbridge was correct in this respect: all ideals must
be subject to a judgment not of this world, to the judgment of a
transcendent personality to whom devotion can be absolute--even if
such a person cannot exist or be said to exist.[31]

Furthermore, suffering, evil, sin and death shatter both purpose and action, and require imaginative inclusion in human life.
They are often integrable with worldly ideals; one is, after all,
willing to work, suffer and die for the establishment of forensic
justice. But these realities do in the end conquer. Some suffering can and does blot out all action and even devotion to secular
ideals. Evil and sin do destroy individual and communal achievement and hope. Death is victor over the individual and it will be
over the race. How are all these facts and possibilities to be
brought into relationship with the goals of human life that they
inevitably destroy? The religious answer is that devotion to God
allows unification of all actions and values, and that even the
realities that threaten all worldly values can be included in and
reversed by devotion to the transcendent. But more: God overcomes
even suffering and death.

The possibility of the religious process is the self-
transcending intention which rests in no object, or the presence
of the self to God in feeling. When the self-transcending intention is no longer simply an ontological fact but a symbolically
and even conceptually appropriated presence, we are not left as
we were. We are turned around when the fact of immediacy becomes
a matter of attentive intention. Conversion is, in the religious
tradition, an instance of *gratia operans*, a "gift," an instance
of God's work in the Holy Spirit. So the experience has been understood by the saints, Aquinas no less than Paul, Augustine and
Calvin. But conversion is also a matter of *gratia cooperans*, of
human striving guided and enticed by grace for the historical
goals to which the vision of the transcendent calls.[32] We see
with the eye of the mind what is already present to the mind.
Religious vision of the transcendent mediates to us the immediate
presence of the whole, which includes all the parts and allows all
the parts to stand as mediators of the whole. Even pain and death
can become for religious faith parts wherein the whole is found.
The Christian symbol of the crucified-in-glory means this.

George Santayana had an exceptional appreication of the distinction between unconditioned and conditioned loves, and of the
religious life which properly orders them.

> Beggars in Catholic and Moslem countries used to beg an
> alms, sometimes, for the love of God. It was a potent
> appeal; because God, according to the Socratic tradition,
> was the good to which all creation moved; so that anyone
> who loved deeply, and loved God, could not fail, by a
> necessary inclusion, to love the good which all creatures
> lived by pursuing, no matter how repulsive these crea-
> tures might be to natural human feeling.

> Thus the absolute love of anything involves the love
> of the universal good; and the love of the universal good
> involves the love of every creature.[33]

Santayana writes of a religious vision which, far from negating
this-worldly loves, reorders them in reference to the unconditioned
object of unconditional love. While unconditioned religious love
relativizes all worldly love and achievement, the one in love
neither rejects the world, nor its goods, nor its values. The one
in love is in a position to embrace the world critically; devotion
to the value that transcends all worldly values and achievements
becomes the condition for self-criticism and world-criticism.

Religious life, then, is a unification of all intentions,
ideals, and actions in the vision of the Transcendent: the love
for the transcendent includes within itself all other loves. As
Woodbridge put it, life is lived for the transcendent; actions and
achievements are not for here but for Elsewhere, for the glory of
God--even if for Woodbridge God is ideal rather than actual.[34]

And religion, considered as a language for human experience,
is the explication of the unity implicit in human intentionality.
Once again, religion says "what for," and points explicitly to
where all actions point implicitly, to their ground and final
cause. Actions become action, now an intentionally unified practice rather than an implicit unity of intentions. But unification
in religion is achieved in devotion to the transcendent which is
beyond all ideas and so capable of containing and ordering them all.

We have, however, more than a few examples of religious visions complicating, disrupting, and destroying the realization of
legitimate political ideals. The critics have repeatedly and vi-
gorously argued traditional religion's unalterable opposition to
freedom of inquiry, scientific method, and political democracy.
What can be said of the relationship between religion and politics
as the chief case of the intersection of the idea of the transcendent and human historical action?

First, religions are political always and everywhere. No
human being, no human institution can situate itself in a non-
political relation to our common life. Second, the politician is
no less possessed by the transcendent in immediacy and no less
possessed of the possibility of vision of the transcendent than is
the priest or the mystic or the prophet. Religious institutions
have no corner on the visions of God or understandings of the mystery of human existence. Third, both religion and politics are
equally subject to ideological manipulation and distortion of

their symbols. Nazism, Soviet and Chinese Communism, and several
American political movements such as Nativism have employed the
symbols of nation and of transcendent meaning to serve unworthy
political goals. Religious figures have again and again employed
the symbols of their own traditions to crush opposition within
their own assemblies, to harass other church assemblies, and to
launch political crusades. Pope Pius IX told Catholics that God
is opposed to democracy and freedom of religion. Pius X told them
that God is opposed to free and scholarly examination of the Bible.
American ministers told their congregations that God is opposed to
rum, Romanism, rebellion, and racial mixing. The contemporary
chaplins of the New American Right are convinced that the policies
of liberals are against the divine will, and that America's enemies
are God's enemies.

Both assemblies, the sacred and the secular, are fundamentally
concerned with the future, with the shape human life shall take.
Their respective symbols are aimed at the creation, maintenance,
and expansion of their communities of meaning and action, and at
the transformation of the community in the light of the ideal. In
both communities the symbols serve to unite citizens for common
action in the realization of common goals. However, the religious
assembly is concerned with a transformation of the present such
that human beings can commonly recognize that all worldly life,
with its promises and its threats, is a gift, while political assembly aims at a transformation of the present in the hope of
achieving a good of order where the needs and desires of the community can be met recurrently and securely.[35] The fundamental
method by which the transcendent is approached by the religious
community is the presentation in prayer and worship of appropriate
symbols, symbols which rivet attention on the all-embracing transcendent. The fundamental method of the secular community in approaching its goals is the presentation of the symbols of the
public good, free communication of understandings of good and the
good of order, and freedom of action in their common achievement.

Religious devotion to the transcendent expressed in liturgical worship and prayer makes possible and necessary a criticism of
political and social ideals from the point of view of the transcendent goal of human life. It also makes possible and necessary
a criticism of the uses of the symbols of religion by religious
persons and, indeed, a criticism of the adequacy of the symbols,
and this for the same reason: meaning and value that is transcendent calls for criticism of its own expressions and carriers.

Where religion's self-criticism is absent, religious faith and
love are prey to ideological, masked political manipulation of the
symbols of its own faith by leaders whose real devotion is not to
the transcendent but to all too worldly aims and achievements of
their own. The need for an inner-religious critique of religious
symbols and their uses is displayed throughout the entire history
of Christianity, as much in its present as in its past. If the
religious vision of the whole is required for a healthy political
and social life, as I believe it is, then equally the religious
vision requires criticism of its own mediating elements and its
claims to authentic humanity. Thus, Hans Küng serves the church
in this as in many respects, and deserves the gratitude of
theologians.

Against this background, my view of the relationship between
religious and political symbols and assemblies can be stated in
three theses.

THESIS I. The Protestant principle: Love toward and loyalty to
the transcendent relativizes all partial and secular loves and
loyalties, values and objectives, and conditions them. Only devotion to the transcendent radically establishes inner freedom and
grounds criticism of all loyalties to conditioned causes. To put
it in religious language: "Let the dead bury their dead....He who
loves father or mother more than me is not worthy of me." Prophetic protest against the inclusive worldliness of the politics of
both church and state stands on this principle.

THESIS II. Religions must answer to political criticism. The
critique of religious life, symbols, and institutions is based not
only on devotion to transcendent value (a *religious* critique of
religions), but also on devotion to worldly values and means (a
political critique of religions). The critique compels the religious community to examine the symbols of the transcendent in the
light of the needs of the good of order in politics, to question
its recurrent subjugation to religiously masked ideologies, and to
prize and transform the actual conditions of existence rather than
to negate them.

THESIS III. The Catholic Principle: the sacred and secular assemblies are reconcilable finally. Worldly history has its origin
and goal in the divine; the sacred accepts and sublates the secular and does not exist without it. The transcendent values such
as self-sacrificing love and the values of the good of order such
as liberty and untrammeled communication merge in the ideal of the

Kingdom of God whose very metaphor is the secular assembly. This
thesis reasserts the unity of all actions in the love for God.

Religious experience, in sum, is a process of intention
grounded in feeling, promoted by symbol, and critically transfor-
mative of the world of human meaning. However, one understands
and decides upon the status-in-existence of the transcendent,
whether ideal or real or illusion, it is intended and it does
unify. Grace is a matter of fact even if it turns out that God
is not.

NOTES

[1]For James' discussion of the divided self and its unification, see the fourth through the tenth chapters of *The Varieties
of Religious Experience* (New York: Collier Books, 1961). The influence of James on the psychology of religion is decisive, but
it must be added that a very broad range of thinkers have, from
several perspectives, found unifications and unities crucial to
an understanding of religion and to the practice of it: James
himself, E. Underhill, and L. Dupre on mystical experience; the
mystics themselves such as the author of the *Cloud of Unknowing*
and Thomas Merton; social scientists such as M. Eliade, C. Geertz,
R. Bellah, E. Erickson, A. Maslow, and P. Pruyser; philosophical
theologians as different in their conceptualizations and contexts
as P. Tillich, K. Rahner, and D. Tracy; and philosophers of religion from quite different traditions, such as J. Royce, W. E.
Hocking, A. N. Whitehead, and E. Cassirer.

[2]Ludwig Feuerbach, *Lectures in the Essence of Religion* (New
York: Harper & Row, 1967); *Karl Marx and Friedrich Engels on
Religion* (New York: Schocken Books, 1964); Friedrich Nietzsche,
Joyful Wisdom (New York: Ungar Publishing, 1968). For a thorough
critical discussion of the masters from a theological perspective,
see Hans Küng, *Does God Exist?* (Garden City, NY: Doubleday, 1980).

[3]*Art as Experience* (New York: Capricorn Books, 1958) 194.
For a comment, see W. Shea, "Qualitative Wholes: Aesthetic and
Religious Experience in the Work of John Dewey," *Journal of Reli-
gion* 60 (1980) 32-50.

[4]Although most of the American naturalists correct Kant on
the important issues in epistemology, they nonetheless take a
qualified Kantian position on the regulative ideal. They have in
common with him the rejection of the possibility that the whole
enters primary experience in any way and the affirmation that the
whole is an idea or Ideal which the subject contributes to experience and the means by which it is unified. For them to deny in-
dependent reality to the whole is a corollary of their denial that
the whole is ever encountered in primary (nonreflective) experience. On Kant, see John Herman Randall's *Career of Philosophy*
(New York: Columbia University, 1965) 2.106-91.

[5]John Dewey, *A Common Faith* (New Haven: Yale University,
1934) 46ff.

[6]For discussions of the intentional character of feelings,
see Magda Arnold, *Emotion and Personality* (New York: Columbia
University, 1960) 1.50-90; and Dietrich von Hildebrand, *Christian
Ethics* (New York: David McKay, 1953) 191ff.

[7]Friedrich Schleiermacher, *On Religion: Speeches to its
Cultured Despisers* (trans. John Oman; New York: Harper and Row,
1958) 26-118, esp. 101ff.

[8]*Foundations of Christian Faith: An Introduction to the Idea
of Christianity* (New York: Seabury, 1978) 50-71.

[9]*The Cloud of Unknowing* (ed. William Johnston; Garden City,
NY: Doubleday, 1973) 54-55.

[10]*The Meaning of God in Human Experience* (New Haven: Yale
University, 1912) 96-99.

[11]On the correlation as argued by contemporary theologians, see K. Rahner, *Hearers of the Word* (New York: Herder & Herder, 1969) and B. Lonergan, *Insight: A Study of Human Understanding* (New York: Harper and Row, 1978.1957) 348-74, 634-86.

[12]On mediation and immediacy, see Lonergan, *Method in Theology* (New York: Seabury, 1972) 76ff., and his unpublished essay, "The Mediation of Christ in Prayer," available at the Lonergan Centre, Regis College, Toronto.

[13]For a naturalistic interpretation of the "sense of presence" see James Leuba, *The Psychology of Religious Mysticism* (Boston: Routledge and Keegan Paul, 1972.1925) 280-99, as well as James, *The Varieties*; for another view, see Joseph Maréchal, *Studies in the Psychology of the Mystics* (Albany: Magi Books, 1964.1927) 57-123.

[14]The images through which the transcendent is intended and thought will depend to a great extent on one's tradition and one's experience, including one's experience of other persons and objects. But the immediacy is nonetheless a universal, a transcendental underlying all attempts at articulation, whether as Yahweh of hosts, Father, Moloch, the Absolute, the Ideal. Religions mediate the presence by means of myth, rite, dogma and law--all shaped by the forces of emotion stirred up between the immediate presence and actual operation. The religions name the objective of our intention, bringing it into focal consciousness, coloring the feelings associated with it and with the symbols, giving it correction as well as expression, or, unfortunately, trivializing, brutalizing, maiming, and distorting it in ways familar to us all.

[15]Canto XXXIII.

[16]For discussions of the status of the symbols from the point of view of philosophical theology of the Platonic tradition, see K. Rahner's "The Theology of the Symbol," in *Theological Investigations* (Baltimore: Helicon, 1966) vol. IV, and his *Church and Sacrament* (New York: Herder and Herder, 1963); and Paul Tillich, "Theology and Symbolism," pp. 107-16 in *Religious Symbolism* (ed. F. Ernest Johnson; Port Washington, NY: Kennikat, 1969).

[17]For the intentionality analysis underlying these propositions, see Bernard Lonergan, *Insight*; for a brief presentation of his views, see his essays "Cognitional Structure" and "Metaphysics as Horizon" in *Collection: Papers by Bernard Lonergan* (ed. F. Crowe; New York: Herder and Herder, 1967).

[18]*Method in Theology*, 64. For Lonergan's discussion of feelings as intentional response to values, see 30-40.

[19]J. H. Randall, *Nature and Historical Experience* (New York: Columbia University, 1958) 258-59.

[20]Paul Ricoeur, "The Symbol Gives Rise to Thought," pp. 347-57 in *The Symbolism of Evil* (Boston: Beacon, 1969).

[21]On the whole and parts in experience, see the fascinating and complex discussion of the issue in D. Tracy, *The Analogical Imagination: Christian Theology and the Culture of Pluralism* (New York: Crossroad Publishing, 1981) Part II.

[22]Joachim Jeremias, *The Lord's Prayer* (Philadelphia: Fortress, 1964).

[23]On the relationship of theology to religion and religious studies, see: Tracy, *The Analogical Imagination*; Schubert Ogden, "What is Theology?", *Journal of Religion* 52 (1973) 22-40, and "Theology and Religious Studies: Their Difference and the Difference it Makes," *Journal of the American Academy of Religion* 46 (1978) 3-18; and Arthur McGill, "The Ambiguous Position of Christian Theology," pp. 105-38 in *The Study of Religion in Colleges and Universities* (ed. P. Ramsey and J. F. Wilson; Princeton: Princeton University, 1970).

[24]Leuba, *The Psychology of Religious Mysticism*, 128.

[25]For example, see Dewey's *A Common Faith* and his "Antinaturalism in Extremis," pp. 1-16 in *Naturalism and the Human Spirit* (ed. Y. Krikorian; New York: Columbia University, 1944).

[26]In its fullest form, the theory of theory and action is argued in *Logic: The Theory of Inquiry* (New York: Holt, Rinehart and Winston, 1938).

[27]*Scepticism and Animal Faith* (New York: Dover, 1955).

[28]See *An Essay on Nature* (New York: Columbia University, 1940).

[29]See *How Philosophy Uses Its Past* (New York: Columbia University, 1963).

[30]Religion presents the ideal of ideals, the transcendent ideal: for Dewey, God is the relation between the ideal and the actual; for Randall, religion provides the connective that enables us to live with evil and transform it to good; for Woodbridge, religion points to an imaginative Elsewhere for the sake of which we act here; for Santayana, religion is the statement in imaginative vision of the deepest values and meanings of the human individual and communal life. Nevertheless, they maintain that a transcendent ideal is incapable of realization; indeed, they think it impossible. Not only do they hold that the ideal cannot be actual, but they also maintain that the ideal cannot be absolutely transcendent if it is to function for human action. I would rephrase the issue: the transcendent ideal cannot be at once realizable and yet relevant to all actions as their unifier. The transcendent is not ideal as opposed to real or existent. Only in a highly restricted sense can it be said to be ideal at all, namely, only in the sense that it serves to unify the plurality of ideals. For all of the eulogistic language of the religions and the not infrequent outbursts of megalomaniacal religious enthusiasm, religious persons do not intend to become God. Again, precisely because the transcendent is absolute and our intention of it points and cannot define, precisely so can the vision of it unify all human actions.

For examples of outbursts, see Norman Cohn, *The Pursuit of the Millennium* (New York: Harper Bros., 1961). The language of mysticism, east and west, can be interpreted to support the claim that religious persons intend to be God. I think that the interpretation is a mistake, for the mystic intends either to love God, thus preserving a distinct personal identity, or to be absorbed into God, thus ending personal identity; see L. Dupre, *The Other Dimension: A Search for the Meaning of Religious Attitudes* (New York: Doubleday, 1972), and W. Johnston, *The Inner Eye of Love* (New York: Harper & Row, 1978).

[31]Woodbridge, *An Essay on Nature* (above n. 28), 321-22.

[32] For the distinction between *gratia operans* and *cooperans*, see Lonergan, *Grace and Freedom* (ed. J. P. Burns; New York: Herder and Herder, 1970).

[33] "Ultimate Religion," in *Obiter Scripta: Lectures, Essays and Reviews by George Santayana* (ed. J. Buchler and B. Schwartz; London: Constable, 1936) 223.

[34] Woodbridge, *An Essay on Nature*, 321-22.

[35] On the meaning of the good of order, see Lonergan, *Insight*, 595ff.

RELIGIOUS IMAGINATION AND INTERRELIGIOUS DIALOGUE

Paul F. Knitter

The focusing theme of the 1981 meeting of the College
Theology Society--and an undercurrent of concern in recent yearly
meetings--has been the necessity of a fertile and active religious
imagination. If our religious imaginations become dull and dry,
our personal religious lives and our institutional religious practices cannot help but lose their animating meaning. We have been
reminded of this from various perspectives.

The following reflections will examine, from the standpoint
of a Christian theologian, the relationship between religious
imagination and interreligious dialogue. Two main claims will be
made: (1) Today Christians must look upon dialogue with believers
from other religions not merely as a promising *possibility* for
nurturing their religious imagination (most people would agree
with that) but as a pressing *necessity*. Christian religious
imagination, in our present age, not only can but *must* be expanded
and cross-fertilized through dialogue with other faiths. (2) Yet
for such interreligious dialogue to be effective and productive it
must use as one of its central tools the very religious imagination it seeks to expand. There is a mutual dependence between
religious imagination and interreligious dialogue.

I. The Necessity of Dialogue

Over the past decades the notion as well as the practice of
religious dialogue has been somewhat trivialized. Today everyone
recognizes the value of other religions, and of course everyone is
willing to dialogue with them. Not to do so would be to rank oneself among those narrow-minded fundamentalists; religious bigotry
is disgusting. So, for educated Christians an openness to other
religions and a willingness to speak with them is among the musts
in their wardrobe of religious attitudes.

The danger here is that such laudable openness easily assumes
the casualness of an evening or weekend away--something one does
on the periphery of one's ordinary and real religious pursuits.
A lecture on Islam or a weekend workshop on Eastern mysticism provides a bit of interesting diversion from one's ordinary religious
fare. Such religious exchange is, naturally, friendly. But the
friendliness easily cloaks a type of lazy tolerance which so
stresses agreement that it fails to take real differences and

conflicts seriously. It is a friendliness which is so comfortable
with one's own religious beliefs and the state of one's own religious imagination, that it excludes any real need to learn from
others. Also, it is a friendliness which tends to look at all
religions as essentially the same--as different ways of talking
about the same thing. For such an attitude, the differences between religions may be interesting, but again, there's not much
to learn from them.

     In this section I would like to suggest two reasons why
interreligious dialogue for Christians cannot be merely a casual
affair or an occasional tickling of their religious imaginations.
Today an expanding of our religious imagination through encounter
with other faiths has become *necessary* for the authenticity of
our Christian identity. The two reasons are grounded in recent
insights from two perspectives which, on first sight, seem strange
bedfellows: epistemology and politics.

Epistemology: Truth Needs the "Other"

     On our shrinking, ever-more intercommunicating and inter-
dependent globe, pluralism has become a fact of life. It's a
fact which is becoming more and more undeniable and bewildering:
there is never just *one* of anything; there are *many* of everything--
cultures, races, religions, philosophies, economic systems. The
ontological reality of multiplicity, of many versions of every-
thing, has been recognized and proclaimed by specialists from various fields; it's part of what is called "historical" or "modern"
culture.[1] This recognition of the pluralistic nature of reality
is also seeping down to the popular level. Many people are sensing
that "(t)oday, the universe of meaning has no center,"[2] or that
"...I (my reason, my consciousness, my being, my nation, my religion) do not exhaust the real nor am I its center--but only one of
its poles, if anything at all. There are others."[3] What's more,
the realization is dawning that such pluralism is not merely a
provisional state of affairs which we have to put up with until
we--all humankind--can get our act together. "Pluralism is not
the mere justification of opinions, but the realization that the
real is more than the sum of all possible opinions."[4]

     This confrontation with and acceptance of pluralism is forcing
a further and unsettling conclusion concerning what it means to
know the truth--the truth about the world around me as well as
about myself. This conclusion is an insight as simple as it is
profound: we can't do it alone. Our modern world's experience of

the reality of pluralism should convince us that no individual person and no individual nation or culture or religion can carry on the pursuit of truth by themselves. To try to "lone it" is to cut oneself off from truth in its fullness, in its variety, and in its quality of dynamic change. We need others to aid us--others who are genuinely other and different in their experience, their history, the way they use their imaginations.

So Charles Davis, following the lead of Jurgen Habermas and the School of Critical Theory, argues that we must affirm but also move beyond a "post-conventional morality or identity." Yes, we must determine values critically and intelligently, on our own and not simply to gain parental or societal approval; only so can we establish a morality and identity that is really our own. Yet if these values are to be not only personal but universal, i.e. not only values for us (ideologies) but also for others, we cannot search for them alone. Today we must recognize the need for a post-conventional, *universalistic* identity. This means that we cannot attain values that will be valuable for all, truth that will be truth for all if we stay only within the backyard of our own culture or nation or religion. We have to step out of our own neighborhood and *together with* people on the other side of the tracks or ocean strive for values which can ground our collective identities. If there is not this effort at universal communication and cooperation in the search for what is true and good, we cannot avoid deceiving ourselves and hurting each other.

> ...human society today cannot achieve a rational identity within the boundaries of any permanent collective body, with its particular territory or organization. Our basic social identity cannot come from membership in a stable collective entity, confronting us as fixed objective reality. Such a social identity is incompatible with our universalistic personal identity. Instead of consisting in membership of a fixed collective body, collective identity at its basic level lies in a process of universal communication, uniting human beings without distinction in the shaping of a new collective will, in the creation of new collective identities at the level of concrete action, in the formation of a new global order.[5]

Wilfred Cantwell Smith calls for the same universal expansion of our experience and imagination when he insists that true knowledge, knowledge that will bring life, is not a matter of cold, individual objectivity but rather, can result only from what he terms "critical, corporate self-consciousness." Self-consciousness, or personal identity, must be critical--we have to apply our intelligence and reason. But it must also be corporate, or what he calls "global" or "transcultural": we also have to use the

experience, the intelligence, the imagination of others. "True
knowledge, in human affairs, is that knowledge that all intelligent
men and women...can share, and can jointly verify, by observation
and by participation. True human knowledge is disciplined and
corporate self-consciousness."[6] Truth which is only truth for me,
which others cannot participate in and profit from is a very sus-
picious truth. Smith puts it succinctly and challengingly: "The
truth of all of us is part of the truth of each of us."[7]

On the more popular level, the attitude towards strangers,
towards the "new kid in town," the fellow with the turbaned head
or different colored skin is slowly changing. No longer are they
seen as threats or adversaries but as potential partners and
friends. The stranger, as Panikkar points out, should be seen no
longer as the "barbarian" but as the "sancta barbara"--the holy
barbarian, someone we need and must respect. The reason is simple:
"Once the assumption that the stranger is inferior is shattered,
then he is experienced *as* a stranger. And once you admit that you
do not understand *him*, you are gradually forced to admit that you
do not understand yourself."[8] We are realizing today, gradually
but with mounting urgency, that in order to answer the perennial
question, "Who am I?," we have to ask and try to answer the question, "Who are you?"

> And this is a radically different question, for it not
> only cannot be answered without *you*, but it requires you
> as a fellow-questioner...and the "you" is the Pygmy, and
> the Muslim, and the woman, and the Communist, and the
> Christian, and the Democrat, and the wife, and the worker,
> and the poor....How can we pretend to deal with the ulti-
> mate problem of Man if we insist on reducing the human
> being to only the American, or to only the Christian, or
> to the black, or the male, or the exclusively hetero-
> sexual, or the healthy and "normal," or the so-called
> civilized.[9]

It must be admitted that many people today, in experiencing
the need and the unsettling complexity of learning from others,
are threatened; they are giving up the effort and are building
even higher fences around their own backyards. There is a resur-
gent nationalism and ethnocentrism among us today. Yet this would
seem to be the last gasp of a dying culture--of an attitude which
must die if a new--a necessarily new--world order is to emerge.
We cannot run away from the persistent truth in Charles Hartshorne's
claim: "The 100 percent American, or Russian, or what have you, is
an enemy to all of us. We need an element of world citizenship in
each person."[10]

If this new epistemology of pluralism is correct, if we cannot know the truth by ourselves, if we need the genuinely other to
truly know both the world and ourselves, then it is evident that
religious dialogue cannot be considered a luxury. Rather, it must
be part of our religious identities, of the way we go about understanding our own faith, our own god. So we witness among Christian theologians a growing "opinio communis" that Christian theology must move beyond its traditional confines if it is to properly
do its job in the contemporary world. Theology today must be a
"World" or a "Global" theology.[11]

What this means first of all is readily accepted by most
people: Christians in general and Christian theologians especially
must know other religions so that their own religious life and
theology can be "enriched" and deepened by the experience and insights of others. This, in itself, is "...an unprecedented task.
Never before in the history of Christianity has this challenge
been raised."[12] But theologians such as Raimundo Panikkar and
Wilfred Cantwell Smith are saying much more and making more dras-
tic demands. When Smith argues for a "world theology" or a "theology of comparative religion," he is presupposing the epistemology of pluralism described above and is suggesting that the
cognitive claims of Christian tradition must somehow be true also
for those of other religions if they are genuinely to be true for
Christians. "...no statement about Christian faith is valid to
which in principle a non-Christian could not agree. Theologians
have not usually adopted such a principle...ideally the theology
of comparative religion, when constructed, should be acceptable
to, even cogent for, all humankind. We may dream, may we not?"[13]

Panikkar is arguing the very same thing with his notion of a
new kind of fundamental theology. If the task of fundamental theology is to critically examine and question the presuppositions of
all theology and Christian life, it will be able to carry out this
task, in our present world, only through a dialogue with other
religions. "The role of fundamental theology is therefore to make
theological affirmations also intelligible outside the culture and
even the religion where they had until then grown and prospered."[14]
Panikkar is working out of the same epistemological framework: if
we cannot make our Christian assumptions clear and in some degree
convincing to people of other religions, we must ask whether they
are really true, really valid for us.

This new epistemology of pluralism, then, is not simply suggesting but *demanding* of Christians that they engage in dialogue

with other religions. There is a kind of Teilhardian evolution at
work here: Christianity, as well as all religions, must evolve out
of the micro phase of religious history in which the various faiths
grew and consolidated in relative isolation from each other; the
direction today is towards a macro phase of history in which each
religion will be able to grow and understand itself only through
interrelating with other religions.[15] Just as we cannot really be
citizens of our own country unless to some extent we are world
citizens, so we cannot truly be intelligent and engaged members of
our own religion unless we are also, in some real way, members of
other religions.

Politics: The Need for a New World Order

In view of the present political and economic condition of
our world, we can say that humankind's persistent dreams of a "new
world" today must be translated into reality. We need a *new* world
order. The present one won't do. Anyone who reads the newspapers
and listens to the daily news cannot avoid, at least occasionally,
the leaden feeling that somehow the world has gone amuck, radically amuck. It's a gnawing fear that the growing and ever more confusing tensions between nations and "isms" are suddenly going to
blow up in a planetary conflagration. We know the problems too
well: starvation and malnutrition, economic inequality, dwindling
resources, exploitation and poverty, official flouting of human
rights. And over all of this tinder hovers the flame of nuclear
weaponry.

For many it seems the maladies afflicting our globe grow from
a sick international system which cannot be remedied through band-
aids and aspirins but only through radical surgery. We are not
indulging in doomsday prophecy when we find ourselves asking
whether biological and human-cultural evolution has brought us to
a critical juncture where the very survival of humankind and the
planet are at stake. Something must be done. Important decisions
must be made.

They are decisions which will construct a new world order.
The central vision of this new order, as it is described by various prophets of hope, is captured in a children's story about the
dinosaurs and all that rubbish. The story deals with a man who
devastated the earth so that he could build a rocket and travel to
a better planet. After he departs, some dinosaurs, who had been
asleep for ages under the ground, rebuild the earth into a planet
flourishing in greenery and abundance. The man in his rocket,

meanwhile, finds himself on a futile journey; all the other planets
are barren. However, he finally finds one that is green and beautiful, and cared for by dinosaurs. In amazement, he realizes it is
the earth he left in devastation. Desparately he pleads with the
dinosaurs for a small plot to live on, "...just a hill, or a tree,
or a flower." Their answer summarizes the spirit of the new world
order:

>   "No," said the dinosaur.
>   "Not a part of it,
>   but all of it.
>   It is all yours,
>   but it is also mine.
>   Remember that.
>   This time the earth belongs to everyone,
>   not part of it to certain people
>   but all of it to everyone
>   to be enjoyed and cared for."[16]

It will be a world in which the earth does belong to all, a
world in which the nations will assume values and structures that
can change the economics of greed into the economics of community,
in which each nation will finally realize that it can prosper only
when it respects and promotes the prospering of other nations. It
will be a world order in which the many communities of individual
nations truly form a *community of communities*.[17] In this community, the word "we" will take on a new meaning; when people say "we,"
they will no longer mean just their family, their neighborhood,
their country. To say "we" will mean to say and to feel all humankind. Only if such a Community of Communities takes form out of
our present fractured and feuding international order does our
future seem possible.

But can such a new world order be fashioned? Has it not been
the unfulfilled dream of humanity during these last few centuries?
Such "realistic" questions do not remove the growing conviction
that today the necessity of a new world order presses more than
ever. Unrealized hopes do not mean unrealizeable hopes. To create a new world will be the imposing task of politicians, philosophers, economists. Yet history seems to attest that their efforts
will flounder if left to themselves.

W. C. Smith speaks for many: "My own view is that the task of
constructing even that minimum degree of world fellowship that will
be necessary for man to survive at all is far too great to be accomplished on any other than a religious basis. From no other
source than his faith, I believe, can man muster the energy, devotion, vision, resolution, capacity to survive disappointment, that
will be necessary--that *are* necessary--for this challenge."[18]

Certainly the hard work of social and economic analysis, the
sagacity of political diplomacy, the charism of inspired leaders
will all be absolutely necessary in struggling towards this Community of Communities. But what is equally and perhaps primarily
necessary is that all these efforts be grounded in and inspired by
a common religious imagination fueled by symbols and myths which
will assure the value of the individual, the meaningfulness of
justice and love, the vision of common fellowship in common origins, and especially the promise that our efforts to promote the
unity of humanity will bear fruit, even if they cost us our lives.

A number of scientists and philosopher/theologians make use
of the implications of biological evolution to argue the necessity
of a religious basis for a new stage in the evolution of humanity.
From the genes of our animal ancestors we humans have inherited
aggression towards outsiders and loyalties towards our own kin
which were essential for survival and for the development of the
most viable genotypes. In the earliest stages of animal-human
evolution, a certain survival of the fittest through aggression
was necessary if there was to be survival and advancement at all.
Today, however, as biological evolution has given rise to cultural
evolution and as cultural evolution has advanced from kinship
interdependencies to the interdependence of nations, the conditions
for survival have changed.

Now cultures and nations will survive not through aggression
and dominance but through cooperation. Yet we are still burdened
with our aggressive, selfish genes. This is where the world religions enter the process of evolution. They will provide not the
"genotypes" but the "culturetypes"--not the new genes but the new
social values--which will enable humans to overcome their natural
selfishness and ethnocentrism. All the major world religions ex-
tol the value of self-sacrificing love for others; all contain
symbols of the universal unity of humanity. The stage is now set
for them to make their evolutionary contribution.[19]

To make this contribution they must work together. But here
many will rightly object: this is precisely what the religions of
the world have not done in the past nor are doing in the present.
We cannot help but share the anger and dismay of former Secretary
of State, Cyrus Vance (in a talk at the Interreligious Peace
Colloquium, 1975), "...that given the presumed strength of the
religious community throughout the world, we should go from crisis
to crisis, from conflagration to conflagration--that the religious
community should have such apparently ineffective input into the

management of our global village."[20] Efforts towards a new collaboration among religions must be preceded and inspired by a
humble confession that in the past and present, the world religions have contributed devastatingly to the divisions of humanity.
Perhaps this egocentric, aggressive posture was part of the micro
phase of religious history when the religions had to establish
their own identity and cohesion.

Today, however, the need for a world community must shake the
religions into reviving their inner vision of love and common
fellowship. Whatever their divisions and aggressions of the past,
world religions share something today that calls them and binds
them together: "...what the various religious traditions have in
common is the fact that each is being carried today by persons who
increasingly are involved in the same problems. Christians, Jews,
Buddhists, Hindus, Muslims, and the others are all faced today for
the first time, by a joint challenge: to collaborate in building
a common world."[21] Their common task is rendered all the more ur-
gent by the consideration that their contribution may be the essential added ingredient or the catalyst necessary for the success
of the efforts of politicians and social engineers.

Again we face the *imperative* of interreligious dialogue. Not
only as an interesting pastime but as a political, moral obliga-
tion, Christians must open themselves, learn from and grow from an
exchange with believers of other faiths. Only if all the religions
of the world form and work out of a Community of Communities among
themselves can they help form such a community among nations.

II. Religious Imagination Integral to Dialogue

After all these arguments for the necessity of interreligious
dialogue, something must be said about how to do it. In recent
years, much has been written on the nature and the method of dialogue.[22] I would like to make a suggestion which might add to and
clarify the discussion: if interreligious dialogue is to lead to a
corporate search for truth and to a Community of Communities, it
must be *based on the use of religious imagination*. At the beginning of these reflections it was said that the expansion of religious imagination is an *end* of dialogue; here we are suggesting
that the religious imagination is also an essential *means* for dialogue. If we understand the imagination as a crucial tool for our
conversations with people of other faiths, we will be able to trace
a middle path between two approaches to dialogue which all too often lead to dead ends: the intellectual and the mystical.

The overly intellectual encounter with other religions,
stressing objectivity, the hard facts, and an *epoche* suspension of
all personal involvement, has for the most part been rejected by
those who have tried it. Panikkar agrees with other specialists
in comparative religions like Mircea Eliade and Wilfred Cantwell
Smith when he states that if interreligious dialogue is mainly a
phenomenology or a philosophy of religions, it will go nowhere.
It will end up with nothing more than further knowledge, further
facts and interesting comparisons; it will not bring about any
truly personal insight or conversion. It will be study rather
than dialogue.[23]

Today most of the practitioners of religious dialogue recognize that their conversations must be based on *religious experience*, on one's personal faith as it tries to touch and be touched
by the faith of another tradition. Interreligious dialogue must
be *intra*religious dialogue; it must involve my entire religious
being and "...proceed from the depths of my religious attitude to
these same depths in my partner."[24] A true encounter with another
tradition cannot take place "from the outside," from my own religious beliefs looking into those of another. Rather, dialogue
must presuppose and operate out of a universalist faith within all
religions; this will enable me, with my own faith experience, to
look from within at the same faith experience in another religion.[25]
Before dialogue can be *communication* about doctrines and beliefs,
it must be a *communion* which comes about when the partners
"...penetrate the ultimate ground of their beliefs."[26]

Yet in trying to grasp more concretely what these authors
mean by "religious experience," "universalist faith," "depths in
my religious attitude," "ultimate ground of beliefs," one often
feels that one is handling something so elusive as to be unusable.
Just what does it mean to ground religious dialogue on common
religious experience? How do you do it? Some, like Frithjof
Schuon and the Perennial Philosophers, will respond that the experience behind and within all religions is so transcendent that
it cannot be expressed; or they would say you can express it any-
way you want, through any symbol or belief; one is as good as
another.[27] Most of the authors we have cited do not go to these
extremes, yet many of them speak under such a mystical "cloud of
unknowing" as to make it difficult for the person in the trenches
of dialogue to know just what they're talking about. Even Panikkar
is somewhat guilty of this when he argues that dialogue should not

proceed primarily out of *logos* or *mythos*, but out of the inexpres-
sible *pneuma* which breathes where it will within all religions--or
when he claims that the mystical experience out of which dialogue
should flow will be a center which is void. "Only a void center
can coincide with all the movements of the circumference."[28]

This is not to deny that the content of any genuine religious
experience will be mystical, always beyond any word or symbol, any
logos or *mythos*. Yet if the *pneuma* of personal faith and religious
experience is the foundation of authentic dialogue, there is a real
danger in talking about this foundation so mystically that one cannot get at it. Unless we are able to offer some definite method
or means of access to religious experience, our own and especially
that of another, we will be hamstringing dialogue in its very
first steps. How can we enter into the always elusive, never
fully defined religious experience of another?

Our religious imagination would seem to provide such a point
of entry into the heart of another's personal faith. The imagination, which bounds beyond the structures of the intellect and yet
does not lose itself in the apophatic clouds of the mystic, offers
a tool for personally entering into the content of the stammering
words and elusive symbols of another person's religious experience.

The first step in attempting to dialogue with another religion would be to prepare the way for letting our imaginations play
or run free with the images contained in that religion's symbols,
myths, doctrines. This preparatory step requires the usual historical, semantic homework necessary for approaching a person or
classic of another time or culture. If we are dealing with a myth
or doctrine, we will first have to try to grasp the basic contours
of its meaning by situating it in its *text*--its place within a
broader literary work--and in its *context*--its historical situation. We then turn this general grasp of its vision and its
images over to our imagination--and let our imagination take us
where it will: possibly to new insights, to new images of the
world, ourselves, our god, to new modes of being in the world, to
surprisingly different perspectives on the symbols and beliefs of
our own tradition.

Various veterans of dialogue, who have achieved notable suc-
cesses in entering other religious worlds, are making such use of
the imagination, even though they may not describe their method in
precisely these terms. Certainly Panikkar, for all his occasional
mystical evasiveness, holds up *mythos* as the main data for dialogue; and the creative way his own imagination plays with the

symbols and images of other religions is evident throughout his
works, especially in his monumental *The Vedic Experience--
Mantramanjari*.[29]

In John Dunne's well known method of "passing over" to other
religions and other persons, the imagination plays a central role.
In his description of this technique, the imagination or use of
images is the point of entry into the feelings of another believer;
the imagination then provides the data for new "theory" or insights
which then must be verified in "praxis": "The technique of passing
over is based on *The Process of Eliciting Images* from one's feelings, attaining insights into the images, and then turning insight
into a guide of life. What one does in passing over is try to
enter sympathetically into the feelings of another person, become
receptive to the *images* which give expression to his feelings,
attain insight into those images, and then come back enriched by
this insight to an understanding of one's own life which can guide
one into the future."[30]

One of the most scholarly and convincing cases for the central role of the imagination in attempting a conversation with a
person or classic foreign to us has recently been made by David
Tracy in his *The Analogical Imagination*.[31] Especially his chapters
on "The Classic" and "Interpreting the Religious Classic" might be
read as a handbook of guidelines on the nature of dialogue with
other traditions and the pivotal role of the imagination in such
dialogue. For Tracy, the effort to interpret and converse with a
classic, either of our own tradition or of another, is essentially
the same as the experience of a genuine work of art. In it we
must risk playing a "game," a game in which we have to abandon our
intellectual control and our own self-consciousness and let our
feelings and imagination take over. "In every game, I enter the
world where I play so fully that finally the game plays me."[32]
This game of conversing with a classic (or another religion) will
lead us into an "intensification process" by which we find ourselves, through our imaginations, participating in a reality which
perhaps we didn't realize existed.[33]

In his epilogue, Tracy explicitly recognizes "...the possibilities of approaching the conversation among the religious traditions through the use of an analogical imagination...."[34] The
analogical imagination will always be a limited tool, for it
recognizes that its images are analogies, telling us something but
never telling us everything; yet it will be *the* means by which we
can gain access to the religious experience and different worlds

of other religions. In fact, our religious imaginations will
compel us to dialogue. Viewing the very different world of
Buddhism, Tracy claims: "...if I have already lived by an analogical imagination within my own religious and cultural heritages,
I am much more likely to welcome the demand for further
conversation."[35]

So it will be our religious (always analogical) imagination
that enables us to respond to the demands of the new epistemology
of pluralism described above. Our imagination will grant us access to other religious traditions and to authentic dialogue with
them, so that together--we with them and they with us--we will be
able to get beyond our own ideologies and carry on the corporate
and never-ending pursuit of truth.

And through such a dialogue based on imagination we will come
to realize, as those experienced in interreligious dialogue are
telling us, that the evident differences between the religions are
not as divisive and exclusive as we may have thought. What has
been achieved so far in dialogue is suggesting "...that the immense variety of what appear to be conflicts...can be transformed
...into *dialogical tensions and creative polarities.*"[36] We will
perhaps discover that the real differences between the impersonal
Brahman and the personal Yahweh, between the Triunity of God and
the Oneness of Allah, between the worldly involvement of the
Judaeo-Christian tradition and the detachment of the East--that
all such differences are ultimately much more complementary than
contradictory. "In all ultimate matters, truth lies not in an
either-or but in a both-and."[37]

And this recognition of the underlying unity among the
religions--which does not deny the real differences--can provide
the basis on which all the religions of the world can work towards
a Community of Communities among themselves and thus contribute to
establishing the needed Community of Communities among nations.

NOTES

[1] Bernard Lonergan, *Method in Theology* (New York: Herder and Herder, 1972) 300-302, 326-29; idem, "The Transition from a Classicist World View to Historical Mindedness," pp. 126-33 in *Law for Liberty: The Role of Law in the Church Today* (ed. J. Biechler; Baltimore: Helicon, 1967); Langdon Gilkey, *Reaping the Whirlwind* (New York: Seabury, 1976) 188-208; David Tracy, *Blessed Rage for Order* (New York: Seabury, 1975) 4-14.

[2] Nicholas Lash, *Theology on Dover Beach* (New York: Paulist, 1979) 71.

[3] Raimundo Panikkar, "The Myth of Pluralism: The Tower of Babel--A Meditation on Non-Violence," *Cross Currents* 29 (1979) 217.

[4] Ibid., 226.

[5] Charles Davis, "Our New Religious Identity," *Studies in Religion* 9 (1980) 36.

[6] Wilfred Cantwell Smith, *Towards a World Theology* (Philadelphia: Westminster, 1981) 102; cf. also 59-79.

[7] Ibid., 79.

[8] Lash, *Theology on Dover Beach*, 71.

[9] Panikkar, "The Myth of Pluralism," 213, 203.

[10] Charles Hartshorne, "Beyond Enlightened Self-Interest," p. 315 in *Religious Experience and Process Theology* (ed. Harry J. Cargas and Bernard Lee; New York: Paulist, 1976).

[11] Smith, *Towards a World Theology*; John Hick, *God Has Many Names* (London: Macmillan, 1980) 1-9, 80-97. Paul Tillich, "The Significance of the History of Religions for the Systematic Theologian," pp. 80-94 in *The Future of Religions* (ed. Jerald C. Brauer; New York: Harper & Row, 1966); John Carmody, "A Next Step for Catholic Theology," *Theology Today* 32 (1976) 371-81.

[12] Ewert H. Cousins, "Introduction," *Cross Currents* 29 (1979) 145-46.

[13] Smith, *Towards a World Theology*, 101, 126.

[14] Raimundo Panikkar, *Myth, Faith and Hermeneutics* (New York: Paulist, 1979) 330; cf. also 325-33.

[15] Thomas Berry, "Religious Studies and the Global Community of Man," *An Integral View* 1 (1980) 35-43; Robley Edward Whitson, *The Coming Convergence of World Religions* (New York: Newman, 1971); Paul Knitter, "The Challenge of the World Religions: A New Context for Theology," *Verbum Svd* 19 (1978) 34-56.

[16] Michael Foreman, *Dinosaurs and All That Rubbish* (New York: Thomas Crowell, 1972) 26-27.

[17] Wilfred Cantwell Smith, "Divisiveness and Unity," pp. 71-85 in *Food/Energy and the Major Faiths* (ed. Joseph Gremilion; New York: Orbis, 1978).

[18] Wilfred Cantwell Smith, "The Christian in a Religiously Plural World," p. 11 in *Religious Diversity* (ed. Willard G. Oxtoby; New York: Harper & Row, 1976). Cf. also the two volumes on the necessary role of world religions in constructing a new world order: *Food/Energy and the Major Faiths* (cf. n. 17) and *World Faiths and the New World Order* (ed. Joseph Gremillion and William Ryan; Washington, DC: Interreligious Peace Colloquium, 1978).

[19] Ralph Wendell Burhoe, "The Source of Civilization in the Natural Selection of Coadapted Information in Genes and Cultures," *Zygon* 11 (1976) 263-303; idem, "Religions' Role in Human Evolution: The Missing Link Between Ape-Man's Selfish Genes and Civilized Altruism," *Zygon* 14 (1979) 135-62; Donald T. Campbell, "On the Conflicts Between Biological and Social Evolution and Between Psychology and Moral Tradition," *Zygon* 11 (1976) 167-208.

[20] *Food/Energy and the Major Faiths*, viii.

[21] Wilfred Cantwell Smith, "Mankind's Religiously Divided History Approaches Self-Consciousness," p. 113 in *Religious Diversity*.

[22] Raimundo Panikkar, *The Intrareligious Dialogue* (New York: Paulist, 1978); *Guidelines on Dialogue with People of Living Faiths and Ideologies* (Geneva: World Council of Churches, 1979); *Truth and Dialogue in World Religions: Conflicting Truth Claims* (ed. John Hick; Philadelphia: Westminster, 1974); *Christianity and Other Religions* (ed. John Hick and Brian Hebblethwaite; Philadelphia: Fortress, 1981).

[23] Panikkar, *The Intrareligious Dialogue*, 25-52; Mircea Eliade, "Crisis and Renewal," pp. 54-71 in *The Quest: History and Meaning in Religion* (Chicago: University of Chicago, 1969); W. C. Smith, "Comparative Religion: Whither--and Why?," pp. 138-57 in *Religious Diversity*.

[24] Panikkar, *The Intrareligious Dialogue*, 50; cf. also 40-44.

[25] W. C. Smith, *Towards a World Theology*, Chapter 6, esp. 111, 125-26.

[26] Thomas Merton, *The Asian Journal of Thomas Merton* (New York: New Directions, 1975) 311, 315.

[27] Frithjof Schuon, *The Transcendent Unity of Religions* (New York: Harper & Row, 1975) xxvii-xxxiii, 31-56.

[28] Panikkar, "The Myth of Pluralism," 193-94; idem, *Myth, Faith and Hermeneutics*, 336-48.

[29] Raimundo Panikkar, *The Vedic Experience--Mantramanjari* (Berkeley: University of California, 1977); cf. also his "Sunahsepa: A Myth of the Human Condition," pp. 97-184 in *Myth, Faith and History*.

[30] John Dunne, *The Way of All the Earth* (New York: Macmillan, 1972) 53, emphasis mine.

[31] David Tracy, *The Analogical Imagination* (New York: Crossroads, 1981).

[32] Ibid., 113-15; cf. also 115-24.

[33]Ibid., 173-74.

[34]Ibid., 449.

[35]Ibid., 451.

[36]Panikkar, "The Myth of Pluralism," 226.

[37]Wilfred Cantwell Smith, *The Faith of Other Men* (New York: Harper & Row, 1972) 80; cf. also John A.T. Robinson's case that all religious truth claims are essentially "two-eyed" or di-polar in *Truth is Two-Eyed* (Philadelphia: Westminster, 1979).

LIBERATION AND METHOD:
THE ANALECTICAL METHOD OF ENRIQUE DUSSEL

Roberto S. Goizueta

A number of North American theologians have become increasingly critical of Latin American liberation theology. Two of
their most common criticisms concern its methodology. They charge
that liberation theology effects an uncritical assimilation of
Marxism and that, as a consequence of this methodological naiveté,
fails to rise to the level of genuine "theology"; that is to say,
it is more "witness" than truly critical reflection.[1] Such blan-
ket critiques often betray a superficial and incomplete knowledge
of the relevant material. By and large, the North American understanding of liberation theology has been hampered by the inaccess-
ibility of many significant works in that field to those who do
not read Spanish. Many of the more technical and specifically
methodological works of, among others, Raúl Vidales, Leonardo and
Clodovis Boff, José Croatto, Juan Carlos Scannone, and Enrique
Dussel have yet to appear in English translation.[2]

In this paper we hope to bring to light but one example of a
major methodological work which has yet to be published in English.
That work is Dussel's *Método para una filosofía de la liberación:
Superación analéctica de la dialéctica hegeliana.*[3] Our aim will
not be to evaluate the success or failure of Dussel's enterprise
by applying external criteria, but rather simply to lay out his
argument and allow it to confront us as one attempt to develop a
critical methodology which, far from settling for an undifferentiated appropriation of one or another ideological "system," seeks
ultimately to go beyond such systems insofar as they limit our
alternatives.

Dussel calls his method "analectical" because it moves beyond
(*aná-*) the dialectical method. As such, he maintains, the analectical method represents a movement toward a truly liberating mediation of the Latin American historical experience. Implicit in
this movement is an openness to the voice of the historical "Other,"
that is, the voice of those victims of history whose experience has
been excluded from the dominant Eurocentered understanding of human
experience. Dussel argues that the dialectical tradition within
European philosophy closes itself off from the Other by imposing
its own conceptualistic framework on *all* of history, thereby blinding itself to the experience of the historical victims of European
culture, such as the Latin American people. He maintains that the

voice of the victims of history will be heard only if it is heard
as the "Other" which is always, to some extent, beyond our concep-
tual grasp. We can never "see" the Other; we can only "hear" him
or her indistinctly. For this to happen, the totalizing concept
must give way to the symbolic imagination in a historical commitment to listen for, and serve, the Other. Only then can one be
open to the *novelty* of the Other. Dussel's method represents,
therefore, a recognition of the totalitarian tendencies inherent
in the rational *logos* and an option for a more open-ended hermeneutical model, one which would always be open to revelations from
outside its own Totality. Thus his method moves toward symbol and
away from concept as the central hermeneutical cipher.

While rejecting the totalitarian tendencies of the *logos*-
oriented dialectical tradition, Dussel does not--and, as he
readily admits, cannot--reject the tradition as a whole. In attempting to go beyond European dialectics he critically appropriates the European tradition in his own project. In *Método para
una filosofía de la liberación* he adroitly weaves his way through
the history of philosophy, commenting on the notion of "dialectic"
and its corollary, the "totalized Totality," as these have been
employed methodologically by great thinkers from the Greeks to the
present. He shows how the dialectic, which in Aristotle was
grounded in the "everyday," becomes increasingly ego-centered.
Beginning with Descartes the dialectic becomes internalized in the
ego, which itself comes to be seen as the measure of all things.
As a consequence, the everyday world is idealized.

With Hegel the ego achieves even greater comprehensiveness in
its self-constituting drive towards absolute self-knowledge. Here
the ego is no longer merely the measure of all things, but, as the
absolute, *is* all things insofar as the totalizing ego embraces all
entities in its drive towards absolute self-consciousness. The
ego would then--at the point of absolute self-consciousness--be
revealed to itself as the all-encompassing monad beyond which no
being exists.

While clearly critical of the conceptualism and egocentrism
characteristic of Hegel's thought--and later reflected in some of
the writings of post-Hegelian philosophers--Dussel does discover,
in some of the post-Hegelians, a movement away from the involuted
Hegelian dialectic and towards a more open dialectic. It is to
these post-Hegelians that he looks, therefore, to find some in-
spiration for his own work. Consequently, Dussel's intricate and
dense discussions of the European philosophers serve to illuminate

the development of his own method which, as creative as it is, does not take shape in an historical vacuum.

He devotes the second part of his book to an elaboration on his method. It is this second part which is the focal point of the book. In order to provide an adequate framework within which to set forth Dussel's analectical method, therefore, we will begin, as Dussel himself does, with a discussion of the European dialectical tradition. Then, in the second part of the paper, we will look at his analectical method.

I. Dussel's Commentary on "Dialectic" and the "Totalized Totality"

According to Dussel, the dialectical method is, in Aristotle, "a method or primary path which, originating in the everyday, opens itself to the fundamental: to being" (30). It is "the art of *dis-covery* or of the truth of being: it is a *dis-covering* of what is covered" (19). Starting from the *a priori factum*, the everyday, the Aristotelian dialectical method moves towards that which can be neither fully comprehended nor described. That which it seeks to grasp can only be understood existentially and, then, only negatively, "by a demonstration of that which is in the 'everyday' and by the impossibility of the 'everyday' being its opposite at the same time, that is, of its being what-it-is-not" (30).

Consequently, dialectics precedes and underlies all demonstrative, apodictic, or scientific knowledge by negating the absolutized everyday and bursting through the world of naive reality. For Aristotle—and in contradistinction to Plato, for whom dialectics is the ultimate, or final form of knowledge—it is a pre-philosophical and pre-scientific attitude which belongs more to the realm of wisdom than to that of knowledge and, as such, undergirds all forms of knowledge, at least normatively or prescriptively (27-29).

Originating in the everyday, dialectics demonstrates those principles which then become scientific axioms, the primary one being that of the impossibility of self-contradiction: something cannot be and not-be simultaneously. Thus, Aristotelian dialectics echoes the words of Parmenides: "being is, non-being is not," and "thinking is the same as being" (31). Dialectical thinking enunciates the oneness of reality. What lies outside that oneness or Totality is non-being. The identification of reality with being is thus already beginning to point towards a concomitant

identification of the Other (i.e., that which lies outside the
oneness of reality) with un-reality, or non-being.

This tendency increases as dialectics becomes increasingly
ego-centered in later European thought. In the modern era the
dialectical method will take as its starting point, not the
"facticity of existential understanding," but rather the rejection
of that very facticity in order to turn inward to consciousness-
as-subjectivity (33).

In Descartes, for instance, the everyday is rejected as incapable of yielding certitude; thus, the direction of the dialectic is definitively changed so that now it moves, not outward
"towards being (which 'im-poses' itself)," but inward "towards
consciousness (which poses being)" (34). This involuted dialectic
begins, then, by denying everyday facticity in order to ground itself in the *cogito* which is both its beginning and end, thereby
completely immanentizing the dialectic and necessarily idealizing
the everyday world. More importantly, in the Cartesian *ego cogito*
the *ego* is totalized and becomes the forerunner of Kant's *ich denke*
and Marx's *ich arbeite* (34, 36, 265).

Some years later, Kant develops a more sophisticated version
of the involuted dialectic. For him all reason is intrinsically
dialectical inasmuch as it is contradictory in itself. The goal
of the dialectical method thus becomes that of demonstrating "the
impossibility of the positive use of reason" (38). The dialectic
as positive is grounded in its own negativity. Given this, Kant
then goes beyond Descartes by enlarging the dialectical circle to
include praxis as well as theory.

> The dialectical movement [according to Kant] originates
> with the sensorial and concludes with the "I think."
> The deduction begins from the "I think": the "I think"
> is definitively conceived of as a free subject....The I
> is active. The *Critique of Practical Reason* closes
> the circle by indicating how the individual alters the
> empirical through moral action. (41)

At the point where Kant employs dialectics to posit the impossibility of a system of pure reason, J. G. Fichte comes in to
uncover what he sees as a latent system within Kant's own thought
and further develops a dialectic which finds its starting point in
pure, infinite, and unconditioned subjectivity. It is this subjectivity, Dussel asserts, which Fichte sees as underlying all of
Kant's thought. Based in this subjectivity, Fichte's dialectic
moves through a process of idealistic abstraction to a knowledge
(*contra* Kant) of things in themselves, but only within a dialectic

that remains thoroughly immanent and anchored in the absolute I,
the "I am I," the "I am I-ness" (*Ichheit*). This I is a pure *act*
of consciousness and, as such, is capable of embracing both the
infinite and finite, something impossible for a dialectic (e.g.,
Aristotle's) grounded in the everyday, the world of *Sein*--or so
opines Fichte (43, 48).

In the second state of Fichte's dialectic, the pure I is
diminished by coming into contact with the "not-I," which opposes
itself to the absolute I, conditioning it, and setting the stage
for the negation of the negation, namely, the reestablishment of
the absolute. This entire movement is immanent within consciousness and is, in fact, that immanence's own auto-development.
Fichte's thought thus marks the triumph of absolute idealism and
of the principle of identity (51, 52).

Drawing on Fichte, the young Schelling further develops the
dialectic by including within it the dialectics of nature. The
universe now becomes absolute. Everything originates in oneness
and returns to oneness (54-55). What is more important, the absolute I now knows itself as an act of pure consciousness, *but* the
not-I, because superfluous, disappears, thus completing the imma-
nentization of the dialectic begun with Descartes.

> From the thing *known* in Descartes' idea, one moves on to
> the thing *believed* by Kant, from there to its disappear-
> ance in the purely antithetical not-I interior to the I,
> to its annihilation even as not-I in the pure immanence
> of the absolute I, which knows itself as autoconsciousness
> [*autoconciencia*]. The involution is complete. (56)

In contrast to Kant's negative dialectic, Hegel's is a positive dialectic which is seen as yielding the highest form of
knowledge, though this by means of negation (38). For Hegel, the
task of dialectics is to discover that fundamental unity, the absolute, which is prior to the apparent contradictions given by our
understanding and which, through its dialectical movement, will
ultimately eliminate those contradictions. Our understanding, as
an inferior faculty, tends to crystallize and absolutize the apparent opposites (72-73, 112).

In positing the starting point of his dialectics, Hegel re-
covers the everyday facticity of Aristotle, though only to negate
it, not in order to locate it in the transcendent, but in order to
attain an involuted Totality (77). In this negation, argues Dussel,
what is negated is "merely natural consciousness"; thus the point
of departure is "non-coincident consciousness" (77, 80). The negation is itself in turn negated in the dialectical drive towards

total coincidence, i.e., the absolute. Coincident consciousness,
as the suppression of all non-consciousness, reaches its climax at
that point where all possibilities of novelty are exhausted, in
the totalized Totality, which point is simply a return to the
genetic absolute. The dialectical process is thus a progressive
involution of an initial and final *Totality* which is, nevertheless,
always *becoming* totalized intra-subjectively (80-93).

This dialectical movement is not merely a logical method, but
is "the real process of consciousness, of the spirit as humanity,
as absolute: God as subject" (84). As such, Dussel contends, it
comprehends both knowing and being and identifies them with each
other. The thinking-being of Parmenides and Aristotle is now retrieved, yet in a more radical way, inasmuch as for Hegel that
identity does not simply equate "thing" with "object," and these
with "thinking," but rather posits that the "entity, the thing as
thing, or the object as such...is the very thinking of them" (90).
The essence of an object *is* its actuality as concept. The subject-
object dualism is thereby collapsed.

One of the key critiques of Hegelian dialectics is that put
forth by the mature Schelling. He accuses Hegel of confusing ontology with logic, reality with mere possibility, which accusation
paves the way for an opening up of the dialectic--a dialectic that
for Hegel, as we have seen, is being's internal process of negating
itself in the form of conditioned entities and then negating these
negations--towards a new and more expansive dialectical horizon of
being, thereby reaching the positive itself. Though never developing it into an explicit methodology, Schelling thus proposes a
"beyond-being," hence initiating a new philosophical era. The
idea-as-God has now been challenged. Beyond the idea, beyond reason, there is the person: "The person seeks out the person"
(Schelling in Dussel, 125). Beyond the science of reason there is
the real exteriority experienced in mythology, etc. as positive
revelation, a real existence experienceable *a posteriori*. The involuted dialectic of Hegel is now directed *outward* (121-27). This
re-direction of the dialectic, Dussel argues, represents a major
advance because it recognizes the possibility of revelation from
outside the dialectical ontology of being as thinking.

Schelling's critique of Hegel is followed by Feuerbach's
critique, which takes two tacks: (1) Hegel's dialectic is exclusively temporal, thus not allowing for that *spatial* dimension
which alone makes the notion of "coexistence" intelligible over
and above that of "succession"; (2) that dialectic represents the

"absolute auto-alienation of reason" inasmuch as the dialectical
process prescinds from sense experience. Feuerbach then moves to
his famous rejection of God, which God--the only one possible for
him in his historical situation--is the inherited Hegelian God of
the absolute auto-alienation of reason. Having rejected Hegel's
divinized ontology, Feuerbach then looks outward from the dialectic, from the Totality, and beyond the Totality finds the sensori-
al, material, spatial. For him, philosophy must return to the
factum as the starting point, not to negate it, but to implant itself in it. With Feuerbach philosophy is again brought down to
earth. It becomes anthropological. The fundamental philosophical material is now not the purely rational, but the human, and
the rational only insofar as it is human (129-36). According to
Dussel, this rejection of the Hegelian God of the Totality leads,
then, to a recognition of the primacy of the human as concrete
existence.

Feuerbach's critique of Hegel is superseded, however, by Karl
Marx. Marx's dialectics, though inspired by the Hegelian dialectical *form*, gives that form a new content: the history of the
forces of production (137).[4] Like Feuerbach, he rejects the
Hegelian intra-rational definition of reality, but, *contra* Feuerbach, identifies the real not with materiality as such, but with
materiality as "that which is produced."

> For Hegel reality is thinking and what is thought;
> Schelling proposes to go beyond the ontology of the
> identity of being and thinking and discovers the trans-
> versality of revelation; Feuerbach goes beyond the
> ontology of being as thinking, opening himself up to
> the ambit of sensoriality, affectivity, the I-thou,
> person-person relationship. Now Marx goes beyond the
> Feuerbachian ambit...describing the real as the pro-
> duced, the labored upon; and the abstract I-thou,
> person-person relationship as that of master (capi-
> talist), exploited.... (139)

Marx thus supersedes Feuerbach's passive anthropology and, by dis-
covering the significance of the forces of production, the economic
base of history, Marx is consequently able to develop the notion of
ideology and to posit the ideological conditioning of philosophy
(144). That conditioned knowledge, moreover, "re-presents reality
but neither identifies itself with nor is an *a priori* of that real
historical reality" (145).

Yet, despite the Marxian reconceptualization of the Hegelian
dialectic, the ontological category of the totalized Totality remains intact. The bourgeois Totality already contains within itself, as a negation, the proletariat; thus the dialectical future

is simply a development of the potentiality *internal* to the bourgeois Totality. Furthermore, as a corollary of his inability to
go beyond the Totality, Marx is also unable to fully supersede the
category of "nation" as his analytical horizon. He is thus incapable of adequately appreciating the position of, for instance,
the Third World (as it is now called) as *outside* of history and as
comprised of cultures "distinct" from European cultures (148).

     After Marx, as Dussel sees it, the ongoing critique of Hegel
takes on a heightened metaphysical sense in the thought of Kierkegaard (149). The Danish philosopher accuses Hegel of a gnostic
reification of reason, and thus of a modern form of paganism.
Such, he goes on, is the paganism that characterizes Christendom.
For Kierkegaard individual existence, Hegel's negation of the Totality, cannot be captured by the idea (recall Kant and Schelling)
and is completely distinct from it. That existence is the ultimate
measure of the individual's stance vis-à-vis the revelatory Other
who lies outside the realm of reason, which stance cannot be rational or speculative, but only existential (149-54).

     The return to the everyday is continued in the thought of
Edmund Husserl and Martin Heidegger, but now in the respective
contexts of the phenomenological subjectivity and the existential
Dasein (the latter being reminiscent of Kierkegaard's philosophy).
With Heidegger the dialectic originates in the *factum* but, rather
than turn inward, moves out through intermediate horizons towards
the ultimate ontological horizon of being which is the foundation
of the ontic and intramundane, there to affirm the *factum*. The
existentiell everyday is transcended by the *existential* dialectical thrust towards the horizon of being beyond all subjectivity.
Yet that ultimate horizon remains onto-logical and, as such, comprehends (as in *légein*) the entire process, imposing itself on
what it comprehends, and thus, because *existential*, revealing the
finiteness of the human person (157-62).

     According to Dussel, Heidegger's notion of the ultimate hori-
zon is further developed by Sartre, who employs it to critique
Hegel's totalized Totality. For Sartre, the horizon precludes any
such totalized Totality since the dialectic--and history--must
always remain open-ended. One cannot situate oneself, as Hegel
does, at the end of history, for history is still in progress; to
do so would be to succumb to the idealism of the identity of
thought and being. The interminability of the dialectic and the
continuous movement of the horizon are precisely the sources of
the anxiety caused when the intrinsically untotalized person either

believes himself totalized or else ceases to reach towards that
totalization, which, to his frustration, is unattainable (164-67).

The philosophical scope of Sartre's interminable dialectic is
later extended by the Spanish existentialist, Xavier Zubiri, to
include the biological dialectic: physico-biological reality, in
its continuous evolution, always exceeds and never exhausts our
ability to understand it (169). Our understanding of that reality
is always "finite, progressive, and dialectic" (170).

After Zubiri the next, and last, key alteration of the dialectic, and one which will be essential to the development of
Dussel's Latin American liberative methodology, is Levinas' threefold discovery that: (1) underlying the entire European philosophical tradition is the Greek notion of being as "what-is-seen"
(*idein* = "to see"); (2) the I-thou relationship, where the thou is
absolutely other, is based on language; and (3) therefore, reality
is "what-is-heard" from afar, issuing from a being who is not em-
braced by *my* Totality and who reveals himself in his *word* (171-72).
This dialectic would be liberating in that it would not subordinate
the entity to being, which subordination (as in Heidegger) would
prove fatal to those entities that refuse to yield to the dictates
of reason (172).

For Levinas, "what-is-seen" is mere appearance; "what-is-
heard" is the truly expressive and always mysterious word, a word
that is never fully internalized (172). Whereas the relationship
of what-is-seen to the seer is wholly impersonal, the relationship
of the speaker to the listener is grounded in the interpersonal
justice characterized by the latter's ability to facilitate the
former's self-expression, a self-expression in which, "without
reciprocity, the person presents himself as *unique*" (Levinas in
Dussel, 173).

The ultimate consequence of being-as-"what-is-seen" is violence, for, as Dussel maintains, what-is-seen is already included
within *my* system; but being-as-"what-is-heard" demands that the
Other be respected as always "other." A new exteriority now
raises its head beyond my horizon, demands that it be respected as
other than me, and reveals its own history. The what-is-heard is
the mystery towards which the dialectic moves but to which it will
never be able to extend as a totalizing force. The speaker will
forever be distinct from the listener and, as such, will be a
source of novelty for the latter's world, a world which, unlike
Hegel's, is not one of complete givenness (173-74).

II. The Analectical Method

While rejecting the totalitarian tendencies of the dialectical tradition, Dussel does not deny the validity of certain elements of that tradition. After examining a number of advances
made by key figures in this tradition, he incorporates them into
his own intellectual enterprise. The first of these is the mature
Schelling's "indication that beyond the dialectical ontology of
the identity of being and thinking...one finds the positivity of
the unthinkable"; that, therefore, the Other's revelation from
"outside" can be considered an "adequate and special source of
knowledge (*Erkenntnissquelle*)" (176-77). Feuerbach's work represents a further advance insofar as Feuerbach rejects the Hegelian
God of the Totality, for

> the atheism of the god of the Hegelian Totality is the
> condition of the possibility of the affirmation of a
> creator God. To reject the human person as only reason
> is to pass from possibility to existence; it is to re-
> discover the sensorial, corporeal, fleshly human person
> whom Descartes had denied. (178)

Dussel also recognizes the following as positive developments:
Marx's critique of Feuerbach's passive materialism, Kierkegaard's
theological notion of the Other who cannot be comprehended except
as the incomprehensible, and the whole scope of Levinas' thought,
though still exclusively European and ambiguous (176-81).

At this point Dussel begins his own attempt to elaborate a
method which will be genuinely liberating and Latin American. His
entire enterprise is an attempt to rediscover the Other not as
Levinas' ambiguous "*absolutely* other," but as the Other which is
represented in the faces of the poor of the Third World, the Other
which "is Latin America with respect to the European Totality,
...the Latin American poor and oppressed with respect to the dominant oligarchies..." (181-82).

The only method that will adequately account for the Other,
asserts Dussel, is what he calls the "analectical method" (*el método analéctico*). Such a method would subordinate the Greek *lógos*
(which carries with it the univocal and thus totalizing sense of
"collecting" or "defining") to the Hebrew word which it translates
(*dabar*) and which carries the plurivocal sense of "dialogue" or
"revelation" (it being no mere coincidence, then, that the Semites
were the first to truly develop the notion of "the Other") (184-85,
205).

The analectical method goes further than, a level beyond
(*aná-*), the *dia*-lectical method. It goes beyond the dialectical

Totality and asserts the freedom of the Other, taking as its
starting point the Other's word, and, with confidence in that
word, "laboring, working, serving, and creating....The face of the
Other is an *anâ-logos*; it is already the first and supreme word"
(182). The analectic serves the Other (and thus, derivatively--
and *only* derivatively--itself), while the dialectic as such serves
only itself.

> The dia-lectical method is the dominating expansion of
> the Totality *from itself*; the passage of "the same" from
> potency to act. The ana-lectical method is the passage
> to the just growth of the Totality *from the Other* and
> in order to "serve him" (the Other) creatively. (182)

The analectic does not merely place the Same and the Other
face-to-face; it also makes the concrete demand that a worker-
creator ("beyond, but assuming, the work that derives from 'necessity' in Marx") be placed at the service of the Other.

> The anthropological analectic is then economic (putting
> nature at the service of the Other), erotic, and politi-
> cal. The Other is never "one alone" but fleetingly,
> also and always "you all." Each countenance in the
> face-to-face is equally the epiphany of a family, a
> class, a people, an epoch of humankind and of humankind
> itself as a whole, and, what is more, of the absolute
> Other. (182)

For the Latin American philosopher and theologian this means
that his "material" will be the anthropological, economic, and
political significance of the Latin American Other: "We say it
sincerely and simply: the countenance of the poor dominated Indian,
of the oppressed mestizo, of the Latin American people is the
'theme' of Latin American philosophy" (182). This philosophy will
be the first to overcome that Europeanism which none of the previ-
ously discussed philosophies has been able to transcend (182-83).

Having thus adumbrated the task of the analectical method,
Dussel goes on to describe its five moments. Philosophical discourse "originates in the everyday" and moves both "dialectically
and ontologically" towards the Totality. Secondly, it provides a
demonstration of the existential possibilities of the entities
beyond their mere identification with thinking (183).

The third stage is the properly analectical in that it represents the point at which one recognizes that the ontic Other cannot be encompassed within the Totality. In this sense, then, the
analectic is negative (183). It is also, however, positive in
that "one thinks of the possibility of interpreting the Other's
revelation from the perspective of the Other" (183).

The Other-as-revealed presents itself as a fourth moment, in that the revelation from outside the Totality has allowed the primary negativity of the Other to question the new, externally-created ontological level. As the discourse enters the realm of ethics, "the fundamental ontological level is discovered as not primary" (183). (One discovers that empathy *is* possible.)

Finally, in the fifth moment, the newly established ethical foundation becomes the catalyst for and judge of the same ontic level of possibilities, which possibilities "as analectical praxis go beyond the ontological order and advance as 'service' in justice" (183). Philosophical discourse hence becomes intrinsically ethical and empathic.

Once we place ourselves face-to-face with the Other as Other we have made a moral commitment, one which implies a denial of our Totality as Totality and an openness to the Other's word: "in this case the philosopher, before being an intelligent person, is an ethically just person; a good person; a disciple" (183). He or she must learn to listen, in order to learn to interpret, in order to learn to serve (184).

The philosopher is able to listen, interpret (though as yet only imperfectly, since the Other is in fact "Other"), and serve only because the Other confronts him, not as *totally* different, but as distinct, as analogue. The analogy referred to here, Dussel points out, is not the *analogia entis*, but the analogy of "being itself"; thus the *entis*, as an expression of being, is doubly analogous. Being itself, as the foundation of the Totality, is no longer the only way to posit being, because now being-as-beyond-the-Totality is an analogue to being-as-the-fundament-of-the-Totality. Consequently, what is outside is neither completely different from nor identical with what is inside; it is *similar*. This similarity both makes possible an as yet imperfect, imprecise, and approximate interpretation of the Other's word and precludes complete comprehension, while at the same time being a condition of the possibility of the acceptance of that word as true through "con-*fide*nce, faith, in the Other: 'because he says so.'"

> To be able to commit oneself on the basis of a *believed* word is...a creative act which travels above the horizon of the All and advances, *on the word* of the Other in novelty. (187-91)

The movement initiated by the philosopher's commitment, the confident advance made possible by the acceptance of the Other's word, leads to that liberative praxis which

> accedes to a new Totality in justice; only then does one arrive at a certain analogical identity...from which,

> only now, the word that was previously understood impre-
> cisely...reaches the possibility of an adequate inter-
> pretation. (192)

As the condition of the possibility of this liberative process,
however, the philosopher must, insists Dussel, know how and where
to place himself so that the Other's revelatory word may be
interpreted correctly.

The liberative process involving listening and interpretation
is also ongoing. The word which the Other, as person (*per-sonare*:
that which makes sounds, not that which is seen), spoke yesterday
is today a dead letter, therefore any philosophy that grounds itself in that word will forever be "remembering." Those who advance
such a philosophy

> forget that philosophy is primarily a listening to the
> historical voice of the poor, the people; a commitment
> to that word; an unblocking or annihilation of the old
> Totality as one and eternal; the taking of a risk in
> beginning to speak what is new.... (193)

Human history is itself nothing but this recurrent movement from
listening, to interpretation, to action; which movement represents
a continuous expansion of our everyday world (193, 270).

* * * * * * *

As the expression of this historical process, philosophy is
then primarily pedagogical: the philosopher begins as disciple
that he may become teacher in the future, which role will again
require discipleship, and so on (194). The philosopher's original discipleship (i.e., his confidence in the word of those whom
European philosophy and society would consider his disciples, his
students) is the condition of the possibility of actually being a
philosopher. In advancing from that origin-al stance in the movement described above, the philosopher participates in the liberation not only of the Other but also of himself. Without that
initial stance, the philosopher becomes a master in the worst
sense of the word. There is no middle ground here: either the
philosopher becomes a disciple, or his students (in both the society at large and the classroom) will be relegated to the status
of slaves.

Any philosophy that considers itself "above" such a listening
process will claim for itself a universality that it does not have
and, in the meantime, will crush those who exist outside that
"universality." For Dussel the emergence of a philosophy of the
oppressed peoples, of international human liberation, signals the
end of Europe's (and her North American and Russian extensions')

"pretended universality" (196-97). The new philosophy will indeed
be "universal," but not in the univocal Hegelian sense; rather, in
the sense of an

> analogical humanity, where each person, each people or
> nation, each culture, can express itself in the analogical
> universality, which is neither an abstract universality
> (totalitarianism of an abusively universalized particu-
> larism) nor a concrete universality (univocal consummation
> of domination). (196)

Within the historical movement, Dussel finds four different
levels: (1) the dialectics of nature, (2) the historical analectic
as such, (3) the dialectical method as fundamental ontology, and
(4) the analectical method itself. The first level involves historical and ongoing evolutionary ontogenesis. The second level is
the real and human analectic itself, which is an ongoing demonstration of the fact that the human individual "never has a final ontological horizon of comprehension in his existential or everyday
life" (200). The third level, the dialectical method, follows the
first two because theory can never exhaust reality. At this level
one is again confronted by one's finiteness and, hence, by one's
inability to become a totalized Totality.

> Not starting from the absolute, which we are not, but
> rather from the *finiteness* which we are, the human in-
> dividual understands himself as projected towards a
> possibility-of-being that includes essentially a
> possibility-of-not-being: his future as realization or
> frustration. (201)

As such, the dialectical method has two key moments: (1) the "negation of the apparent security of the obvious everyday world"; and
(2) the ongoing attempt to comprehend what is being progressively
revealed in each horizon (201-202). At the dialectical level,
then, the conceptualized All is reimplanted "as transcendence in
the preconceptual All which is both com-prehended and future" (202).

This dialectical level of the historical liberative movement
poses two options for Latin Americans. First, some would opt for
no method at all, instead ardently defending the status quo. The
dialectical level would force these people into a crisis of skep-
ticism in order to "open them to new historical horizons" (203).
Secondly, others have already adopted interpretative systems and
look to dialectics for a method of explaining revolutionary change,
without however "being careful to clearly posit the *conditions of
the possibility* of such a method, and without even imagining the
possibility of its being superseded" (203). For Latin Americans,
the condition of the possibility is, at the very least, a thorough

knowledge and appreciation of the Latin American historical experience (203). It is at this point that Marxism, according to Dussel (citing Sartre), falls short. By resorting to the use of abstract universals (e.g., "the universal class") and making symbols of concrete individuals and circumstances Marxism eventually winds up suppressing the very people it wants to help.

Finally, at the fourth level of the historical movement is the analectical method itself, encompassing the dialectical method, but going beyond it to encompass a liberative dimension as well. The superiority of the analectical method over the merely dialectical thus makes possible a new method for philosophy and all the human sciences (204).

The analectical method offers a clearer insight, for instance, into theological and scriptural questions. It can enable us to see, for example, how the biblical stories which explain the origins of evil in the world really point to one "original sin."

> Cain killed Abel and when Cain killed Abel he could not but become closed in upon himself, become the one and only; that is the only human sin: to kill one's brother. When he killed his brother he committed "the" sin, which is explained in the Adam myth. The serpent is "the Other which tempts," nothing more than "the Other" which tempts. "The Other" which tempts proposes to Adam that he be like God; in order to be God one has to be the Totality and in order to be the Totality one has to be alone. In order to become God it would be necessary to kill the Other....The "death of God" begins with the death of the brother. (271-72)

This original sin then affects all human beings in that every child finds himself in a world--the horizon of being in which the child understands whatever he confronts--that has been denying the Other, killing the Other, in many different ways; therefore, that evil, that original sin, becomes a part of every individual's understanding of being. The person who, therefore, becomes open to the word of the Other and loves him as the Other is the prophet, who will inevitably die as a martyr at the hands of the Totality. The prophet's *conversion to* the Other will always be viciously counteracted by the Totality's *aversion from* the Other (272-74).

                          * * * * * * *

Dussel's exposition of the relationship between the dominant and the dominated then moves to a discussion of the levels at which the relationship may be considered paradigmatically, and the ways in which these levels may be altered as a means of overcoming the oppressive relationship. Dussel defines three such levels: (1) the erotic (man/woman, where the revelatory word may be "I love you"); (2) the pedagogical (parent/child, where the revelatory word may be "Child, obey me"); and (3) the political (brothers and sisters, where the revelatory word may be "I have a right to a just wage") (189).

In patriarchal societies the erotic level has been manifested in the domination of the woman by the man, the woman being the Other in this case. The woman lies outside the Totality of the man. The man/woman bipolarity can only be superseded by positing the possibility of existence beyond the bipolarity, so that the dualism may be truly overcome rather than merely reversed (as some feminists would have it). To a certain extent, Marx's classless society also represents an attempt to attain liberation for the Other only within the dualism, rather than beyond it. For true liberation we must look to a third ambit, beyond those of the bipolarity (275-76).

In this third ambit the man/woman paradigm would be better expressed in the term "the couple." As the couple, they would recreate a common interest in the context of *eros*, being nevertheless careful to remain always open (277).

Within the erotic relationship there then arises something new, a child, and the second level is entered. This child is not, however, the Platonic child "who is 'the Same' as the parents, but rather the child who is truly Other" (277). Once the parents discover the child's otherness they are forced to respect him and to develop a new pedagogy (e.g., Paulo Freire's), so that the *new* child will be able to teach the parents as well as learn from them. The parents, the "teachers," give the child only the "form," "in the sense that they do not give *being* to the Other but rather the ability to think about what already is" (277). The parents cannot tell the child what he is; the *child* must tell *them*. In the new parent-child, or teacher-student, relationship the idea of the disciple as a depository in which "knowledge" is inserted, memorized, and then simply "remembered" (a paradigm common to the Platonic pedagogy and the Hegelian and Heideggerian ontologies) would be replaced by one in which the teacher or parent assumes the role of the "creative nothing" (277-78).

In this new mutuality the parents and children form a new Totality: the home. Ontologically, the house becomes an extension of the body, the door, for instance, being "that by which the home is opened or closed to the Other" (278). As such, however, the home is in danger of becoming simply another Totality closed in upon itself, with the house, furniture, etc. being identified as

"possessions" that are as truly a part of the family as are the
parents and children themselves: the house becomes part of the
very being of the family members, who then exclude the Other from
it as surely and instinctively as they would defend themselves
against physical violence (278-79).

When the family remains open to other families, however, it
enters into a third level at which the dominant/dominated relationship may be overcome. At this level each family treats all
other families with love and respect. When one leaves one's house
one does so to go out to others, to serve them, not to dominate
them by attempting to bring their homes within the ambit of one's
own. Yet even this relationship of mutual respect is always in
danger of becoming closed in upon itself in the name of, for instance, nationalism (279).

It is at this level, the international level, that Dussel
discusses the concrete situation of Latin America vis-à-vis Europe,
the United States, and the Soviet Union, and shows how the aliena-
tion/liberation dialectic acquires a specifically Latin American,
or Third World, sense. A genuinely Latin American liberation, he
argues, would

> reject the ontology of Totality in which liberal capi-
> talism, modern individualism, and modern orthodox and
> European Marxism are rooted, and formulate an Other-
> oriented analectic of real novelty...so that we may
> clear a path beyond capitalism, towards a socialism
> which will define itself as Latin American, a social-
> ism which we are beginning to conceive of, and enun-
> ciate. (279)

The Latin American analectic would have to be grounded in the
Latin American colonial experience. Latin America was born precisely as the bipolar Other which was oppressed by its European
masters in their attempt to re-create the European historical
project and experience in the "new" setting. Europe then became
the reference point for Latin American self-identity, without
which reference point Latin America would simply fade into nothingness (or so thought the Europeans and the Europeanized Latin Americans). As the European shackles are broken Latin America enters
into the process of discovering itself as *new*, as dis-tinct from
the very beginning. It enters into the adolescent phase of its
history (281). This pedagogical process is incomprehensible to a
Heidegger, for example, since he conceives of "being-in-the-world"
as proceeding univocally from the individual human being, at the
same time overlooking the fact that the individual's world is
given its meaning by the Other--e.g., parents, teachers, culture

(281). Only in relationship to others does one discover oneself
as new: "When I discover myself as Other from all Others, I discover myself as new" (280, 281).

As long as the Other is not new, he will be as nothing in the
eyes of the dominant Totality. This has historically been the
case in Latin America, which has been seen as nothingness vis-à-vis
the European Totality. The legendary Argentine folk hero Martín
Fierro expresses the Latin American experience with his simple
eloquence: "In my ignorance I know that I am worthless"--a worthlessness learned only from the dominant Totality (273). If the
feeling of worthlessness ever gives way, "if some day it occurs to
Fierro that he is worth something, then the war begins," a war
which is characteristic of the inherently bipolar Totality (273).

As Latin America comes of age it begins to see itself as
a people.

> "A people" is the "nation" as the totality of a histori-
> cally, geographically, and concretely given political
> and cultural system. "A people" in its strong sense is
> hegemonically and principally the oppressed and working
> classes. (226)

Here Dussel emphasizes the categorial superiority of "a people"
(though neither Hegel's *die Vielen* nor Heraclitus' *hoi polloi*)
over the Marxist category of "class." The Marxist concept of an
international proletarian class does not adequately explain either
the modern international reality of "center" and "periphery" countries, or the existence of noncapitalist countries (e.g., China)
that are apparently able to skip the capitalist phase of historical
development: "Marx's analysis can only interpret the bourgeois-
proletariat, working class-capitalist class opposition" (224).
Marx, then, cannot adequately account for either the qualitative
difference between the working classes of oppressed and oppressor
countries, or the emergence of *national* liberation movements which
arise in the context of a national culture existing outside the
bourgeois capitalist system. These realities can best be explained
by the use of the category "a people" (224-27).

The use of this category permits Dussel to uncover three sets
of oppositions that are key for Latin America today: (1) that between the oppressed and oppressor classes, (2) that between center
and periphery countries, and (3) that between the youth, or non-
establishment groups (recall the parent/child relationship), and
the bureaucratic establishment, or "gerontocracy" (225). The existence of these three levels allows for greater tactical flexibility
in the overall liberation movement, since at different times

different levels may need to be emphasized over others (225). The
long range goal, however, remains clear.

> Ultimately, strategically, what should be attained is the
> liberation of the oppressed in its strong and unequivocal
> sense; what should be procured is the liberation of the
> "working classes," be they peasantry or labor and every
> other kind of salaried worker. (225)

The analectical method demands that this triple-tiered social
liberation be progressive and that its levels be interdependent,
thus yielding a truly new system, in a way that the dialectical
method as such would not and could not.

> It is because of this that those who theoretically or
> practically use only one dialectical method in the strict
> sense cannot but propose: either a national bourgeois
> dictatorship which will ultimately join anew with the
> powers of the "center" and thus remain dependent, or an
> "unhinged radicalism"...which, analyzing everything from
> the category of "class," wants to complete, in only one
> revolution, the long and progressive stages of the lib-
> eration of the oppressed peoples.... (228)

Liberation will thus involve several interdependent stages, none
of which can, in the long run, be sacrificed if an authentically
popular and indigenous liberation is to be achieved.

Such a liberation must be born of the experience of the people.
That experience is, in turn, replete with meaning-full myths and
symbols (in Latin America, especially of a religious nature). A
Latin American liberation must therefore go beyond the reductionist
economic-political revolution of Marx to include an affirmation of
the subversive content and liberative implications of transcendent
symbols. If the liberation movement fails to embrace this transcendent dimension, the dominant classes (especially in the offi-
cially "Catholic" countries of Latin America) will surely appropriate the popular symbols for themselves and turn them into ideological tools of oppression (258).

In the final analysis, then, this Latin American liberation
will arise from "a people" whose culture is truly Other and must
embrace the entirety of that culture. This is a liberation from
outside, not from below. "Liberation from below" is the false
liberation of the dialectical Totality, where someone can rise
only if someone else falls (cf. Adam Smith, Ricardo, and Marx).
Such a reversal of positions is *ontologically* necessary in the
dialectical Totality, as Marx demonstrates when he argues that an
individual is free only when that individual is the *exclusive* de-
terminant of his or her being. I am free, according to Marx, only
when the Totality in which I exist is the Totality of "myself."

This does not allow for an otherness which will be truly other rather than merely "the Same." Consequently, the only kind of "liberation" the dialectical method can envisage is one in which the master and slave exchange places (283).

In the analectical method, on the other hand, liberation emerges not from below, but from outside, from the Other. Here, liberation is "the movement by which the otherness of the oppressed is reconstructed" (285). The Other can be liberated only in his or her otherness. The Latin American liberative project must emerge, then, from the otherness of Latin America itself. It cannot and must not be imposed from the European Totality. Yet that project, as analectic, "does not include the death of the oppressors but rather admits their conversion, because in turning to the more authentic self they can become reintegrated without having to disappear" (286). As both an indigenous and analectic project it would recognize that one should not profit at the expense of another; thus it would strive for a socialist order, but one which would be *new*, born within Latin America and therefore "*criollo*" (288). Latin American liberation will indeed be genuinely liberating only if it is genuinely Latin American, and vice versa.

Conclusion

Dussel's enterprise, as outlined above, represents both a highly nuanced and scholarly reflection on the dialectical method as confronted by the contemporary Latin American experience, and an equally nuanced attempt to set forth a method adequate to that experience. In developing his analectical method, Dussel is careful to avoid an uncritical assimilation of any body of thought, including that of Marxism. As we have seen, for instance, while accepting such Marxian philosophical advances as the critique of Feuerbachian materialism, Dussel explicitly rejects that Marxian dualism which, as a reflection of Marx's inability to escape the totalized Totality, evidences inherent totalitarian tendencies. Dussel is thus anything but reticent about attacking Marx and rejecting aspects of Marxian thought as fundamentally deficient.

Whether his critique of Marx, or of any other thinker, is warranted and accurate is beyond the scope of this paper. What we hope to have shown here is that Dussel, a prominent Latin American liberation thinker, employs a method which is both critical in general, and critical of Marxian thought specifically. As such, the method frees us from the methodological straightjacket of the

conceptualistic Totality and opens us to the possibility of
plurivocity. Though not always explicitly, Dussel moves in the
direction of a symbolic framework in which the imposition of concepts on reality is replaced by an openness to the novel in the
form of the Other.

In its groundbreaking creativity, *Método para una filosofía
de la liberación* is, finally, but one example of the richness of
the intellectual ferment taking place in Latin America today, a
richness whose roots have been tapped only minimally by North
Americans. It is our professional responsibility, as North American academicians, to explore that richness in at least as serious
and concerted a way as we have studied the great wealth of European
intellectual systems. Until we have done so, our reading of Latin
American philosophy and theology will likely remain superficial
and, what is perhaps more damaging in the long run, will continue
to be interpreted as such by our counterparts in Latin America.

NOTES

[1]See, e.g., Schubert Ogden, *Faith and Freedom: Toward a Theology of Liberation* (Nashville: Abingdon, 1979) 33-34; Michael Novak, "Theology of Liberation," *National Catholic Reporter*, 21 November 1975, p. 12.

[2]See, e.g., José Severiano Croatto, *Liberación y libertad: pautas hermenéuticas* (Buenos Aires: Ediciones Mundo Nuevo, 1973); Clodovis Boff, *Teología de lo político: Sus mediaciones* (Salamanca: Sígueme, nd); Raúl Vidales, *Cuestiones en torno al método en la teología de la liberación* (Lima: Secretariado Latinoamericano, 1974); Juan Carlos Scannone, *Teología de la liberación y praxis popular* (Salamanca: Sígueme, 1976); Enrique Dussel, *Para una ética de la liberación* (I-II, Buenos Aires, 1973; III, Mexico, 1977; IV-V, Bogotá, 1979-80); Enrique Dussel, et al., *Liberación y cautiverio: Debates en torno al método de la teología en América Latina* (Mexico City: Comité Organizador, 1975).

[3]Enrique Dussel, *Método para una filosofía de la liberación: Superación analéctica de la dialéctica hegeliana* (Salamanca: Sígueme, 1974). All page references in the paper are to this volume. The translations are mine.

[4]This idea is developed in "Marx and Hegel's Method," an unpublished essay by Joseph O'Malley.

PART II

SELF-TRANSCENDENCE IN THE SPIRITUAL LIFE:
THERESE OF LISIEUX

Joann Wolski Conn
Walter E. Conn

A recent symposium on "The Relations of the Psychological and
the Spiritual" posed the question: "Does the 'self' of the Gospels
and the 'self' of psychology refer to the same reality?" Are we
"speaking in the same universe of discourse when we commend the
self-actualization of the individual and when it is said that the
individual should deny himself and take up his cross"? Are humanistic psychology and Christian spirituality basically together,
moving in the same direction, the symposium leaders were in effect
asking, or are they at odds, pulling in opposite directions? Most
of the participants in this particular symposium were convinced
that the self of humanistic psychology and the self of Christian
spirituality are different and incompatible.[1]

Granting the difficulties of definition, the purpose of this
paper is to suggest that the dichotomy is unnecessary--that the
introduction of a *tertium quid* offers a reconciling possibility
beyond the dilemma of self-fulfillment versus self-sacrifice. Our
candidate as the *tertium quid* is self-transcendence. Our suggestion might be put in the following thesis form: Christian spiritual
life is realized in the dynamic *extreme* of self-transcendence beyond the static *means* of self-fulfillment or self-sacrifice. While
we will suggest that there are authentically human and Christian
understandings of both self-fulfillment and self-sacrifice in
terms of self-transcendence, we will claim that common understandings of these ideals are both anti-human and anti-Christian.

After brief considerations of self-fulfillment and self-
sacrifice (Part I), we will examine the reality of self-transcendence (Part II), focusing on those special instances of self-
transcendence named conversions, as highlighted in the life of
Thérèse of Lisieux (Part III).

I. Self-Fulfillment and Self-Sacrifice

Self-Fulfillment

If this is the century of the ego, as Norman Mailer suggested
some ten years ago, it might well have reached its culmination
during the seventies, the period Tom Wolfe has tagged for posterity
as the "me" decade. This was the time (and is there any reason to

think it has ended?) when self-fulfillment, self-enhancement, self-promotion, self-liberation were promoted from the paperback racks of every supermarket in America: *Looking Out for #1*, *Success!*, *How to Be Your Own Best Friend*, *Power! How to Get It*, *How to Use It*, *Your Erroneous Zones*, *Breaking Free*, *Pulling Your Own Strings*, *How to Get Whatever You Want Out of Life*, and, of course, *I'm OK--You're OK*.   Jerry Rubin may not be typical, but how many of us completely escaped the self-absorbed spirit of his testimony of search: "In five years, from 1971 to 1975, I directly experienced est, gestalt therapy, bioenergetics, rolfing, massage, jogging, health foods, tai chi, Esalen, hypnotism, modern dance, meditation, Silva Mind Control, Arica, acupuncture, sex therapy, Reichian therapy, and More House--a smorgasbord in New Consciousness."[2]

The contemporary search for self-fulfillment has recently become a favorite target of social and cultural critics.   Christopher Lasch's devastating critique of what he calls *The Culture of Narcissism* is only the best known of several attacks.[3]   Paul Vitz, in his *Psychology as Religion*, argues that humanistic psychologists Abraham Maslow, Erich Fromm, Carl Rogers, and Rollo May have supplied the theoretical justification for what he calls "The Cult of Self-Worship."[4]   And, most recently, social researcher Daniel Yankelovich points to the inherent contradiction he finds in the search for self-fulfillment--a search he characterizes as authentic grass-roots experimentation, involving in one way or another perhaps as many as eighty percent of adult Americans.   While the traditional ethic of self-denial and sacrifice has been replaced by an ethic that denies people nothing, Yankelovich found in his interviews that "many truly committed self-fulfillment seekers focus so sharply on their needs that instead of achieving the more intimate relationships they desire, they grow farther apart from others."[5]   This reflects something of "the narcissistic character disorder" of current psychiatric literature--the self-centered affliction, as Robert Coles describes it, of "one whose central, controlling ways of getting on give evidence of a strong avoidance of lasting attachments to other people, accompanied often by a hunger for just such human bonds...."[6]

Insofar as critiques of self-fulfillment are aimed at the pseudo-humanism of consumer oriented "pop psychology," they seem entirely appropriate.   For while the explicit goals of many self-fulfillment therapies appear humanistic in their interpersonal and social orientations, the implicit understanding of the person informing the starting-points of these approaches is self-destructive

in its naive individualism.   The self of "pop psychology" is essentially a bag of desires, and self-realization means fulfilling
as many of these desires as possible.   "You can never do enough
for yourself."   The pervasiveness of this view in the mass media
would be laughable if it were not tragic.   People throw themselves
into intense, self-absorbed navel gazing, runnoff in every direction (sometimes at once) to gratify their every impulse, and end
up deeply frustrated.   Yankelovich cites countless divorces and
wrongheaded career changes as part of the confusing fallout from
the very risky search for self-fulfillment.   Unfortunately, people
fail to perceive the paradoxical truth that authentic realization
of their deepest human desires occurs only when they turn their
primary attention from their own interests and desires and genuinely involve themselves in the needs and desires of others.
Everyone would be a big-game hunter in the jungle of life; to
appreciate that the prey of self-realization and happiness is lost
in the kill is a difficult lesson.

Self-Sacrifice

The "pop-psychology" of self-fulfillment, of course, is only
the latest edition of the guide for the self-seeker.   Through the
ages there have been as many versions as there are forms of self-
delusion.   And the traditional Christian response has always been
the one rooted in the Gospel injunction to renounce onself and
take up one's cross in following Jesus (Mark 8:34).

Unfortunately, the Gospel call to follow Jesus has too often
been (mis)understood as requiring the sacrifice or denial of the
self's authentic realization.   Indeed, several recent studies argue that this misinterpretation of the Gospel has been involved in
legitimating the traditional relegation of women to subordinate
roles of passive, obedient service: self-sacrifice is holy; self-
assertion is sinful.[7]   It takes the artistry of a Mary Gordon to
begin to do justice to the ambiguity of this reality.   The heroine
of her *Final Payments*, Isabel Moore, has sacrificed her young
adulthood to the care of her invalid father, and does not regret a
moment of it.   Though adolescent guilt over a discovered fling with
a boyfriend plays a key part in her relationship to her father,
Isabel looks back on her sacrifice "not with self-pity but with
extreme pride."   Gordon, in fact, sees sacrifice rooted in affec-
tion as having an immense importance in life, though she is at the
same time deeply intrigued by the phenomenon of otherwise powerful
women who suddenly buckle to the authority of a male.[8]

If a misunderstood sacrifice of self has proved devastating
for centuries in the lives of women, the effects on the preaching
of the Gospel have been equally severe, though in a less personally destructive way. For many men throughout the Western world,
Christianity is a "woman's religion." And what else can a patriarchal society expect after using a distorted Gospel to glorify
women in a state of passive, obedient subjection for so long? Beyond male and female relationships, the distortion of the Gospel
has been extended as an ideological justification to every situation of oppressive servitude. As long as this perversion of the
Gospel for the justification of oppression continues, Nietzsche's
judgment will stand: Christianity is a religion for slaves.

This is precisely the kind of interpretation of self-sacrifice
which must be rejected as anti-Christian. Jesus calls us to loving
service of the neighbor as friend, not to self-destructive servitude to a master as slave.[9] Indeed, no authentic Christian interpretation can recommend the denial or sacrifice of the self as the
conscious, creative, critical, responsible, free, and loving personal subject. Such a policy would have Jesus being followed by
an army of robots. No, to follow Jesus genuinely in his life for
others requires the commitment of the very self such sacrifice
would destroy. To follow Jesus, of course, means to live one's
life as authentically as he lived his. It has nothing to do with
being a "follower," everything to do with being a leader. A reader of the Gospels need not "psychologize" Jesus to realize that
the Christian life of creative and responsible love requires courageous assertiveness as much as realistic humility.

What, then, is an authentic Christian understanding of self-
sacrifice, if it is not the sacrifice of the self? Quite simply,
Christian self-sacrifice consists in the denial of all those
(otherwise perhaps quite legitimate) desires, wishes, and interests of the self which interfere with the singleminded commitment
to follow Jesus in love. Such commitment demands not the sacrifice of the self or its authentic realization, but the sacrifice
by the self of anything which stands in the way of loving the
neighbor (in the extreme, even the sacrifice of life itself). From
the viewpoint of Christian commitment to the neighbor and genuine
self-realization, the "to-be-filled-bag-of-desires-self" of "pop
psychology" is really a bag of snakes. The list of possible desires is endless, and particular desires are often mutually contradictory. Many of the goods sought by seekers of self-
fulfillment, of course, are not only legitimate but positively

worthwhile.   Part of the grace of the Gospel, however, is the insight that the search for such genuinely personal goods through
focusing on the self is fundamentally illusory.   Indeed, it is
precisely the renunciation of such fulfillment-seeking that allows
the possibility of authentic self-realization in a loving service
which makes no demands and draws no lines, the service to all
which Jesus calls us to join him in.

II. Self-Transcendence

If the static means of self-fulfillment and self-sacrifice,
as commonly understood, are deadly for the authentic Christian
life of loving service, a living image has been drawn from the
tradition by such contemporary theologians as Reinhold Niebuhr,
Paul Tillich, Karl Rahner, Bernard Lonergan, John Macquarrie and
David Tracy: the dynamic extreme of self-transcendence.

As an image suggestive of the authentic dynamism of the
Christian spiritual life, self-transcendence stands in total opposition to the image of self-sacrifice understood as a denial, renunciation, abnegation, repudiation, sacrifice, or other negation
of the self.   Only a self affirmed in the reality of its subjectivity, and realized in its essential potentiality for objectivity,
is capable of transcending itself.   In the simplest terms, without
a transcending self, there is no self-transcendence.   The self is
not negated through transcendence; rather, it is realized in its
authentic being.   Self-transcendence is authentic self-realization.[10]
Understood as a sacrifice of the self in its essential dynamism for
an intelligent and responsible life of loving service, the image of
self-sacrifice must be rejected by an understanding of the Gospel
in terms of self-transcendence.

At the same time, the image of self-transcendence stands firmly against any image of self-fulfillment which focuses on the self
as a collection of desires to be fulfilled.   Whatever the appearance of surface activity may be, the image of the self whose desires are to be fulfilled is essentially a passive receptacle, a
self whose happiness consists in being filled "to the brim."   Even
if this image were accurate, in a limited world of finite persons
such a self would condemn most people to anxious frustration.   The
cruel truth, of course, is that from the point of view of fulfilling desires the self is not a receptacle, but a bottomless pit.
Thus even the most talented and successful elite will find only
endless frustration in the search for self-fulfillment.   In contrast, the self implicit in the image of self-transcendence,

exactly the opposite of a passive receptacle, is a dynamic spring,
a self that is realized only in its active movement beyond itself.
Freed from the illusion of quantitative fulfillment, such a self
senses the peace of authentic realization in the very activity of
realistic knowing, responsible choosing, and genuine loving.

Like the Gospel, the image of self-transcendence suggests the
paradoxical view that authentic self-realization results not from
a self-centered effort to fulfill one's desires, but from a movement *beyond* oneself in an attempt to realize the good of others.
Indeed, such realization of the self through transcendence is a
form of self-fulfillment. But it is a fulfillment of the fundamental desire for truth, value, and love constitutive of us as
distinctively personal beings. While its fulfillment in self-
transcendence brings a sense of peaceful happiness, the very nature of this basic human desire defies any self-centered striving
for happiness through fulfillment. In fact, the fulfillment proper to the radical personal desire or drive for self-transcendence
can require that one "empty" oneself in the sense of sacrificing
the fulfillment of otherwise legitimate desires. In the ultimate
case, as we have already noted, this self-emptying can mean the
giving of one's very life for the neighbor. One will save the
life of one's true self, the Gospel makes clear, only if he or she
is ready to give up everything else, even life itself, in loving
service of the neighbor.

Though self-transcendence has been developed most extensively
as an image of authentic personhood by theologians, its reality
can be found in the works of many psychologists, most explicitly,
perhaps, in that of Victor Frankl. Frankl discusses self-
transcendence throughout his many works, but even in his early
treatment of the fundamental human dynamism, *Man's Search for
Meaning*, we find an arrestingly direct statement of one of this
paper's basic theses: "Human existence is essentially self-
transcendence rather than self-actualization. Self-actualization
is not a possible aim at all, for the simple reason that the more
a man would strive for it, the more he would miss it." For only
to the extent that a person is committed to life's meaning, Frankl
asserts, is he or she actualized. In other words, "self-
actualization cannot be attained if it is made an end in itself,
but only as a side effect of self-transcendence."[11]

Even when the reality of self-transcendence is not named as
such, it can play a central role in the interpretation of human
existence. From the particular perspective of Christian

spirituality, Henri Nouwen conveys the dynamism of the different
dimensions of self-transcendence through the image of "reaching
out." For Nouwen, the spiritual life is the relationship between
three constant movements of reaching out: to ourselves (moving
from loneliness to solitude), to others (moving from hostility to
hospitality), and to God (moving from illusion to prayer).[12]

Perhaps the most detailed and comprehensive articulation of
the image of self-transcendence is that of Bernard Lonergan. Over
the course of a professional lifetime Lonergan has attempted to
map the route of self-transcendence in its many dimensions. This
is not the place to examine his charts in detail, but a brief re-
connaissance of the main lines of Lonergan's analysis will throw
some light on our question of the role of self-transcendence in
the spiritual life.[13]

For Lonergan, self-transcendence occurs in our effective response to the radical drive, the dynamic exigence of the human
spirit for meaning, truth, value, and love. Though single in
source and ultimate goal, this questioning drive of the human
spirit manifests itself in multiple, interconnected questions: the
drive for understanding seeks meaning in questions for intelligence; but not any meaning, for once attained, meaning is critically scrutinized by the drive for truth in questions for reflection heading toward realistic judgment. And when understanding
and judgment are within a practical pattern oriented toward action,
there follows the further moral question for deliberation: given
my judgment of the situation and required action, what am *I* going
to do about it? Finally, this practical questioning oriented
toward action occurs within a matrix of affectivity which must be
strong enough to support the required action over the obstacles of
conflicting interests. What, in the last analysis, am I going to
commit myself to in love?

In this view, every achievement of creative understanding,
realistic judgment, responsible choice, and genuine love is an instance of self-transcendence. Among all the possible realizations
of human potential, such cognitive, moral, and affective self-
transcendence is the criterion of authentic self-realization. The
Gospel demand calling us to intelligent, responsible, loving service of the neighbor requires no more and no less than the fulfillment of this fundamental personal drive for self-transcendence. As
the criterion of personal authenticity, self-transcending love is
also the norm by which every other personal concern, interest,
need, desire or wish must be judged--and, if necessary, sacrificed.

Fidelity to this law of the human spirit, this radical dynamism
for self-transcending love sums up the demand of the Christian
life because it is a response to the divine within us--God's gift
of love.

III. Conversion

While self-transcendence occurs in every instance of intelligent, responsible loving, the crucial instances of self-transcendence are those special, life-transforming events we call conversions.[14]   In simplest terms, a conversion is an about-face, a re-
orientation of one's life. We will consider the possibility of
conversions as key instances of self-transcendence in the cognitive, moral, affective, and religious dimensions of life. None of
these conversions introduces the reality of self-transcendence to
a person's life. Rather, they bring the drive for self-
transcendence to center stage and give it a starring role. They
turn the possible and sporadic into the probable and regular.

Most broadly, *cognitive conversion* consists of an insight
into one's knowing which allows one to take clearer possession of
it and thereby transform one's life. For example, Thérèse of
Lisieux manifests a cognitive conversion insofar as she gradually
came to the judgment that her own experience and understanding
were a truly valid basis for interpreting her own spirituality as
authentic. Her locus of cognitive authority shifts from others to
herself and her own interpretation of Scripture and spiritual masters. In the 19th century French Carmelite milieu which perpetua-
ted social conformity and adherence to external religious authority, Thérèse shows, in her letters and autobiography, a gentle but
firm trust in her own judgments despite the fact that these con-
victions were misunderstood or not shared by those around her.

Putting in summary form what is a very complex process in
Thérèse's life, her cognitive conversion can be seen by noting the
remarkable difference in the locus of authority for Thérèse's
thinking at three points in her life. Her autobiography recalls
how she thought in 1884, four years before entering Carmel.

> All my teachers looked upon me as a very intelligent
> student, but it wasn't like that at Uncle's house....
> [Uncle and Aunt] often spoke highly of the intelligence
> of others in my presence, but of mine they never said a
> word, and so I concluded I didn't have any and was re-
> signed to see myself deprived of it.[15]

What Thérèse judges to be true is only what others say or imply.
Later, in 1891, during her third year in Carmel, she demonstrates

some beginning of trust in insights she developed on her own. It
is a meager beginning, still dependent on a confessor's reassur-
ance, but very understandably meager, remembering that the insights were theological, and Thérèse, with no more than a ninth
grade education, was an eighteen year old novice thinking about
God in a way that differed from every Sister in her community.
When Thérèse told her Prioress that the retreat confessor for that
year understood her and explicitly confirmed her attraction to a
God who could completely accept a person full of faults, the
Prioress was shocked at this uncommon view of God and forbade
Thérèse to return to speak with that priest. Obediently, Thérèse
never spoke to him again, yet she firmly retained this image of
God.[16]

Still later, she demonstrates a pattern of consistently trusting her own insights and experience. She becomes a kind of "ex-
plorer" into Scripture, for example. "I am constantly discovering
in [the Gospels] new lights, hidden and mysterious meanings. I
understand and I know from experience that 'the kingdom of God is
within you.'"[17] When she shared her insights with those dearest
to her they consistently misunderstood or disagreed with her.
Thérèse made a basic effort to clarify her views, but when misunderstanding continued she peacefully persevered in her own vision, for example, of spiritual development as spiritual liberty,
not as counting acts of virtue or searching for the more difficult
act.[18]

Secure in her judgment that her insight into her experience
of the "little way" of trusting love was true, she was faithful to
this way even in the darkest trial of faith and eventually became
a source of strength for many others.

In its most fundamental form, *moral conversion* is the choice,
based on a realization of the difference between "value" and
"what's good for me," of value over satisfaction as the criterion
for decision.

The one event in her life which Thérèse explicitly designated
as a "conversion" fulfills the criteria of a moral conversion.
Many years after the event, Thérèse recalled that on returning from
Midnight Mass on Christmas, 1886, she overheard her father express
annoyance that at age thirteen Thérèse was still planning to be the
center of Christmas customs typical of small children. Thérèse's
sister, aware of how unusually sensitive Thérèse was and knowing
Thérèse heard their father's remarks, was amazed to see Thérèse
joyfully carry on as though she had heard nothing.[19]

Why does Thérèse call this "my complete conversion"? Because
a dramatic change happened, she says, "in an instant." The permanent change in direction is from being a girl who "was really un-
bearable because of [her] extreme touchiness" to a "strong and
courageous" young woman whose "source of tears was dried up and
has since reopened rarely and with great difficulty." She who
"wasn't accustomed to doing things for [herself]" now experienced
"the need to forget [herself] and to please others." She now had
a great desire to work for "the conversion of sinners."[20]

Although Thérèse gives this conversion a religious interpretation, it is really more accurately understood as a moral conversion. This is not to deny genuine religious aspects and implications to the event. Rather, it is to affirm that the basic change
of direction Thérèse describes corresponds more closely, in three
ways, to that of a moral conversion.

The primary characteristic of moral conversion is the shift
from concern for self-satisfaction to a desire for a life devoted
to value. Thérèse speaks principally of this event as marking a
change in her criterion of decision from self-pity to concern for
others. Second, moral conversion is an experience of more adult
decision-making. A movement out of childhood is precisely the
process that Thérèse identifies as most characteristic of this
event; it marked her "growing up." Third, the qualities of
strength and freedom of decision--characteristics of moral conver-
sion--are singled out in Thérèse's later interpretations of this
conversion.[21]

Unfortunately, moral conversion is not moral perfection.
Moral conversion is more a beginning than an end, more a challenge
than an achievement. To opt for value as a criterion for decision
is one thing; to consistently choose according to it is quite
another. If the choice of a life of value is to be effective in
the long term, and not be just a short bloomer, it must be supported by *affective conversion*. For Lonergan, affective conversion is a falling-in-love. Through affective conversion one becomes a being-in-love. To a greater or lesser extent love establishes itself as a first principle, takes over one's life, and
from it "flow one's desires and fears, one's joys and sorrows,
one's discernment of values, one's decisions and deeds."[22] Just
as one can live for the good of one's beloved, or of one's children, where no sacrifice is too great, one's love can also extend
to the entire human family. Jesus' example of a vision in which
no one is a stranger can become a reality in one's own life.

Thérèse's life is marked by an ever deepening and expanding and maturing love. At her adolescent moral conversion she said, "I felt charity enter into my soul," a love she wanted, at that time, to express through work for the conversion of sinners. This youthful love was characterized by a certain condescending attitude toward these sinners--she would reach down to "snatch them from the eternal flames." Nine years later she has become a woman who, in the dryness and darkness of her trial of faith, can lovingly identify herself in a relationship of sisterhood with these sinners, these unbelievers at whose table she is content to eat the bread of sorrow.[23]

The reality and development, over the years, of her affective conversion is clear when Thérèse declared that the particular grace of the year 1896 (the year before her death) was to finally understand perfectly what charity was. When meditating on John 15:13, she said, "I understood how imperfect was my love for my Sisters. I saw I didn't love them as God loves them," in their faults and weakness. "I understood above all that charity must not remain hidden...." The "more united I am to [Jesus], the more also do I love my Sisters."[24]

A life committed to the Gospel call of loving service to the neighbor is the route--long and difficult--to fully *religious conversion*, to falling-in-love with God without limits or qualifications or conditions or reservations. In fulfilling our capacity for self-transcendence, such an unrestricted being-in-love with God is experienced as other-worldly joy, peace, bliss.[25] Falling-in-love involves surrender, and falling-in-love with God involves the most profound surrender--the surrender of one's deepest (though unadmitted) pretense to absolute autonomy. Such unrestricted, loving surrender allows God to move from the periphery to the center of one's life. Now all of one's life--indeed, all of reality--is seen as gift.

In the same year in which Thérèse wrote the autobiographical narrative of her Christmas conversion, she committed herself to an action that epitomized the definition of religious conversion: total, permanent, unconditional self-surrender in love. On Trinity Sunday, June 9, 1895, she felt strongly inspired to make a total offering of herself to God's Merciful Love in the form of an Act of Oblation.

In order to live in one single act of perfect Love, I OFFER MYSELF AS A VICTIM OF HOLOCAUST TO YOUR MERCIFUL LOVE, asking You to consume me incessantly, allowing

> the waves of *infinite tenderness* shut up within You to
> overflow into my soul, and that thus I may become a
> *martyr* of Your *Love*, O my God![26]

The surrender's totality is conveyed through the image of martyr-
dom. Permanence is implied in the desire that love consume her
incessantly. The oblation is framed precisely in terms of Love,
a framework radically different from most offerings made by nuns
in Therese's day who gave themselves to God's justice as victims
of reparation for outrages of atheism and secularism.

    Conversion is normally a prolonged process, though its ex-
plicit acknowledgment may be concentrated in a momentous decision
or declaration.[27] So it is in Thérèse's case, where her earlier
poetry, letters, and autobiographical manuscript manifest an ever-
deepending love of God. The Act of Oblation becomes the concentrated declaration of that total, loving abandon.

    Conversion also means something new that later fructifies in
a cumulative sequence of developments.[28] In Thérèse's case, there
is a new perspective at the time of the Oblation; then, later,
still newer developments. Thérèse affirms that "the grace" of the
Act of Oblation was a new understanding about how much Jesus desires to be loved, and a new beginning of being penetrated and
surrounded by Love. Her surrender was also a principle of later
dramatically new experience and insight: the sudden experience, at
Easter 1896, of a plunge into a radical trial of faith; and the
remarkably new insights this generated regarding the fact of authentic unbelief and her own affirmation of a relationship of sisterhood with unbelievers. She who formerly was afraid of soiling
her baptismal robe could later peacefully declare identity with
unbelievers and speak of sinners as "us."[29]

    Thérèse's surrender in love also exemplifies qualities of the
particular type of religious conversion that is Christian.[30] For
Christians, conversion is God's own love flooding our hearts.
Thérèse understands this love to be the focal point of her experience. Christian conversion is rooted in confidence. On her death
bed, her hand barely able to hold a pencil, Thérèse wrote, "I go
to Him with confidence and love." Heroism is not required for
Christian conversion. Rather, the model is a child who takes for
granted that it will receive. These are exactly Thérèse's own
sentiments: "I am only a child, powerless and weak, and yet it is
my weakness that gives me the boldness of offering myself as a
victim of Your Love, O Jesus!"[31]

    Dying in great pain and the darkness of her trial of faith,
Thérèse's last writings are, nevertheless, permeated with a sense

of being fulfilled--filled with the immensity of love--and of
missionary concern to draw everyone in the world with her into the
immensity of this love.   Even in emptiness she is fulfilled by
reaching out in love.

NOTES

[1] Symposium sponsored by the Catholic Commission on Intellectual and Cultural Affairs, New York University, October 25, 1980.

[2] Jerry Rubin, *Growing (Up) at Thirty-seven* (New York: Evans, 1976) 20.

[3] Christopher Lasch, *The Culture of Narcissism: American Life in an Age of Diminishing Expectations* (New York: Norton, 1978). For an analysis of the effect of the cultural shift from the ideal of self-sacrifice to that of self-realization on the meaning of love (from "tragic-mythic" to "exchange"), see Ann Swidler, "Love and Adulthood in American Culture" (pp. 120-47 in *Themes of Work and Love in Adulthood* [ed. N. J. Smelser and E. H. Erikson; Cambridge: Harvard University, 1980], esp. pp. 136-39, "Self-Realization Versus Self-Sacrifice"). For a study of the different conceptions of the self constitutive of child-rearing patterns in early America (evangelical: the self suppressed; moderate: the self controlled; genteel: the self asserted), see Philip Greven, *The Protestant Temperament* (New York: Knopf, 1977).

[4] Paul C. Vitz, *Psychology As Religion: The Cult of Self-Worship* (Grand Rapids, MI: Eerdmans, 1977). Vitz, a Christian convert and proponent of "scientific" psychology, finds little practical difference in the last analysis between such theorists as Maslow, Fromm, Rogers and May, and the purveyors of "pop psychology." Perhaps because an objectified, conceptualized Transcendent is either ignored or viewed negatively, Vitz finds no hint of transcendence in their work.

If narcissism is not really self-love, but a manifestation of self-hatred, as the contemporary psychoanalytic literature suggests, it is necessary to challenge the attacks on serious theorists of the self who promote self-acceptance and a sense of self-worth in the therapeutic context. Because impotent selves do not significantly transcend themselves, we cannot in the present cultural context afford the luxury of misunderstanding necessary remedial therapeutic attention to the self as infantile indulgence and self-worship. Of course, the operative understanding of the self remains crucial. Authentic acceptance of oneself means that one accepts not only one's present limitations, but also one's real exigence for self-transcendence. For explicit treatment of self-transcendence in humanistic psychology, see, for example, Abraham H. Maslow, *Religions, Values, and Peak-Experiences* (New York: Viking, 1970) 67.

[5] Daniel Yankelovich, "New Rules in American Life: Searching for Self-Fulfillment in a World Turned Upside Down," *Psychology Today* 15/4 (April 1981) 35-91, at 40; essay adapted from his *New Rules* (New York: Random House, 1981).

[6] Robert Coles, "Unreflecting Egoism," *The New Yorker*, August 27, 1979, pp. 98-105, at 98. See Heinz Kohut, *The Analysis of the Self* (New York: International Universities, 1971).

[7] See, for example, Madonna Kolbenschlag, *Kiss Sleeping Beauty Good-Bye* (Garden City, NY: Doubleday, 1979); Joann Wolski Conn, "Women's Spirituality: Restriction and Reconstruction," *Cross Currents* 30 (Fall 1980) 293-308.

[8]See Diana Cooper-Clark, "An Interview with Mary Gordon," *Commonweal* 107/9 (May 9, 1980) 270-73; and Le Anne Schreiber, "A Talk with Mary Gordon," *The New York Times Book Review*, February 15, 1981, pp. 26-28.

[9]See Sandra M. Schneiders, I.H.M., "The Foot Washing (John 13:1-20): An Experiment in Hermeneutics," *Catholic Biblical Quarterly* 43/1 (January 1981) 76-92, at 84-88.

[10]For a sustained argument of this thesis, see Walter E. Conn, *Conscience: Development and Self-Transcendence* (Birmingham, AL: Religious Education Press, 1981). Though self-realization, self-fulfillment, and self-actualization are sometimes distinguished in the literature, we are considering them here as roughly equivalent. The key distinction in our thesis is between the realization, fulfillment, or actualization of the self which is directly sought, and that which occurs indirectly through self-transcendence.

[11]Victor Frankl, *Man's Search for Meaning* (New York: Washington Square, 1963) 175. For a consideration of self-transcendence in the work of Erik Erikson, Jean Piaget, and Lawrence Kohlberg, see Conn, *Conscience: Development and Self-Transcendence*.

[12]Henri J. M. Nouwen, *Reaching Out: The Three Movements of the Spiritual Life* (Garden City, NY: Doubleday, 1975).

[13]See Bernard Lonergan, *Method in Theology* (New York: Herder and Herder, 1972) 104-105, for a quick sketch; selected essays in *Collection* (ed. F. E. Crowe; New York: Herder and Herder, 1967) esp. 211-67, and *A Second Collection* (ed. W.F.J. Ryan and B. J. Tyrrell; Philadelphia: Westminster, 1974) esp. 69-86, 165-87; and for an extended analysis of cognitive self-transcendence, *Insight: A Study of Human Understanding* (2nd ed.; New York: Philosophical Library, 1958).

[14]For Lonergan on conversion, see *Method in Theology* (237-43) and "Natural Right and Historical Mindedness," *Proceedings of the American Catholic Philosophical Association* 51 (1977) 132-43, at 140. In the cognitive dimension, Lonergan focuses on the profound but relatively rare experience of intellectual conversion (philosophical self-appropriation); here we will deliberately consider cognitive conversion in the wider sense of one's discovery of oneself as a knower.

[15]*Story of a Soul: The Autobiography of St. Thérèse of Lisieux* (trans. John Clarke, O.C.D.; Washington, DC: Institute of Carmelite Studies, 1975) 82.

[16]*Autobiography*, 173-74; Jean-François Six, *Thérèse de Lisieux au Carmel* (Paris: Editions du Seuil, 1973) 141.

[17]*Autobiography*, 179.

[18]Letters of 6 July 1893 and 12 July 1896 in *Collected Letters of St. Thérèse of Lisieux* (ed. Abbé Combes; trans. F. J. Sheed; New York: Sheed and Ward, 1949); *Autobiography*, 207.

[19]*Autobiography*, 98.

[20]Ibid., 97, 99.

[21] Ibid., 77, 97; Letter of 1 November 1896 in *Collected Letters*.

[22] Lonergan, *Method in Theology*, 105.

[23] *Autobiography*, 99, 212.

[24] Ibid., 220-21.

[25] Lonergan, *Method in Theology*, 243.

[26] *Autobiography*, 277.

[27] Lonergan, *Method in Theology*, 130.

[28] Ibid.

[29] *Autobiography*, 180-81, 212.

[30] For an elaboration of these characteristics, see Hans Küng, *On Being a Christian* (Garden City, NY: Doubleday, 1976) 249-50.

[31] *Autobiography*, 181, 259, 195.

THE SIGNIFICANCE FOR THEOLOGY OF THE
DOCTOR OF THE CHURCH: TERESA OF AVILA

Keith J. Egan

The saint will remain an ineffective image in our culture as
long as there is a failure to recognize the rich and varied levels
of symbol that emerge from the lives of those uniquely touched by
God. Yet, the doctors of the church have fared even less well
than the saints. The role of these doctors has not ignited the
imagination; in fact, their significance has been ignored. The
title, doctor of the church, has largely been an idle one, perceived exclusively at a literal level. Indeed, theologians have
not been and are not now excited by this designation. The fourth
centenary in October 1982 of the death of St. Teresa of Avila, the
first woman doctor of the church, is an opportunity for an excur-
sus into the significance for theology of this doctor of the
church and a chance to suggest further discussion of the meaning
for theology of the doctors of the church.

As she lay dying, Teresa of Avila relished her affiliation
with the church. Witnesses to her last days report various versions of the sentiment: "I am dying, Lord, a daughter of the
church."[1] How she would have greeted the news that she would one
day be declared a doctor of the church is anyone's guess. Teresa
had a profound reverence for the authority of the church, but she
did not take herself too seriously. Moreover, her reactions were
hardly predictable. The news of her doctorate might well have
elicited the kind of humor that prompted her to chide those who
referred to her as a saint.[2] In any case, the question of the
meaning of her doctorate is not ours, not Teresa's. How are we,
especially those in the theological community, to interpret the
action of Pope Paul VI, who on 27 September 1970 declared Teresa
of Jesus to be the first female doctor of the church?[3] Was the
pope's action only a reward for faithful devotees and Carmelites
or merely a conciliatory gesture to the women's movement? I suggest that Paul VI's designation of Teresa as a doctor of the church
has a significance for theology that emerges through reflection
upon the history of what it has meant to be a doctor of the church
and from reflection upon Teresa's prolonged candidacy for the
doctorate.

There are thirty men and two women whom the Roman Catholic
Church considers doctors of the church.[4] The other woman is St.

Catherine of Siena who was declared a doctor of the church on 4
October 1970,[5] one week after Teresa was so honored. The steps
leading to these declarations for Teresa and Catherine were intimately connected. However, the limitations of this paper make it
possible to investigate only the theological significance of the
doctorate of Teresa of Avila. (Happily Catherine's role as a woman
of the church received extensive attention on the occasion of the
six hundredth anniversary of her death in 1980.[6]) Nothing short of
two monographs could adequately explore the two aspects of this
inquiry, the development of the notion of a doctor of the church
and a study of Teresa's candidacy for the doctorate. A selective
rather than an exhaustive look at moments in both of these aspects
must suffice for this paper.

Teaching has always been an important function in Christianity. Jesus is called teacher more often than any other title in
the New Testament.[7] He was a teacher in the rabbinic tradition,[8]
who taught with authority.[9] As soon as Christianity began to interpret the Word of God in the Jewish scriptures and then in the
writings that would become its own scriptures, it was inevitable
that certain teachers would achieve special authority, e.g., Jesus
and St. Paul. For the Jews the teacher was a revealer. In the
Greek culture which had so decisive an effect on the early church,
the teacher had more intellectual qualities.[10] The teacher and
his doctrine became key features of Christianity. Luke tells us
that "...in the church at Antioch there were prophets and teachers."[11]
Throughout the early church we hear of the activities of teachers,
e.g., from the *Shepherd* of Hermas, the *Didache*,[12] Hippolytus,[13] and
St. Cyprian,[14] to name but a few instances.

The eventual attribution of the title *doctor ecclesiae* to
specially designated teachers in the church has its roots in the
Latin Bible's widespread use of the Latin word *doctor* for teacher
(Greek: διδάσκαλος). In addition to the numerous occurrences of
docere (to teach) and *doctrina*, the word *doctor* appears fifteen
times in the Latin Old Testament and eleven times in the New Testament.[15] Some instances of the word *doctor* had more impact than
others. That Mary and Joseph found Jesus seated *in medio doctorum*
may be such an instance. In the prolog to his *Sic et Non*, Peter
Abelard made this event an authority for his method of questioning.[16]
The Latin Bible also made known to the West St. Paul's doctrine of
the charisms in the Body of Christ. One hears that "...God has
appointed in the church first apostles, second prophets, third
teachers (*doctores*)....Are all apostles? Are all prophets? Are all

teachers (*doctores*)?"[17] The writer of Ephesians says that
Christ's gifts "...were that some should be apostles, some prophets, some evangelists, some pastors and teachers (*doctores*)."[18]
Surely the long perceived attribution of Paul calling himself
"teacher of the Gentiles (*doctor gentium*) in faith and truth"[19]
enhanced the word *doctor*.

Besides the Latin Bible, another process led to the designation of special teachers as doctors of the church. That process
was the search for tested authorities in understanding the scriptures and the church's tradition. In the first centuries of the
church, the title Father was accorded to bishops as an acknowledgment of their role as teachers and witnesses of the traditions of
the church.[20] By the last half of the fourth century the title
Father was used for ecclesiastical writers in a way that is now in
common usage.[21] At the same time a determination of authentic
doctrine was being attained by argument based upon agreement among
ecclesiastical writers of the past, an argument later to be known
as *consensus patrum*.[22]

The Christian church was working out a way of selecting authorities for its doctrine. A list of post-biblical authorities
occurs in the compilation known as the *Decretum Gelasianum*,[23]
probably a document from the early sixth century.[24] Venerable
Bede (d. 735) broke new ground in this process with his letter to
Acca, bishop of Hexham, concerning the Gospel of Luke, in which he
listed as particularly significant interpreters of this gospel
those writers who would later be called the Four Latin Doctors of
the Church: namely, Ambrose, Jerome, Augustine, and Gregory the
Great. In this leter Bede also refers to St. Paul as a distinguished teacher (*doctoris egregii*).[25] J. de Ghellinck showed that
these four doctors, from Bede's time on and with the weight of his
prestige, were regularly listed as *the* Latin authorities. Occasionally St. Cyprian and St. Hilary of Poitiers were listed along
with these four.[26] The Third Council of Valence in 855 speaks of
St. Paul as *doctor gentium* and lists the "doctors" Cyprian, Hilary,
Ambrose, Jerome, and Augustine as "very lucid expositors of sacred
scripture."[27] Meanwhile, in the East since the ninth century there
had been a feast to honor the three Hierarchs and Universal Teachers, Sts. Basil, Gregory Nazianzus, and John Chrysostom.[28]

In the patristic era and in the Middle Ages, the process of
designating authoritative teachers from the church's tradition
played a critical role in the eventual naming of doctors of the
church. However, it was scholasticism in the twelfth and

thirteenth centuries that had an immediate impact on this naming
of doctors of the church. First of all, early scholasticism
wrestled with the meaning of authorities for doctrine. One thinks
immediately of Peter Abelard, especially of the prolog to his *Sic
et Non*, where Master Peter, in setting forth his method of working
with the dialectical character of opposing authorities, speaks of
Augustine as that "most diligent, blessed doctor of the church";
"the venerable doctor"; and "the spiritual doctor." He also refers in this prolog to Jerome as *doctor*.[29] The sorting out of
authorities continues with Gratian's *Decretum* (*Concordantia dis-
cordantium canonum*)[30] and Peter Lombard's synthesis of authorities in his *Sententiae in IV libris distinctae*.[31]

The dialectical impulse of scholasticism called for a confrontation and reconciliation of authorities, a vigorous discussion much in the air during the twelfth century. A letter from
Innocent II (1130-43), concerning the salvation of an unbaptized
priest, cites the authority of the holy fathers Ambrose and Augustine (*ex auctoritate sanctorum patrum Augustini atque Ambrosii*).
The inquirer is instructed to adhere to the teachings of the *doctorum patrum*.[32] The concern with the relative merit of authorities continues into the thirteenth century. Bonaventure speaks of
Augustine as that "...so great a Father and most especially authentic doctor among all expositors of sacred scripture."[33] In the
determination of a question regarding the baptism of Jewish children whose parents oppose the baptism, Thomas Aquinas argues
against the baptism on the grounds of the custom of the church.
In doing so, he measures the authority of certain teachers, saying
that the practice of the church outweighs the teaching of the doctors (not yet an official title) because the "...doctrine of catholic doctors has its authority from the church." Aquinas adds: "The
authority of the church overrides that of Augustine or Jerome, or
any doctor whatsoever."[34]

Degrees awarded in the medieval universities and titles acquired there also had an impact on the use of the word *doctor* for
special teachers in the church. Since classical times *magister*
designated a teacher. In the twelfth century it acquired a specialized sense and was used for the distinguished teacher of theology, often in the form of *magister in sacra pagina*, which later
"gave birth," in the words of Chenu, to *magister in sacra theolo-
gia*.[35] The word *doctor* was also used in classical times for a
teacher, and in that sense is applied to the teacher by Augustine
in his *De doctrina Christiana*.[36] In the last half of the twelfth

century the word *doctor* took on a more specialized sense in academic circles. At Bologna we hear of the *Quatuor Doctores* who followed in the footsteps of Irnerius.[37] Thomas Aquinas describes the teacher of theology in the prolog to his *Summa theologiae* as *Catholicae vertatis doctor*.[38] Gradually in the Middle Ages, and certainly by the end of the sixteenth century,[39] the title *doctor* replaced that of *magister* for the terminal degree in the university. The custom among scholastic authors of designating contemporary and past authors with descriptive compounds of *doctor* also made the title *doctor* popular and available for those considered special teachers in the church. Among the many descriptive titles used by the scholastics, perhaps the best known to us are *Doctor Angelicus* for Thomas Aquinas and *Doctor Seraphicus* for Bonaventure.[40]

The official recognition of doctors of the church dates from the action of Boniface VIII in 1295, when he declared that throughout the church the feasts of the twelve apostles, the four evangelists, and the four "illustrious doctors of the church, blessed Gregory, who...bore the care of the apostolic see, Augustine and Ambrose, venerable bishops, and Jerome, priest" be celebrated liturgically with an office of the double rank. Boniface's honoring of these four Latin writers under the appelation of *doctor* and his extolling of them as a group gave the Latin church, for the rest of the Middle Ages, its four doctors of the church. His action was not a declaration of who were doctors of the church, but rather a liturgical honor for four teachers long regarded as great authorities in the church. Boniface's document, *Gloriosus Deus*, was published in the *Liber sextus decretalium* and commented on by canonists like Johannes Andreae (d. 1348),[41] and thus had the effect of giving common currency to these four doctors of the church.

The papacy did not again accord the liturgical honors due a doctor of the church until 1567, when Pius V, a former Dominican, so honored Thomas Aquinas,[42] an action which certainly had some impact on the church's official espousal of Thomism in the nineteenth and twentieth centuries. In the following year the same pope accorded these liturgical honors to four teachers from the East: Athanasius, Basil, Gregory Nazianzus, and John Chrysostom.[43] Bonaventure was the last person in the sixteenth century to be acknowledged among the doctors of the church when Sixtus V, a former Franciscan, included Bonaventure in 1588 among those whose feasts were to be celebrated as doctors of the church.[44] In the seventeenth century no such designations were made. While there

were four in the eighteenth, nine received this honor in the nineteenth and nine so far in this century. The last male to be included in the church's liturgical calendar as a doctor of the
church was Lawrence of Brindisi, upon whom this honor was conferred
by John XXIII in 1959.[45] In 1970, Teresa of Avila and Catherine of
Siena, the former a Carmelite nun and the latter a lay woman, became the first female and last named doctors of the church. Of the
thirty-two doctors of the church, twenty-four were Westerners and
eight were Easterners. Among the thirty male doctors, two were
popes and eighteen were bishops. All of the males were priests,
with the exception of Ephraem the Deacon.[46]

     The modern designation of doctors of the church originated in
the years during which the papacy was implementing the teachings
of the Council of Trent and is, I believe, a sign of papal efforts
to dominate Catholic theology in the era of the so-called Counter
Reformation. The naming of the church's first female doctors occurred in the aftermath of Vatican II and may be a sign of a new
attitude toward women in the church. Pope Paul VI, whose image
grows steadily as a leader who struggled to cope authentically
with the ambiguities of his time, turned around a long and persistent tradition against women as doctors of the church. His naming
of Teresa of Avila and Catherine of Siena as doctors of the church
was no empty gesture. The implications of his action may well
have unforseen beneficial consequences for the church. At the
time of Paul's so honoring of Teresa and Catherine, Dom Jean
Leclercq was convinced that it might well signal important changes
in the attitude of the church toward women.[47] However, there had
been little sign of any such change in Teresa's day, unless her
activities are perceived as prophetic. In Teresa's time the attitude of churchmen toward women was patronizing. Felipe Sega,
papal nuncio to Madrid considered Teresa "...a restless and gad-
about woman teaching as a Mistress against the orders of Saint
Paul who has forbidden women to teach in the church...."[48] While
not all traces of this attitude have disappeared, there have been
significant changes. One day the doctorates of Teresa of Avila
and Catherine of Siena may be looked upon as a landmark in the
evolution of the place of women in the Roman Catholic Church.

     The requirements for being named a doctor of the church were
formalized by Cardinal Prospero Lambertini, later Benedict XIV.
These requisites appear in a work that emerged from his experience
as *promotor fidei* and *assesor* of the Congregation of Rites: *De
servorum Dei beatificatione et beatorum canonizatione* (1734-38).

To be a doctor of the church one must be a person of eminent doctrine (*eminens doctrina*) and outstanding holiness of life (*insig-
nis vitae sanctitatis*), and one must be designated a doctor of the
church by a pope or a legitimate general council of the church.[49]
Benedict XIV took for granted that a female could not be a doctor
of the church, a point to be commented on below.[50] The positive
requirements for this honor have remained the same from Benedict's
time until the present.[51] So it is appropriate now to situate
Teresa of Avila within this tradition of the doctors of the church.

There is a wealth of documentation about the long years, in
fact centuries, that led to the doctorate for St. Teresa.[52] Even
in her lifetime, there was abundant critical evaluation of her
doctrine by theologians. Domingo Bañez, O.P. (d. 1604), who examined Teresa's autobiography for the Spanish Inquisition, concluded that "...her experience, discretion and humility enabled
her to say rightly things about prayer that sometimes very learned
men are not able to do."[53] Teresa's beatification in 1614 and
canonization in 1622 were further occasions for statements, official and unofficial, in praise of her doctrine. These statements
served to initiate more than three centuries during which she was
often unofficially spoken of as doctor and even as doctor of the
church.[54] At her beatification there was inserted into the col-
lect prayer of the liturgy, taken from the common of a Virgin, the
following phrase: "that we may be instructed by (her)...heavenly
doctrine."[55] Both during her lifetime and afterwards, the emphasis has been on Teresa's holiness and doctrine, those elements
that constitute the requisites for the doctorate.

Although there was an interest shown in Teresa as an official
doctor of the church at the time of the third centenary of her
death in 1882,[56] it was not until the twentieth century that the
Holy See was petitioned to declare Teresa of Avila a doctor of the
church. The three hundredth anniversary of Teresa's canonization
in 1622 provoked this request. In that year the University of
Salamanca conferred on Teresa the posthumous title, *doctor honoris
causa*. At the ceremonies King Alphonsus XIII bestowed upon a
statue of Teresa the regalia of a doctor.[57] At this time the
bishop of Avila sought from Pius XI a declaration that Teresa be
named a doctor of the church. The Discalced Carmelites also sub-
mitted a confidential petition to the pope with the same request.
A response was relayed to the Carmelites from Pius XI: "Obstat
sexus." (Her sex stands in the way of her being named a doctor of
the church.) However, the pope's message left open some hope for

the future: "I leave the delicate question to be decided by my successor."[58]

Pius XI's reply reflects a long tradition on the way certain texts from St. Paul and from one of the Pastoral Epistles were interpreted concerning the place of women in the church: 1 Cor 11: 2-16, 1 Cor 14:34-35, 1 Tim 2:8-15. In this tradition Thomas Aquinas posed the following question: "Does the gift of speaking wisdom and knowledge pertain even to women? (*gratis sermonis sapientiae et scientiae*)." Thomas distinguishes: women may exercise the gift of speech privately for one or a few but not publicly by speaking to the whole church.[59] In the same century a related question was raised in the schools: "May a woman as a preacher or as a teacher merit the honor of being a doctor?"[60] The negative response was a matter of overkill, as a woman could not participate in the public life of the church or in any way whatsoever in the functions of the university.

Some nine years after Pius XI's negative response in regard to the doctorate for Teresa of Avila and still during his pontificate, a Jesuit, Père Gustave Desbuquois, was advised by his superior general to desist from advocating that another Carmelite woman, St. Thérèse of Lisieux, be declared a doctor of the church, a desire that was receiving widespread support.[61] Almost certainly the same reason given by Pius XI in 1923 for Teresa of Avila was behind the advice given Desbuquois, i.e., a woman could not be named a doctor of the church.

For the sake of brevity, but also because of the pertinence of the material to an understanding of Teresa of Avila's doctorate, I shall now confine myself to a consideration of the evolution of Teresa's doctorate during the pontificate of Pope Paul VI, whose naming of Teresa of Avila and Catherine of Siena as doctors caught everyone by surprise, yet aroused little theological interest. These declarations of 1970 quite clearly caught off guard a British theologian who published the following statement in 1967.

> No woman has been proclaimed [doctor of the church], although St. Teresa of Avila has popularly been given the title because of the influence of her spiritual teaching; it would seem that no woman is likely to be named because of the link between this title and the teaching office, which is limited to males.[62]

Only seven weeks after the close of the Second Vatican Council, Pope Paul VI instructed Cardinal Larrone, prefect of the Sacred Congregation of Rites, to have his congregation investigate the following question: "May the title and cult of doctor of the

church be granted to holy women, who by their holiness and outstanding doctrine have greatly contributed to the common good of
the church?"[63] Four theologians were charged with researching
this question independently of each other. Pietro della Madre de
Dio, O.C.D., Alexis Benigar, O.F.M., Charles Boyer, S.J., and
Alvaro Huerga, O.P., reported back to the congregation unanimously
that nothing stands in the way of a woman being named a doctor of
the church so long as she meets the same requirements laid down
for men,[64] that is, meets the criteria of Benedict XIV: outstanding doctrine, distinguished holiness, and a declaration by a pope
or a general council.[65] The position of the four theologians was
unanimously endorsed by the Sacred Congregation of Rites on December 21, 1967. Their endorsement was confirmed by the pope on
March 21, 1968.[66]

Pope Paul, at least in this matter, was a man in a hurry. He
anticipated the endorsement of the congregation by a few months.
On October 15, 1967, the feast of St. Teresa, in a homily addressed
to the Third World Congress of the Lay Apostolate and with members
of the synod of bishops present, the pope spoke for the first time
in public of his intention of reversing the tradition against women
as doctors of the church. In the Spanish segment of his homily, he
said: "We intend one day to accord her [St. Teresa] and St. Catherine of Siena the title of doctor of the church."[67] The pope carried out his intention when, on 27 September and 4 October 1970 re-
spectively, he solemnly proclaimed Teresa of Avila and Catherine
of Siena doctors of the church. The once unthinkable, the designation of a woman as doctor of the church, had now taken place
twice over.

What can be said about the significance for theology of the
evolution of doctors of the church and the joining of Teresa of
Avila to their ranks? First of all, nothing that I say or that
anyone else may say changes one iota the worth and character of
Teresa's doctrine. Pope Paul VI recognized this fact when, in the
homily at the Mass for the proclamation of Teresa's doctorate, he
began by saying: "We have conferred--rather we have acknowledged--
St. Teresa of Jesus' title of doctor of the church."[68] Just as
saints are not created by canonization but their holiness of life
is thus recognized by the church, so too doctors of the church are
not made by the church but the eminence of their doctrine and
their holiness are acknowledged by the church. The church's recognition does not alter Teresa or her doctrine. Designation as a
doctor of the church is, indeed, an honor for the recipient, but

effectively it is a grace for the community. Pope Paul spoke to
this point in the homily just quoted.

> The significance of this act is very clear. It is de-
> liberately intended to be enlightening, and might be
> symbolically represented by a lamp lighted before the
> humble and majestic figure of the saint. It is enligh-
> tening because of the ray of light which the lamp of the
> title of Doctor of the Church throws on her, and it is
> also enlightening because of the other rays which the
> same title casts over us.[69]

The naming of a doctor of the church is an ecclesial event
through which the church acclaims one of her especially holy members as a significant teacher with eminent doctrine. Moreover, a
number of themes converge to enlarge our understanding of a doctor
of the church: the Pauline doctrine of the Body of Christ and that
of the charisms, along with help from the tradition of *lex orandi
lex credendi*, and some contemporary considerations of the notion
of the Christian classics.

The doctrine of the Body of Christ and its later elaboration,
the community of saints, are the ecclesial setting for the doctors
of the church. The church selects saints to be emulated by earthly
members of the church. The saints have a service or ministry to
the earthly church. What the saints were on earth, they continue
to be in heaven, a revelation of God's love for His people. Through
beatification and canonization the church points out significant
heavenly members. So too, through its declarations, the church
points out from among its heavenly members significant teachers
whose doctrine reveals an authentic doctrine of God's relationship
to His people. The doctors of the church continue the mission
they once carried out on earth, teaching their fellow members.
The doctors of the church are in a very special way the teachers
of the Body of Christ.[70]

The doctors of the church are gifted teachers in the Body of
Christ. Teresa of Avila was declared a doctor of the church in
1970 after the restoration to respectability by Vatican II of the
doctrine of the charisms[71] and after Karl Rahner's thoughts on
this matter had become influential.[72] In the very first paragraphs
of his apostolic letter, *Multiformis Sapientia Dei*, issued on the
occasion of the declaration of Teresa's doctorate, the pope situated his action within the teaching of St. Paul and the Council on
the Body of Christ and charisms. Later in the same letter, the
pope states that Teresa's doctrine "demonstrated the presence and
power of a singular charism of the Holy Spirit."[73] In his homily

for the day of declaration, Paul returned to the theme of charisms, a theme always related to the doctrine of the Body of Christ.

> St. Teresa of Avila's doctrine shines with charisms of
> truth, of conformity to the Catholic faith and of useful-
> ness for the instruction of souls. And we might mention
> another particular point, that charism of wisdom, which
> makes us think of the most attractive and at the same
> time most mysterious aspect of St. Teresa's title of
> Doctor: the flow of divine inspiration in this prodigious
> mystical writer.[74]

We ordinarily speak of the charisms of the earthly members of the
Christian community. However, it makes no sense to deny the activity of the Holy Spirit upon the heavenly members of the community. Can we not speak of the charism of the doctors of the
church as being both *gratia gratum faciens* and *gratia gratis data*,
the former the ongoing growth in holiness and the latter the bene-
fits that accrue to the earthly church from both the holiness and
the doctrine of the doctors of the church?

The declaration of St. Teresa as doctor of the church was
made, however, by a pope who felt that the church's hierarchical
teaching office could clearly be separated from the charismatic
teaching role in the church. In his homily for 27 September 1970,
the pope said:

> We must add two observations which seem to Us to be im-
> portant. The first is that St. Teresa is the first woman
> upon whom the Church has conferred the title of Doctor.
> This has not been done without reference to St. Paul's
> severe words: "Let women keep silence in the churches."
> This still signifies today that woman is not meant to
> have hierarchical functions of teaching and ministering
> in the church. Has the Apostle's precept been violated,
> then?

> We can give a clear answer: No. In reality, it is not
> a matter of a title entailing hierarchical teaching
> functions; but at the same time We must point out that
> this does not in the least signify a lesser appreciation
> of the sublime mission which woman has in the midst of
> the People of God.[75]

With all the respect that is owed to such statements, I suggest
that the *magisterium(a)* and theologians have barely begun to
scratch the surface of the relationship between the charismatic
and the hierarchic in the church. With the doctorates of Teresa
of Avila and Catherine of Siena, new ground has been broken, I
think, in advancing the discussion about this relationship. The
full significance of these declarations has by no means been fully
disclosed.

A brief word on the aphorism *lex orandi, lex credendi* (praying and believing shape each other), a little understood and much

abused tradition. Geoffrey Wainwright has recently tried to un-
pack the potential of this doctrine, but has only begun a discussion in English that has far to go.[76] Investigation of the cultic
implications of canonization and of the naming of the doctors of
the church may provide a better understanding of this tradition.
Since Boniface VIII's directions for the celebrating of the feasts
of the Four Latin Doctors of the Church[77] and for the centuries
that the Congregation in charge of beatifications and canoniza-
tions has screened candidates for the doctorate, the naming of
doctors of the church has been connected with cult. I agree with
Père Droulers, in perhaps a wider sense than his words seem to
imply, that the "question of the doctorate is essentially a question of cult...."[78] The lives of the saints and the doctrine of
the doctors are meant to be celebrated in the Christian community.
A Christian community where holiness and doctrine are so celebrated is being formed in right belief, not in the narrow sense
of orthodoxy but in an enlarged sense. A community being formed
in such a way would likely relish a dialog with theologians who
are also concerned with the fostering of right doctrine in its
deepest meaning. The celebration of the lives of the saints and
the doctrine of the doctors of the church may not only enlarge
belief, but may also make possible a more vigorous dialog between
such a community and those interested in theological discourse.
One may suggest this as another way to promote faith seeking understanding. Further exploration of the tradition of *lex orandi*,
lex credendi in connection with the saints and the doctors of the
church may lead to new horizons.

Teresa of Avila has always been recognized as a good teacher
but now, with her doctorate, the church offers her as a teacher
with special authority. No one needs to be reminded that authority in the church, in theology, and elsewhere has been abused. In
theology authorities have often enough been marshalled like so
many soldiers on display to defend positions. "Theological notes"
have at times been applied rigidly and mathematically.[79] Yet,
theologians as well as the *magisterium(a)* recognize the need for
authorities in developing solid doctrine. A concern common to the
church and to theologians is the discovery of authorities. David
Tracy has indicated that theologians have three publics--society,
the academy, and the church.[80] Does not the church also have
various publics among whom surely are the theologians? Is not the
church proposing to theologians texts of the doctors of the church
as especially significant for inquiry into their "excess of

meaning"?[81] Are not theologians asked by the church to consider
and re-consider these texts which the church proclaims as classics
with permanent and universal value? The classics overcome particularly and are common, public property to be explored creatively.
The naming of the doctors of the church is part of the church's
search for authoritative teachers. For the church, these doctors
are classical teachers with classical doctrine.

In naming Teresa of Avila a doctor, the church has designated
her writings as classics, beneficial to ecclesial life and theological dialog.[82] Too often the mystical classics have served a
very narrow concern and have not been part of theological discussions. As a result, mystical theology has become dessicated and
lost a sense of mystery, and theology has lost a rich resource.[83]
The religious classics are not glass enclosed relics to be rever-
enced only with awe, but rather are rich resources to be explored
anew by each generation in the church and among theologians. The
fourth centenary of Teresa of Avila's death serves as a reminder
that her classical texts await this exploration.

Despite all the quite human and, at times, less than noble
motivation that lies behind the processes of canonization and of
the naming of doctors of the church, both processes are capable
of calling attention to the classical lives of the saints and the
classical doctrine of the doctors of the church. Yet, not all
saints are as universally inspiring as others. Not all doctors of
the church are of the same stature. Gifts vary. Not every age
has an Augustine or an Aquinas. Moreover, among the writings of
the doctors there are both major and minor classics and some writings of only passing interest. Perhaps for these reasons there is
such a variety of saints and doctors. Their seasons vary, but
anniversaries serve at least as an opportunity to recall the depth
and variety of the Christian tradition. Such was the grace of
1974, when the writings of Aquinas and Bonaventure were reviewed
on the occasion of the seven hundredth anniversary of their deaths.

Before bringing this paper to a close, I wish to say that I
am aware that this discussion of the doctors of the church has the
air of an in-house theme for Roman Catholics. That is unfortunate.
The potential for collaboration in this matter among Christian
churches and other religious groups and theologians is enormous.
The sharing of "saints" and of the texts of the significant teachers of the various traditions, while common to some theologians,
needs to be fostered to a greater degree and would surely enrich
ecumenical and interfaith activities. It is another instance of

the need that the churches and the theologians have for each
other.

     The meaning of the classics cannot be exhausted, and this
paper has by no means exhausted the meaning of Teresa of Avila's
doctorate. Rather it intends to be suggestive of various ways of
retrieving the meaning of her doctorate and those of others
through reflection on the evolution of the naming of doctors of
the church that seems rooted in the search for authorities, in the
biblical doctrine of the Body of Christ and its charisms, in the
tradition of *lex orandi*, *lex credendi*, and finally in the contemporary recovery of religious classics. The Roman Catholic tradition has recognized Teresa of Avila as a public, charismatic
teacher in the Body of Christ, whose doctrine has relevance for
the teaching and the learning church and for theologians. Karl
Rahner has taught us to view dogma not as a finished product but
as a place to begin. So, too, the doctrine of Teresa of Avila is
not a fence to protect an overly anxious concern for orthodoxy,
but an open field with broad horizons for the exploration of divine activity in human life. Teresa of Avila died delighted to be
a daughter of the church. She may well now be proud to be the
first daughter of the church to be a doctor of the church and
happy to know that her doctorate enriches both the church(es) and
theology. [84]

NOTES

[1]Efrén de la Madre de Dios and Otger Steggink, *Tiempo y vida de santa Teresa* (2nd ed.; Madrid: Biblioteca de Autores Christianos, 1977) 983-84.

[2]*The Letters of Saint Teresa of Jesus* (trans. E. Allison Peers, II; Westminster, MD: Newman Press, 1950) 697.

[3]*Acta Apostolicae Sedis* 63 (1971) 185-92 (henceforth: *AAS*).

[4]For list of the doctors of the church, see H. Rahner, "Kirchenlehrer," *Lexikon für Theologie und Kirche* 6 (1961) cols. 230-31; *The New Catholic Encyclopedia* 4 (1967) 938; *Enciclopedia Cattolica* 4 (1950) cols. 1905-6; E. Simmons, *The Fathers and Doctors of the Church* (Milwaukee: Bruce, 1959) 182-84 (this book is a popular collection of sketches of the Fathers and Doctors).

[5]*AAS* 63 (1971) 674-82.

[6]See issue in her honor: "Catherine de Sienne," *La vie spirituelle* 134 (Septembre-décembre, 1980).

[7]John L. McKenzie, *Dictionary of the Bible* (Milwaukee: Bruce, 1965) 870.

[8]Ibid., 870, 718.

[9]Matt 7:29; Mark 1:22, 11:18.

[10]McKenzie, *Dictionary of the Bible*, 870.

[11]Acts 13:1.

[12]Robert M. Grant, *The Apostolic Fathers* I (*An Introduction*) (New York: Thomas Nelson, 1964) 160.

[13]Hippolytus, *La tradition apostolique* (SC 11[2]; 2nd ed; trans. B. Botte; Paris: Editions du Cerf, 1968) 68, 76, 125.

[14]Cyprian, *Opera omnia* III(1), ed. G. Hartel, "CSEL" (Vienna, 1868) Epistola 29.

[15]*Novae concordantiae bibliorum sacrorum iuxta vulgatam versionem critice editam* (ed. B. Fischer; Stuttgart-Bad Cannstatt: Frommann-Holzboog, 1977) II, cols. 1488-90. Latin text of Bible used for this paper: *Biblia sacra iuxta vulgatam versionem*,(ed. R. Weber et al.;(Stuttgart: Württembergische Bibelanstalt, 1975).

[16]Luke 2:46. Peter Abelard, *Sic et Non, a Critical Edition* (ed. B. Boyer and R. McKeon; Chicago: University of Chicago, 1976-77) 104.

[17]1 Cor 12:28-29. Revised Standard Version used for English quotations from the Bible.

[18]Eph 4:11.

[19]1 Tim 2:7.

[20]Otto Bardenhewer, *Patrology* (2nd ed.; trans. T. J. Shahan; St. Louis: B. Herder, 1908) 1.

[21] E. Amann, "Pères de l'Eglise," *Dictionnaire de Théologie Catholique* 12 (1), col. 1192.

[22] Ibid., col. 1199.

[23] Denziger-Schönmetzer (34th ed.), nn. 350-54.

[24] Ibid., editor's note.

[25] *Patrologia Latina*, 94: col. 689.

[26] J. De Ghellinck, "Les premières listes des docteurs de l'Eglise en Occident," *Le mouvement théologique du XIIe siècle* (2nd ed.; Paris: Desclée-de Brouwer, 1948) 514-17.

[27] Denziger-Schönmetzer, n. 625.

[28] H. Rahner, "Kirchenlehrer," col. 230.

[29] Peter Abailard, *Sic et Non*, 90, 93, 99, 94. See references to the doctors in the letters of Abelard and Heloise, edited by J. T. Muckle, *Mediaeval Studies* 12 (1950) 163-213; 15 (1953) 47-94; 17 (1955) 240-81; 18 (1956) 241-92 (ed. by T. P. McLaughlin). See especially: "praecipui doctores Ecclesiae...Origines..., Ambrosius atque Hieronymus," 17 (1955) 279; "maximus ecclesiae doctor... Hieronymus," 18 (1956) 289 (and also 250, 263, 279, 292).

[30] Edited by E. Friedberg (Leipzig, 1879; reprint: Graz, 1959).

[31] Third edition (Quaracchi: Editiones Collegii S. Bonaventuae, 1971, 1981).

[32] Denziger-Schönmetzer, n. 741.

[33] Bonaventure, *Quaestiones disputatae*, IV, *Opera omnia* (Quaracchi, 1891) V, 23, cited by J. Pelikan, *The Growth of Medieval Theology, 600-1300* (Chicago: University of Chicago, 1978) 271.

[34] Thomas Aquinas, *Summa theologiae* IIa, IIae, q. 10, a. 12, cited by "St. Thomas Aquinas, Angelic Doctor for Our Age," *The Pope Speaks* 19 (1974-75) 301 n. 33.

[35] M.-D. Chenu, *Toward Understanding Saint Thomas* (trans. A.-M. Landry and D. Hughes; Chicago: H. Regnery, 1964) 242, see also 253, 302. See Walter Principe, "Thomas Aquinas' Principles for Interpretation of Patristic Texts," *Studies in Medieval Culture*, VIII-IX (1976) 111-21.

[36] "Corpus Christianorum, Series Latina, XXXII," ed. by J. Martin (1962) IV, IV, 6; X, 24.

[37] Stephan Kuttner, "The Father of the Science of Canon Law," *The Jurist* 1 (1941) 14.

[38] With this phrase Thomas is clearly describing the teachers of theology for whose students the *Summa* was composed.

[39] C. Lefebvre, "Docteur," *Dictionnaire de Droit Canonique* 4 (1949) cols. 1326-29. See Gabriel le Bras, "Velut Splendor Firmamenti: le docteur dans le droit de l'eglise medievale," *Mélanges offerts a Etienne Gilson* (Toronto: Pontifical Institute of Mediaeval Studies, 1959) 373-88.

[40]Bonaventure, it seems, received the above title from John Gerson (d. 1429); for a long time before, he had been called *Doctor Devotus*. Bonaventure, *The Soul's Journey into God*, etc., trans. by Ewert Cousins, "The Classics of Western Spirituality" (New York: Paulist, 1978) xiii. For lists of these medieval titles, see *Enciclopedia Cattolica*, 4, cols. 1900-1; E. Pace, "Doctor," *The Catholic Encyclopedia* (1909) 5:74-75; E. Valton, "Docteur," *Dictionnaire de Théologie Catholique* 4 (2), cols. 1507-9; J. Vansteenkiste, "Doctor (Scholastic Title)," *The New Catholic Encyclopedia* 4:936-38.

[41]*Corpus iuris canonici*, ed. by E. Friedberg, II, Liber sextus, lib. III, Tit. XXII, cols. 1059-60. For a sequence in honor of these four doctors from at least the early fifteenth century, see *Analecta Hymnica Medii Aevi*, ed. by C. Blume, 55 (1922) 403-4.

[42]J. J. Berthier, *Sanctus Thomas Aquinas, Doctor Communis Ecclesiae* I (Rome, 1914) 97-99.

[43]H. Rahner, "Kirchenlehrer," col. 230.

[44]Bonaventure, *Opera Omnia* I (Quaracchi, 1882) XLV-LII.

[45]H. Rahner, "Kirchenlehrer," cols. 230-31.

[46]Ibid.

[47]Jean Leclercq, "Deux nouveaux Docteurs de l'Eglise," *La vie spirituelle* 123 (1970) 135-46.

[48]Otilio Rodriquez, "Saint Teresa of Jesus: First Woman Doctor of the Church," *Spiritual Life* 16 (1970) 215.

[49]The above text available to me only in the following synopsis: Benedict XIV, *Doctrina de servorum Dei beatificatione et beatorum canonizatione* (ed. E. de Azevedo; Brussels, 1840) 294.

[50]Pp. 13-14.

[51]*AAS* 51 (1959) 460; 63 (1971) 191.

[52]E.g., *Ephemerides Carmeliticae* 21 (1970); *Carmelus* 18 (1971), and *Fe y magisterio ecclesiastico I; Doctorado de santa Teresa II*, "XXVIII semana española de teología" (Madrid, 1971).

[53]Rodriquez, p. 215.

[54]Valentino Macca, "Il Dottorato di santa Teresa, sviluppo storico di una idea," *Ephemerides Carmeliticae* 21 (1970) 61-95.

[55]Ibid., 68; *Santi del Carmelo* (ed. L. Saggi; Rome, 1972) 342.

[56]Macca, p. 97.

[57]Enrique del Sagrado Corazon, "Datos históricos sobre el 'doctorado' de Santa Teresa de Jesús," *Fey y Magisterio...Doctorado de santa Teresa*, 367.

[58]Macca, pp. 103-4; Rodriquez, p. 218.

[59]*Summa theologiae*, II^a, II^{ae}, q. 177, a. 2. The Bollandists in 1845 published an opinion that St. Teresa could not be named a doctor of the church. Macca, p. 96.

[60]Leclercq, p. 138.

[61]Paul Droulers, "Le doctorat de sainte Thérèse de Lisieux propose en 1932," *Ephemerides Carmeliticae* 24 (1973) 123.

[62]Bernard Forshaw, "Doctor of the Church," *The New Catholic Encyclopedia* (1967) 4:939.

[63]Macca, p. 105; Rodriquez, p. 221.

[64]Macca, p. 106; Rodriquez, p. 221.

[65]Note 49 above. No such action has ever been taken by a general council.

[66]Rodriquez, p. 221.

[67]*AAS* 59 (1967) 1047; *The Pope Speaks* 12 (1967) 341.

[68]*AAS* 62 (1970) 590; *The Pope Speaks* 15 (1970-71) 218.

[69]*AAS* 62 (1970);590; *The Pope Speaks* 15 (1970-71) 219.

[70]Note 17 above.

[71]*Lumen gentium*, n. 12; *Apostolicam auctuositatem*, nn. 3, 30; *Ad gentes*, n. 23.

[72]Karl Rahner, *The Dynamic Element in the Church* (trans. W. J. O'Hara; New York: Herder and Herder, 1964); see "The Charismatic Element in the Church," pp. 42-83.

[73]*AAS* 63 (1971) 185, 188.

[74]*AAS* 62 (1970) 591; *The Pope Speaks* 15 (1970-71) 219.

[75]*AAS* 62 (1970) 593; *The Pope Speaks* 15 (1970-71) 221.

[76]Geoffrey Wainwright, *Doxology; the praise of God in worship, doctrine and life* (New York: Oxford University, 1980) chaps. VII and VIII.

[77]Note 41 above.

[78]Droulers, p. 88 n. 4.

[79]Johann Finisterhölzl, "Theological Notes," *Encyclopedia of Theology; the Concise Sacramentum Mundi* (ed. Karl Rahner; New York: Seabury, 1975) 1679-85.

[80]David Tracy, *The Analogical Imagination; Christian Theology and the Culture of Pluralism* (New York: Crossroad, 1981) chap. 1. My discussion above of the classics is dependent upon Tracy's exposition in chaps. 3,4,5, and Part II, passim, of this book.

[81]Ibid., 102.

[82]Ibid., 176, where Tracy speaks of Teresa of Avila's writings as classical.

[83]Keith J. Egan, "The Prospects of the Contemporary Mystical Movement: a Critique of Mystical Theology," *Review for Religious* 34 (1975) 904.

[84] For a discussion of the relationship of Teresa of Avila's writings to theology, see (Cardinal) G.-M. Garrone, "Santa Teresa Dottore della Chiesa," *Ephemerides Carmeliticae* 21 (1970) VIII-XVI.

THE TREE OF LIFE IN HINDU AND CHRISTIAN THEOLOGY

John Borelli

The tree of life may be either upright or upside down, de-
pending upon the particular tradition out of which it emerges.[1]
Generally the tree stands upright in the Christian tradition but
hangs inverted in the Hindu tradition. This does not necessarily
mean that the tree of life has an entirely equivocal significance
in these traditions. Nor does it mean that comparative theological analysis is necessarily precluded. It is my intention to
illustrate, quite to the contrary, that the tree of life symbol
does have theological significance which, at least to some extent,
is cross-cultural and which can be uncovered through comparative
analysis. For both traditions, the tree of life focuses the religious imagination towards God as the source of life--as humanity's
true abode.

To illustrate this contention, I will focus on the Vedānta
tradition of Hinduism and Bonaventure's Christian theology. After
a few introductory remarks, I will examine the occurrences of the
tree of life symbol in the respective scriptures and then demon-
strate how its several meanings function theologically. Needless
to say, this symbol is a rich and complex image in both traditions.
Obviously, it is not possible here to offer an exhaustive treatment of its significance or history in either tradition; furthermore, although our questioning turns around the evident differences,
particularly the location of the roots, my aim is to focus attention on the important convergences.[2] For example, the tree of life
is a manifestation of divinity in both traditions. In the *Bhagavad
Gītā*, it represents Brahman's lower nature. In Christian sources,
the cross is the "tree of life" upon which the mystery of Jesus'
salvific act unfolds. The tree of life also serves as an image of
the human condition for both traditions.[3] The humanity of Christ
is the focal theme for Bonaventure's meditation in the *Lignum
Vitae*. In the *Gītā*, Kṛṣṇa employs the image to teach Arjuna how
one escapes the cycles of life and death (*saṃsāra*). Consequently,
the tree of life provides a way of imagining the mystery of divinity's entrance into the human world. In both traditions the tree
of life is closely associated with death. Although in the Christian tradition both the tree in the garden of Eden and the cross
provide access to life, they are also paths to death. In the
Hindu tradition, the tree of Brahman and the tree of *saṃsāra* are

one and the same--divinity's manifestation which is ultimately
rejected.

Finally, in both traditions the tree of life functions as an
image of divinity's relation to the cosmos. In the *Bhagavad Gītā*,
the themes of the cosmos as a manifestation of God and of Kṛṣṇa's
entrance into the cosmos to defeat evil and support good interact.
Kṛṣṇa is at once supreme Lord and first principle. He is both the
Lord who triumphs and the divinity which orders. Kṛṣṇa's roles as
friend, charioteer, teacher and Lord of Arjuna originate from his
divine reality as the origin of all creation. For example, in
4:6-9, Kṛṣṇa gives this instruction:

> Though unborn, though I am eternal,
>   Though the Lord of beings,
> Resorting to my material nature,
>   I come into being by my own power.
>
> For whenever righteousness wanes,
>   Son of Bharata,
> And unrighteousness arises,
>   Then I send myself forth.
>
> For protection of the good,
>   For the destruction of evil-doers,
> To make a firm footing for righteousness,
>   I come into being age after age.
>
> My divine birth and actions,
>   Whoever knows them as they truly are,
> On leaving the body, he does not go to rebirth;
>   He goes to me, O Arjuna![4]

Once again, the Christian tradition offers a parallel. The
tree of life grows at the center of creation in the garden (Gen
2:9) and of the new Jerusalem which descends from the sky (Rev
22:2),but the tree also stands at the center of the Christian life
as the cross (Mark 8:34-35). Bonaventure's exemplarism, through
which he describes every living creature as reflecting the divine
exemplars and being drawn back to God in a divinely ordered scheme,
and his view of Christ as the chief exemplar, combine in the image
of the tree of life. In Bonaventure's theology, the tree of life
represents both a divinely ordered cosmos and the crucified Lord.

Jesus is not God in human form, as Kṛṣṇa is. Jesus is at
once divinity, humbled and emptied, and humanity, glorified and
uplifted. Profoundly moved by the double implication of the incarnation, Bonaventure composed these lines:

> Oh, if you could feel in some way
> the quality and intensity of the fire sent from heaven,
> the refreshing coolness that accompanied it
> the consolation it imparted;
> if you could realize the great exhaltation of the Virgin Mother,
> the ennobling of the human race,
> the condescension of the divine majesty.[5]

Kṛṣṇa is clearly not Jesus; Jesus is not Kṛṣṇa. Yet, the
Christian and Vaisnava presumption is shared--there is a salvific
mode through which divinity enters and partakes of the human world.

I. The Tree of *Saṃsāra*

The most complete description of the inverted tree of life in
the Hindu tradition occurs at the beginning of chapter 15 of the
Bhagavad Gītā. The entire chapter develops several themes associated with the tree, but the first six verses are the actual depiction.

> The Blessed Lord said:
>
> Root aloft and branches below,
> The undying tree they call the aśvattha,
> Whose leaves are the sacred hymns.
> He who knows it knows the Vedas.
>
> Below and aloft its branches spread
> Strengthened by the causal factors; sense objects,
>   the sprouts.
> Below too its roots extend everywhere
> Attached through actions in the world of men.
>
> Its form is not perceived here,
> Nor its end, nor its beginning, nor its frame.
> Chopping with the strong ax of detachment
> This fully grown and firmly rooted fig tree,
>
> One thus should seek that quarter
> To which those who have gone do not return:
> "I take refuge in that first spirit
> From whom the ancient emanation poured forth."
>
> Without pride and delusion, conquerors of harmful
>   attachments,
> Being devoted to the supreme spirit, desisting from
>   pleasures,
> Liberated from dualities known as joy and sorrow,
> Unperplexed, go to that deathless quarter.
>
> The sun does not illumine it,
> Nor the moon, nor fire.
> Where those who have gone do not return,
> That is my supreme domain.

Kṛṣṇa mentions immediately afterwards that a part of himself
becomes a living soul (*jīva*) and appropriates to itself a mind and
senses (vs. 7). This means that he becomes immersed in the world
of materiality, in which spirits are imprisoned to wander from one
body-mind complex to the next. Those who are disciplined discern

the true spiritual self (*ātman*) which experiences through the
body-mind complex, but the deluded and undisciplined remain ignor-
ant of their true identity (vs. 11). Using images of light, such
as the sun, the moon and fire, and images of life, Kṛṣṇa claims to
be both the splendor and living essence of creation. Finally, at
the conclusion of the chapter, he mentions two spirits (*puruṣau*),
the perishable and the imperishable. The former is the spirit in
materiality; the latter, the purely conscious, unchanging spirit.
Kṛṣṇa declares that he is a third spirit, above these two, the
supreme and highest spirit (*puruṣottama*).

The image of the inverted tree is aptly located in chapter 15,
for it follows immediately after two important teachings. In chapter 13, the twofold character of human existence (materiality and
spirituality) is discussed, and chapter 14 explains matter's causal
factors, the motivating and distinguishing factors of existence,
known as the three strands (*guṇās*): clarity, energy, and mass. The
tree of life, growing out of Kṛṣṇa's supreme domain, is strengthened
and nourished by these causal factors.

The description of the upside down tree in the *Bhagavad Gītā*
recapitulates a series of passages from the Vedas and other
sources. It resembles most clearly a passage in the *Katha Upaniṣad* (6.1) where a tree of Brahman is described. It is the same
fig tree with root above and branches below. It is pure, immortal,
matrix of all worlds, and without limits. The opening lines are,
for all practical purposes, identical with those of chapter 15 in
the *Gītā*. *Mahābhārata* 14.47.12-15 describes a primeval tree of
Brahman also. It, too, is composed of material elements emanating
from Brahman. One is encouraged to chop it down for the same reason Kṛṣṇa prescribes in the *Gītā*--the attainment of immortality.
This freedom from death and rebirth again results from knowledge
as the sword which severs the tree. Closely related is this brief
passage from *Taittirīya Āraṇyaka* (1.11.5):

> He who rightly knows the tree,
> With root aloft and branches below,
> Would by no means believe
> That death would kill him.

There are many other passages too. In *Taittirīya Upaniṣad*
1.10.5, the true self is identified as the living essence of the
cosmic tree and then described further as pure, like the sun, immortal, and wise. *Śvetāśvatara Upaniṣad* 3:7-9 says that Brahman,
the supreme person hidden in all, embracing all, inhabiting every
body, is also like a tree which is established in heaven and fills

the universe. *Maitrī Upaniṣad* 6.4 states that Brahman is called
the one holy fig tree. Three-quarters of it are aloft as root;
its branches are the created material elements. This recalls a
famous passage in the *Ṛg Veda* (10.90.3-4) where the one great person is divided into the cosmos with three-quarters forming the
gods and heaven. Furthermore, the same Veda asks the question
(10.31.7 and 10.81.4): "What is the wood, and what the tree, of
which they created heaven and earth?" In *Taittirīya Brāhmaṇa*
2.8.9.6 is a response: "The wood was Brahman, Brahman the tree,
of which they created heaven and earth: it is my teaching, you who
know, that there stands Brahman, supporting the world."

        In his *Gītārtha Saṅgraha*, Yāmuna (tenth century) summarized
the overall intention of the last six chapters (13-18) of the
Bhagavad Gītā: "Topics separate from the foregoing discussions of
action, thought, and devotion, such as nature, spirit, the manifest, the Lord of all, are discussed in the final instructions."[6]
He stated further that "in the fifteenth instruction, the supreme
spirit is said to be different because he is pure and is not consciousness mingled with what is unconscious and because he is
pervader, maintainer, and Lord."[7] All Vedānta commentators agree
that chapter fifteen is on God as the highest spirit, and the
chapter is so designated as the teaching or discipline concerning
the supreme spirit (*puruṣottama-yoga*). The image of the tree
serves as a transition from discussion of manifest creation to
instruction about God in himself as source and abode.

        Earlier in the *Gītā* (10:26), while Kṛṣṇa was identifying him-
self with the best and most representative member of scores of
classes of beings, he declared: "Of all trees, I am the holy fig."
At the conclusion of chapter four, in which Kṛṣṇa educates Arjuna
in yoga as the secret knowledge of salvation, he urges Arjuna
with the following words.

> Therefore with your own sword of knowledge
> Cutting that doubt which is born of ignorance
> And which abides in the heart,
> Practice yoga and arise, heir of Bharata!

Through knowledge, one discriminates materiality, body and mind,
from the spiritual self. Thus, knowledge is the cutting edge of
salvation.

        The highest domain of God is the supreme spirit. Generally
for Hindus, he corresponds to the absolute Brahman. In chapter 7
(4-6), a section of the *Gītā* in which Kṛṣṇa encourages devotion to
his personality, he distinguishes between his lower and higher

natures. The lower nature is composed of the material elements
which constitute all nonspiritual phenomena, and his higher nature
is distinguished as the living soul of this world. Chapter 15 recalls these two natures as perishable and imperishable spirits re-
spectively, but a third spirit is distinguished. Though it is
essentially connected to the soul of the world as its source as
well as the source of materiality, it is identified as the supreme
spirit.

In chapter 10:8, Kṛṣṇa claims that he is the origin of all
things and that all things emanate from him. In chapter 9:17-18,
Kṛṣṇa calls himself father and mother of the world, for he is both
receptacle and undying seed. Chapter fifteen clarifies this with
a discussion of the three spirits. God's emanating materiality is
his lower and feminine nature and the condition in which all living
souls are immersed. His higher nature as immovable, witnessing
spirit and life of the world is actually distinct from the lower
as its origin. Finally, the one root or highest nature of God is
the supreme spirit, both unified totality of spirit and origin of
the perishable and imperishable natures.

The fig tree, resplendent in evergreen foliage, with the
Vedas as its leaves, corresponds to God's feminine materiality
enlivened and witnessed by his spiritual nature. Like all of nature, the human person is a living soul inhabiting a body-mind
complex. Discriminating spirituality from materiality and ensouled
spirituality from originating spirituality, the disciplined devotee
of God severs the tree from its root and seeks the supreme abode
of God above. This is the deathless quarter beyond the sun, moon,
and fire. It is described paradoxically as both the dark source
of light and the brilliance at the center of light.

It is worthwhile to take stock of the various associated
images, namely: the sun; father and mother; the one great person
filling the universe; and the spreading out of branches or rays
below. There is an homology between the inverted tree and the
sun, for the branches and rays extend below. Also, at the root
of the tree, sun, moon, and fire do not shine; they illumine the
world below. From the one reality, root or sun, there is an ema-
nation and diffusion of beings. In the case of the tree, this is
growth filling out the cosmos. Kṛṣṇa declares himself to be
father and mother, seed and womb, the unified fecundity of his
higher and lower natures; and so he is the one divine person extending to the ends of the universe. In a sense, Kṛṣṇa is the
androgynous person reproduced throughout all of creation.

The inverted tree, then, signifies the axis of creation, the
scale of being, the organic whole of creation, and the reproduction of the whole of creation in each of its parts, especially in
persons. The ways to climb inverted trees are through the severing knowledge of discrimination, nonattachment to materiality of
both body and mind, and faith in God. One should keep in mind
that upside down trees are still trees and therefore imply meanings usually associated with the tree of life symbol.[8]

The kind of fig tree which represents the tree of life in
Hindu sources is the *aśvattha*. There are two theories on the
derivation of its name, which M. B. Emeneau discusses at the conclusion of his monograph, "The Strangling Figs in Sanskrit Literature."[9] In the *Taittirīya Brāhmaṇa* (3.8.12.2), Agni is said to
have fallen from the region of the gods and then to have taken the
form of a horse. He seeks out this particular kind of tree and
hides in it. Thus the tree is called "where the horse stands"
(*aśva-sthā*).

In *The Quarterly Journal of the Mythic Society* (1938), Ananda
K. Coomaraswamy published the most extensive study to date on the
inverted tree. His derivation refers to a different passage, one
in the *Taittirīya Saṃhitā* (4.1.10), but to essentially the same
story.

> The word *Aśvattha* is understood to mean the "station of
> the Horse" (*aśvasthā*), the Horse being Agni or the Sun,
> and that this is the proper interpretation is placed
> almost beyond doubt by the repeated expression "as unto
> the standing horse" (*aśvāyeva tiṣthante*) with reference
> to offerings made to Agni kindled at the navel of the
> earth....[10]

Coomaraswamy cites a number of other texts which connect horse to
tree, for example, Odhin tethering his horse to Yggdrasil, the
evergreen cosmic tree of Scandinavian mythology.

None of the Vedānta commentators whom I have studied derive
aśvattha from horse (*aśva*). All seem to share Śaṅkara's (eighth-
ninth centuries) view, basing their interpretation on *śvas* (tomorrow) and *sthā* (stand). "The "a" at the beginning of the word
functions as a negative prefix. Hence the whole word means "not
standing until tomorrow: "The *aśvattha* does not abide even until
tomorrow; when they speak of the *aśvattha*, they tell us about it
perishing every instant."[11] Emeneau interprets this second derivation to mean "*non in se constans*." On the one hand, he notes
the tremulous character of the *aśvattha* leaves; on the other hand,
he points out that the tree can begin as an epiphytic bush on a

host tree. Emeneau's study of strangling figs indicates that the
epiphytic feature of this fig partially explains why the root is
aloft.

According to Śaṅkara, a tree whose root is above, with
branches extending below, was chosen by Kṛṣṇa to teach Arjuna
about the path to the true spiritual self. For Śaṅkara and his
school of Nondual Vedānta, the highest self is the ultimately real;
the remainder, souls and the world of materiality, are products of
a veil of illusion covering the one spiritual reality. Therefore,
citing the *Mahābhārata* passage on the tree, Śaṅkara identified the
primeval tree of Brahman with the cosmic tree of *saṃsāra*. Knowledge of this tree manifested below is inferior to the knowledge
which unifies one with Brahman. Śaṅkara believed that the cosmic
tree is depicted in the *Gītā* to cause nonattachment to ordinary
and illusory existence (*saṃsāra*).

Rāmānuja (eleventh century) agreed with Śaṅkara only so far
as the fig tree is to be cut from its root with the sword of nonattachment; however, the tree is symbolic of creation which is
real and derived from Brahman according to Rāmānuja. After him,
Vallabha (sixteenth century) suggested that through the tree the
greatness and causal primacy of God is known. The tree symbolized
for Vedānta theologians, except the Nondualists, both rootedness
in God as Brahman and separate but real creation from him.

Madhva (thirteenth century), referring to the *Taittirīya
Upaniṣad* passage, stated that Viṣṇu, the supreme God of whom Kṛṣṇa
is a manifestation, is aloft as the inciter of the tree, for what
is aloft is supreme. Some passages refer to the tree as eternal,
and others to it as undying. Puruṣottama (seventeenth-eighteenth
centuries) stated that the tree is undying in that God's creativity
abides eternally. Madhva interpreted differently: "Even so, the
streaming forth is not forever. At a former time, it abided in
Brahman; and so in a sense it is eternal."[12]

The tree of *saṃsāra*, rooted in Brahman, streaming forth from
above, and manifesting Brahman, is an image of the chain of being
in the Hindu tradition. Śaṅkara explains:

> From man down to the inanimate and from him up to the
> abode of Brahmā, the creator of all, the results of
> knowledge and action, depending upon what kind of knowl-
> edge and what kind of action, are wide-spreading branches
> reaching out like the branches of this tree. They are
> nourished and fed by the causal factors, clarity, energy
> and mass, which constitute the material basis; the sense
> objects, such as sound, are the buds, as it were,
> sprouting from the branches which are physical and other
> bodies resulting from actions.[13]

The abode of Brahmā, a god with four faces who serves as a demiurge, is the Hindu designation for the highest tier of creation.
The upper world is the highest rung, and branching out from it,
the lower worlds descend. But, Śaṅkara was emphasizing the human
condition more so than the scale of being. Rāmānuja provided
this description:

> It has a root above beginning with four-faced Brahmā,
> who presides over the seven worlds, and its branches
> reach below extending down to all beings inhabiting this
> wide world: men, domestic and wild animals, birds, worms,
> insects, flying insects, and plants.[14]

In Vedānta theology, therefore, the chain of being is associated with the inverted cosmic tree. The organic unity of the
tree, vitally connecting all parts and layers with divinity, is a
positive value of the image. On the other hand, the dreadful
qualities of the Hindu chain of being are ceaseless rebirth and
the suffering of souls bound to the tree through their good and
bad actions producing buds for further growth. Ignorance of the
spiritual root of the tree and of the inner connection between
each aspect of the tree and its source is the cause of suffering.

Ananda Coomaraswamy believed that the inverted tree image
communicates duality--higher and lower natures of Brahman, root
and branch, immortality and endless death. He pointed out that
the theme of two trees, as in paradise with the tree of life and
the tree of the knowledge of good and evil, is ancient and can be
associated with the inverted tree image. Confusion of the two
trees brings death; distinction brings immortality. Hence, dualism or polarity is its final meaning. Its implication is in the
severing of the tree from its root. He concluded:

> The felling of the Tree, or taking flight from its
> summit involves, in other words, the usual substitution
> of the *via remotionis* for the *via affirmativa*; the great
> transition involves a passing over from the Taught
> (*saikṣa*) to the Untaught way (*asaikṣa mārga*), the
> Spoken to the Unspoken Word. The Brahma-tree (*brahma-
> vṛkṣa*), the Brahman in-a-likeness, as *saṃsāra-vṛkṣa*, is
> an indispensable means to the knowledge of Brahman, but
> of no more use than any other means when once the end
> of the road has been reached; it is a Tree to be used,
> and also to be felled because whoever clings to any
> means as if they were the end can never hope to reach
> the end.[15]

The same elements which compose the cosmic tree also constitute the personal body-mind complex inhabited by spirit. The
spirit which enlivens creation and connects all living things is
also present within each person. Inverted trees are not only

trees of life and divine trees, but also images of the human person. Through nonattachment and discriminating knowledge, one comes to realize spirit within and its relationship to spirit above. One transcends this world and this body-mind complex and rests unified in the true spiritual abode.

II. Lignum Vitae

Placing the chain of being and the tree of life together is reminiscent of Bonaventure. This comes to mind particular because of Ewert Cousins' recent translation of Bonaventure's *Itinerarium Mentis in Deum* and *Lignum Vitae*.[16] The structure of the *Itinearium* is based clearly on the chain of being proceeding from God, who is at once self-diffusive goodness and perfect being. Bonaventure guides the reader through a spiritual ascent to God by means of a generalized ladder of being--nature, souls, and God. In the "Prologue," the symbol of a six-winged angel, a seraph, in the likeness of the Crucified, unites the scale of being and the cross as the Christian axis of the spiritual life. The lower two wings represent all things within nature as vestiges of God. The middle wings stand for the soul as the image of God. The upper two wings represent the divine aspects of goodness and perfect being.

The chain of being is connected even more intimately by Bonaventure's doctrine of exemplarism. All realities are formed according to the divine patterns of which Christ is the first or chief exemplar. This exemplarism is dynamic because the divine processions within the Trinity form the basis of creation. As in the Vedānta tradition, one finds in Bonaventure the themes of hierarchy, chain of being, intimate connection between God and creation, and coincidence of all reality in God with real differences of particular beings.

Although Bonaventure did not employ the image of the inverted tree, I know of two examples in the Christian mystical tradition. The first is found in a vision of the Flemish Beguine, Hadewijch, a contemporary of Bonaventure. On the Sunday after Pentecost, sometime in the early thirteenth century, the Eucharist was brought to Hadewijch because she was too ill to attend church. Upon reception of communion she was taken up into a vision of a meadow, which she described as a "place of perfect virtue." Several trees stood in the meadow. Her guide was a throne, one of the angels charged with discernment.

In the garden, Hadewijch was led to seven trees in this order:
(1) the tree of self-knowledge, (2) the tree of humility, (3) the
tree of perfect will, (4) the tree of discernment, (5) the tree of
wisdom, (6) the tree of the knowledge of God, and (7) the tree of
the knowledge of love. It was the sixth tree, in this order of
mystical perfection, the tree of the knowledge of God, which was
inverted and near the center of the garden.

> There stood a tree with its roots upward and its summit
> downward. This tree had many branches. Of the lowest
> branches, which formed the summit, the first is faith,
> and the second is hope, by which persons begin. The
> Angel said to me again: "O mistress, you climb this tree
> from the beginning to the end, all the way to the pro-
> found roots of the incomprehensible God! Understand that
> this is the way of the beginners and of those who perse-
> vere to perfection." And I understand that it was the
> tree of the knowledge of God, which one begins with
> faith and ends with love.[17]

From this tree, the mystic was led to the seventh tree, where the
angel departed, and Hadewijch turned around to a vision of God.
She saw through a crystal cross to a great space. In front of the
cross was a seat in the shape of a brilliant disc, more radiant
than the sun. The seat was supported by three pillars which stood
for the names of God. Important to our discussion is the fact that
the inverted tree is here associated with the knowledge of God, the
brilliance of the sun, and the cross.

The other instance of an inverted tree image is in the work
of John of Ruysbroeck (1293-1381), who was quite familiar with the
writings of Hadewijch. His example is found in *The Adornment of
the Spiritual Marriage* and is coupled with the story of Zaccheus,
the short tax collector who climbed a sycamore tree to catch a
glimpse of Jesus (Luke 19). Speaking of the perfect follower of
the spiritual life who has a desire to see the Bridegroom, John
counsels:

> then he must do as the publican Zaccheus did, who longed
> to see Jesus, who He was [sic]. He must run before the
> crowd, that is the multiplicity of creatures; for these
> make us so little and so low that we cannot see God.
> And he must climb up the tree of faith, which grows from
> above downwards, for its roots are in the Godhead. This
> tree has twelve branches, which are the twelve articles
> of faith. The lower speak of the Divine Humanity, and of
> those things which belong to our salvation of soul and
> body. The upper part of the tree tells of the Godhead, of
> the Trinity of Persons, and of the Unity of the Nature of
> God. And the man must cling to that unity, in the high-
> est part of the tree, for there it is that Jesus must
> pass with his gifts.[18]

Faith has the same function in both Hadewijch's and Ruysbroeck's visions, for through it one ascends the tree. Inverted
trees cannot be scaled physically. The ascent is spiritual. There
are connections, too, between Ruysbroeck's tree and Bonaventure's
tree of life. In both, the number twelve is significant, and
Jesus' humanity is an initial focus in prayer and meditation for
the ascent.

Although Bonaventure's *Lignum Vitae* does not have an inverted
tree image, it provides a close parallel with the *Bhagavad Gītā's*
inverted tree. In his mystical treatise, Bonaventure takes the
major scriptural passages on the tree of life, combines them with
his meditations on Jesus' life, death, and glorification, and unfolds his Christology with special reference to the humanity of
Jesus.

In the *Gītā* and *Lignum Vitae*, the trees of life are considered deadly in their implications. The rejection of the tree
of life in the garden by Adam has led to death, and especially to
the death of the savior.

> "With Christ I am nailed to the cross,"
> from Galatians, chapter two.
> The true worshiper of God and disciple of Christ,
> who desires to conform perfectly
> to the Savior of all men
> crucified for him,
> should, above all, strive
> with an earnest endeavor of soul
> to carry about continuously,
> both in his soul and in his flesh,
> the cross of Christ
> until he can truly feel in himself
> what the Apostle said above.[19]

Bonaventure reiterates that the Crucified is the center of Christian life and emphasizes this by superimposing Jesus' life, passion, and glorification on the twelve-branched tree of life.

First, Bonaventure turned to Rev 22:1-2 for a description of
the tree of life growing in the new Jerusalem.

> And he showed me a river of the water of life, clear
> as a crystal, coming forth from the throne of God and of
> the Lamb. In the midst of the city street, on both sides
> of the river, was the tree of life, bearing twelve fruits,
> yielding its fruit according to each month, and the
> leaves for the healing of nations.

The text is from the Latin Vulgate which was used by Bonaventure.
This tree is watered from above, that is, from the river flowing
from the throne of God. It bears fruit, and its leaves are not
the chants of scriptures but the healing substances for all nations.

Even so, the tree with its fruits and leaves is envisioned in such a way by Bonaventure that each leaf corresponds to one of the mysteries of Jesus' origin, passion, and glorification. This is no inverted tree but an upright one; however, it is interesting to note that it grows in the new Jerusalem which *descends* from above (Rev 21:2).

Next, Bonaventure structured his text according to the twelve fruits. Each of the fruits is exemplified by four events in Jesus' life and are depicted as leaves surrounding each fruit. The twelve fruits become titles for twelve chapters.

    (1) His Distinguished Origin
    (2) The Humility of His Mode of Life
    (3) The Loftiness of His Power
    (4) The Plentitude of His Piety
    (5) His Confidence in Trials
    (6) His Patience in Maltreatment
    (7) His Constancy Under Torture
    (8) Victory in the Conflict of Death
    (9) The Novelty of His Resurrection
   (10) The Sublimity of His Ascension
   (11) The Equity of His Judgment
   (12) The Eternity of His Kingdom

Ewert Cousins, the recent translator of the treatise, writes: "In *The Tree of Life*, Bonaventure situates his meditation on the humanity of Christ within the context of his speculative theology of the Trinity, thus making the link with the mystical Christ of *The Soul's Journey*."[20] Bonaventure reminds the reader of Jesus' humility, poverty, meekness, his wounds, and his body dripping with blood. Here is a special link of intimacy to humanity, in addition to the link of Christ to all creation through exemplarism, in that Jesus is at once human and the divine son.

In his "Prologue," Bonaventure also mentions the other instance of the tree of life in the Bible.

> I call these fruits because they delight with their rich
> sweetness and strenghen with their nourishment the soul
> who meditates on them and diligently considers each one,
> abhoring the example of unfaithful Adam, who preferred
> the tree of the knowledge of good and evil (Gen 2:17) to
> the tree of life. No one can avoid the error unless he
> prefers faith to reason, devotion to investigation, sim-
> plicity to curiosity, and finally the sacred cross of
> Christ to all carnal feeling or wisdom of the flesh.[21]

The temptation of dualism is overcome with reconciliation; polarity resolves in the coincidence of opposites. The trees at the center of the garden are juxtaposed in Jesus' death on the tree of life. Adam's choice of the tree of the knowledge of good and evil over the tree of life was the cause of suffering. Death is the consequence for those who continue to reject the tree of life.

This ambivalence of themes which Bonaventure resolved in his own way was evidently characteristic of medieval lore about the cross. Gerhart Ladner, in a recent article on symbolism in *Speculum*, commented:

> A resolution of duality into unity is characteristic of the tree symbolism of the Christian Middle Ages, the principal source of which was of course the Bible. I am referring here above all to the relationship that was established between the tree of Paradise and the Cross of Christ, which in fact comprises two symbolisms.[22]

Ladner notes that the tree of the knowledge of good and evil was an instrument of sin, "but according to medieval Holy Cross Legend it later furnished the wood for the Cross of the Savior."[23] He observes further that this tree is not the only prefigurement of the cross--so too is the tree of life. Consequently, Ladner contends that the cross effects a unification of themes; it sums up two symbolisms as well as the role of Christ's suffering.

In the development of the Vedas there were two sets of gods, *devās* and *asurās*. Eventually, the *devās* ousted the *asurās* as the ruling powers. The latter became demons. R. C. Zaehner, in his book *Hinduism*, suggested that, had not the popular gods, Viṣṇu, Kṛṣṇa, Śiva, and their associates, swept away the Vedic pantheon, Vedic religion might have gone the way of Persian dualism.[24] Coomaraswamy, who made much of the two trees theme in his study of the inverted tree, indicated that the two trees may represent two aspects of the same tree.

> Both of these Trees are "in the midst of the garden" (Genesis II, 9), which is as much as to say "at the navel of the earth." One is tempted to ask if these Trees are not in reality one, a Tree of Life for those who do not eat of its fruits, and a tree of life-and-death for those who do....[25]

Bonaventure requests devotees to draw near and partake of the fruit of the tree of life. Vedānta theologians caution readers that such contact with the tree of life means further immersion in life-and-death (*saṃsāra*), but they paradoxically identify the tree of life and the tree of Brahman as the two natures of Brahman.

Dualism is avoided by Bonaventure in two significant ways-- through his Christology and through his exemplarism. His greater emphasis on the humanity of Christ in the *Lignum Vitae* enabled him to effect the intimacy of these two coincidences with the human condition. Bonaventure's description of Jesus, too, as the fruit which hangs on the Christian tree of life, unites the themes of Christ's origin, the centrality of the tree, and the brilliance of

the sun: "This is the fruit that took its origin from the Virgin's
womb and reached its savory maturity on the tree of the cross
under the midday heat of the Eternal Sun, that is, the love of
Christ."[26]

The association of the sun, spreading its rays down to earth,
with the inverted tree was seen in the Hindu sources. Bonaventure
visualized the importance of the cross standing upright under the
true Sun.

> Then when the innocent Lamb, who is the true Sun of
> justice, had hung upon the cross for the space of three
> hours, and when the visible sun, out of compassion for
> its Maker, had hidden the rays of its light, now that
> all things were consummated, at the ninth hour that
> Fountain of Life dried up.[27]

In the *Gītā*, at the end of the description of the tree, we are
told that sun, moon, and fire do not illumine the highest domain
of God. Here, in Bonaventure, the true Sun of God hangs upon the
tree, and the sun darkens at the moment of death.

A prominent tenet of Bonaventure's theology is that Christ is
the true light, equally as brilliant as the Father: "From the
Eternal Light which is at the same time measureless and most
simple, most brilliant and most hidden, there emerges a coeternal,
coequal, and consubstantial splendor, who is the power and wisdom
of the Father."[28] The lower nature of Brahman is not coequal with
its higher nature; nevertheless, the out-flowing of light and life,
symbolized by the downward-growing tree, represents a procession
out of the supreme spirit.

From Christ, there is further outpouring of life. After his
death, when the fountain flowing from heaven dries up temporarily
and when he is pierced upon the cross, the fount of life then issues from his side.

> . . . there
> apply your mouth
> to draw water from the Savior's fountain
> for this is the river
> arising from the midst of paradise
> which, divided into four branches
> and flowing into devout hearts,
> waters and makes fertile
> the whole earth.[29]

Bonaventure stated further that this fountain issued from Jesus'
side so that the Church might be formed. His blood mixed with
water, flowing as the price of salvation, gives power to the
actions of the Church.

In the final sections of the *Lignum Vitae*, Bonaventure com-
bined the images of fountain and light with Christ as the super-
essential ray and the fountain-ray of light.

> You soul devoted to God
>   whoever you are,
>   run
>   with loving desire
> to this Fountain of life and light
> and with the innermost power of your heart
>   cry out to him:
> "O inaccessible beauty of the most high God
> and the pure brightness of the eternal light,
>   life vivifying all life
>   light illuming every light,
> and keeping in perpetual splendor
> a thousand times a thousand lights
>   brilliantly shining
> before the throne of your Divinity
>   since the primeval dawn!"[30]

The Christian tree of life is the cross on which hangs the divine
fruit, and the glorified Christ is the completion and full maturity of that fruit. The glorification of Christ takes him beyond
the fact of the cross to his divine source.

There is no denial of the cross and no denial of the world
in which it stands, for Christ is the eternal fountain of all
life. Nor is there denial of Christ's humanity, for it is precisely the existential reality of his humanity and suffering,
symbolized in the cross, which draws the faithful to the divine
source.

The tree of life is scaled by a faithful, ascending meditation on the Crucified. Humanity is exalted through Christ. But,
the Vedānta and Bonaventurian traditions are quite close on a
major point--beyond the cross, just as beyond the inverted tree,
is the source, the most high God. At the root of the inverted
tree and at the fountain source of life is God himself, the highest spirit, who is humanity's true abode.

NOTES

[1]The tree of life is a major archetypal symbol; I have found images of it in a wide range of sources: Hindu religious literature, Platonic and Neoplatonic philosophies, Gnostic and Manichaean sources, Kabbalah literature, alchemical printed materials, Renaissance thought and poetry, Romantic poetry, and Christian mystical writings.

[2]John Arapura ("The Upside Down Tree of the Bhagavadgītā Ch. XV," *Numen* 22/2 [August 1975] 132) cautions that "parallels with the Cosmic Tree in other parts of the world known to us through the history of religion can mislead one into thinking that the *Gītā* is talking about the visible universe, its creation, implying the creator behind it, etc." I disagree to the extent that the image carries with it several levels of meaning. While Arapura exploited one level in his interpretation, following the Vedānta of Śaṅkara, no single theme or level of meaning appears alone in any of the inverted tree's traditions. Śaṅkara offers only one Vedānta interpretation as I shall point out in this study.

[3]Mircea Eliade (*Patterns in Comparative Religion* [trans. Rosemary Sheed; New York: Sheed and Ward, 1958] 273) writes: "In the *Bhagavad Gītā*, the cosmic tree comes to express not only the universe, but also man's condition in the world."

[4]Translations from Sanskrit throughout this study are my own. The standard editions of texts have been used.

[5]In deference to my teacher and friend, Ewert Cousins, who has brought out recently a translation of three of Bonaventure's works (*The Soul's Journey into God, The Tree of Life, The Life of Francis*, The Classics of Western Spirituality [New York: Paulist Press, 1978]), I am quoting his translation verbatim throughout this study.

[6]Yāmuna, *Gītartha Saṅgraha* 4.

[7]Ibid., 19.

[8]Eliade, 266-67, notes these: (1) stone-tree-altar, (2) image of cosmos, (3) cosmic theophany, (4) symbol of life, (5) center and support of the world, (6) mystical bond, and (7) resurrection and rebirth of life.

[9]*University of California Publications in Classical Philology* 13/10 (1949) 369-70.

[10]A. K. Coomaraswamy, "The Inverted Tree," *The Quarterly Journal of the Mythic Society* 29/2 (1938) 12.

[11]*Śaṅkarabhāṣya* 15.1.

[12]*Mādhvabhāṣya* 15.1.

[13]*Śaṅkarabhāṣya* 15.2.

[14]*Rāmānujabhāṣya* 15.1.

[15]Coomaraswamy, 35.

[16]See note 5 above.

[17]Hadewijch, *The Complete Works*, The Classics of Western Spirituality (trans. Mother Columba Hart, O.S.B.; New York: Paulist Press, 1980) 266.

[18]John of Ruysbroeck, *The Adornment of the Spiritual Marriage* (trans. Dom C. A. Wynschenk; London: J. M. Dent & Sons, 1916) 48.

[19]Cousins, 119.

[20]Ibid., 14.

[21]Ibid., 122.

[22]*Speculum* 54/2 (April 1979) 235-36.

[23]Ladner, 236.

[24](Oxford: Oxford University, 1962) 27-32.

[25]Coomaraswamy, 8.

[26]Cousins, 121.

[27]Ibid., 153.

[28]Ibid., 126.

[29]Ibid., 155.

[30]Ibid., 171.

COSMOS AND CONSCIENCE IN THE HISTORY
OF RELIGIOUS IMAGINATION

Robert Kress

Both religion and philosophy have traditionally understood the world which human beings experience in their everyday lives to depend upon and reflect another world beyond, ruled by supernatural forces (deities). This "beyond," known by the Greek as *apeiron*,[1] the unlimited and boundless which precedes and encompasses immediately experienced everyday life, has preoccupied and puzzled Western thought from its very beginning. About its existence there has been unanimous agreement, about its nature unanimous disagreement. Even modern atheistic theories cannot entirely escape the *apeiron*. For some it is a godless nothingness (*Nichts*; *Néant*), whose innerworldly consequence is Nihilism. For others like Nietzsche, refuge is taken in the myth of the eternal return, hoping thereby to avoid the otherwise inevitable nihilism. A classic theistic interpretation of the *apeiron* is provided by the biblical assertion that "God said 'Let us make man in our own image, in the likeness of ourselves...'" (Gen 1:26). Philosophically the relationship of the created human world to the creating divine world has been formulated in terms of finite and infinite.

However, this relationship is not a concern of philosophy alone. The experience of finitude is coextensive with human being itself, evoking that wonder (admiration) which is the beginning of all thinking and which finds expression in all the "works of man." Thus, "the philosopher and poet are similar...both are concerned with the admirable (*miranda*)."[2] Likewise, John N. Findlay has insisted that the Platonic myths "represent, with some decorative devices, a very serious ontology, cosmology, rational psychology, and theology which we moderns would do well to take seriously, since they may be true."[3]

Among the *miranda* which excite human wonder is the experience of not only finitude and contingency but also failure and guilt. In regard to these latter two, myth has excelled in that unveiling of being which is the truth (*aletheia*).

In the universal search to reveal the meaning of being, cosmos and conscience have been key concepts and symbols. Indeed, the coupling of cosmos and conscience, as well as their relationship to the *apeiron*, is as old as Western thought itself and predates by far its division into philosophy and myth, as the famous

saying of Anaximander strikingly shows: "But whence the origin of
the things that are, thither of necessity also their dissolution
(passing away); for they must do penance and pay the penalty to
one another for their unrighteousness, according to time's order"
(*taxis*: determining decree).[4] How the unrighteousness, which must
be compensated, arises in cosmos and conscience has long tortured
the human consciousness. For Plato, conscience was "an oracle,
a sign...a kind of voice...imposed on me by god...in which the
will of the divine power was...intimated...[I]t always forbids but
never commands me to do anything...[M]y great and only care was
lest I should do an unrighteousness or unholy thing...dishonorable
and impious and wrong."[5]

Now inevitably arise the critical questions about the nature
and relationships of *apeiron*, cosmos and conscience. Is the cosmos a prison of blind necessity with *No Exit*, as Sophocles and
Sartre seem to suggest? Is conscience but one more homogeneous
part of the cosmic *taxis*, subject to the determinations of an in-
exorable fate as blind as the blinding exile it automatically
exacts from even indeliberate violators? Is the *apeiron* of this
cosmos, and conscience within it, the impersonal tyrant of *heimar-
mene*,[6] itself as unfree and unloved as the cosmos it has produced
and tyranically rules? Or is the *apeiron* the very dear Father-God
(Mark 14:36), whose creative power and healing love have called
forth a world in his image and likeness in which there is forgiveness of failure (Luke 23:34), the promise of paradise (Luke 23:43)
and the lavishing of life to the fullness (John 10:10), so that
even failed, finite cosmos and conscience do not fade into nether-
worldly nothingness, but are exalted into the never fading, ever
resplendent freshness of the new Jerusalem. Cosmos would, then,
be destined to become not exile and hades, but a new heaven and a
new earth, conscience the beautiful bride of the *beingfull*, personal *apeiron*--and, all together, the new creation wholly transformed
into the Holy City of God (Apoc 21:22: passim).

Myth, philosophy and theology reveal that human wonder has
pondered both possibilities. Indeed, the history of human thinking
is the history of human wrestling with the messengers of different
*apeiron*s. For the interpretation of humanity's history, can more
effective hermeneutical principles be discovered than cosmos and
conscience?

I. Oedipus: Cosmocentric Conscience

Where better begin our consideration of human history than
with one of the great cosmos-conscience wrestlers of all time,

Oedipus Rex? What is the point of this masterpiece of religious
imagination? Is this tragedy a morality play which preaches the
fall of the mighty and narrates the preordained punishment of the
prideful hero? Hardly, although Oedipus was certainly "a man most
masterful; not a citizen who did not look with envy on his lot."[7]
Is it an ascetical exhortation to a stoic endurance of life in
this cosmos, where we may "count no mortal happy till he has
passed the final limit of his life secure from pain"?[8] Is it an
early example of Existentialist *Angst* proclaiming that "not to be
born surpasses thought and speech"?[9] That is closer to the truth,
for, as Freud correctly perceived, "The *Oedipus Rex* is a tragedy
of fate...the conflict between the all-powerful will of the gods
and the vain efforts of human beings threatened with disaster."[10]
But Freud incorrectly suggested that it was a prolepsis of his own
psychoanalytic philosophy, wherein our fate and destiny and nature
are revealed to us in "the basic (primeval) wish-phantasy of our
childhood," namely parricide and incest.[11] For the pious Sophocles,
the Oedipal drama may well not be "an accusation agaisnt destiny
and the gods."[12] But it need not, on that account, be merely servile submission. It is really a wondering and questioning about
the nature of the "God in whose hands all these things are."[13]
Freud's offhanded dismissal that "the form which it (the Oedipus
fable) subsequently assumed (in Sophocles) was the result of a mis-
conceived secondary elaboration of the material, which sought to
make it serve a theological intention"[14] can be dismissed with the
ease with which it was made.

     The intention is clearly theological. Paul Ricoeur has re-
cently come close to acknowledging this, suggesting that Oedipus
is "the tragedy of truth...the tragedy of self-consciousness, or
self-recognition."[15] He is correct in asserting that "the core of
the tragedy is not the problem of sex, but the problem of flight."
However, his own "antithetic reading" breaks down in his assertion
that "Oedipus becomes guilty precisely because of his pretension
to exonerate himself from a crime that, ethically speaking, he is
not in fact guilty of." The "disaster" is not "this impure passion with respect to the truth, his hubris...his passion for non-
knowing." Ricoeur is right insofar as the tragedy of *Oedipus Rex*
is not about Oedipus' libidinal guilt. But he is wrong when he
asserts that Oedipus' guilt is "in the sphere...of self-
consciousness: it is man's anger as the power of nontruth."[16]
Oedipus Rex is certainly "the tragedy of truth," and, we might
well add, of "guilt" too. But the tragic truth and guilt are not

Oedipus'. Sophocles himself was at least troubled by the prospect
that the tragedy and guilt might inhere in Oedipus' conscience.
Ricoeur seems to know that they cannot, but then he wavers, seem-
ingly compelled to find Oedipus tragically guilty in some way or
other--part, perhaps, of his Freudian heritage, although he is
also clearly aware of the dangers of the psychoanalytic "reductionist hermeneutic."[17]

If not in the person of Oedipus, whether orphan-son or
husband-king, where is this tragedy and guilt, of which there is
certainly aplenty, located? It is in the pre-given cosmos inhabited by Oedipus' conscience, not in his personal conscience. The
Sophoclean drama is decisively ontological not psychological, philosophical not psychoanalytical. Neither Oedipus, the truth
seeker, nor Teiresias, the truth speaker, was guilty of that psychoanalytic "reductionist hermeneutic" about which Ricoeur elo-
quently warns, but from which he seems not to have escaped entirely. Nor is Sophocles' tragic truth "ethnological," like
Freud's.[18] His quest was not historical, for an original parricide at the beginning of history, but philosophical, for an
originating Father at the beginning of a "logos-tic" cosmos.
Sophocles' drama would be tragic only insofar as it would peacefully acquiesce in Oedipus' "guilt." It is tragic insofar as he
could not clearly discover at the source of the cosmos a God who
is father not fate, creator not tyrant. Not Oedipus, but the
cosmocentric cosmos of classical Greek thought, is guilty.[19]

This cosmos is "guilty" because it does not adequately arti-
culate man, cosmos and deity. Consequently the human conscience
is subsumed into the cosmos, the cosmos itself considered an absolutely necessary and inviolable order (*taxis*) bent on avenging
all violations of itself. This cosmocentric objectivist ontology,
typical of Greek thought, does not really allow for a conflict
between "the all-powerful will of the gods and the vain efforts of
human beings...between fate and human will." It cannot even allow
for "the attempt to reconcile divine omnipotence with human responsibility,"[20] for it does not allow for human responsibility at
all. Consequently, it does not allow for conscience. This stage
of (Greek) thought had not yet accorded human being that ecstasy
(*ek-stasis*) which enables it to stand out from the pre-given
material cosmos. Human being is, then, but one more homogeneous
part of the pre-given material cosmos. On this account Oedipus
cannot truly repent. Nor can he ask forgiveness, for he cannot
sin. He can only petition mitigation of the consequences of the

violation of the pre-given order of nature. Guilt is not, however, properly present, for the distinction between *actus hominis*
and *actus humanus* has not yet been accomplished.

In this whole drama the guilt is not really Oedipus', for he
remains noble, endures heroically, and finally, at Colonus, is
freed from agony. The tragic truth is not in the conscience of
Oedipus, but in the cosmos which does not allow him to have a
conscience in the proper sense. As noble as he may well be,
Oedipus is not yet a subject. He remains an object, a homogeneous
part of the pre-given material cosmos. The tragedy is that conscience is subsumed (a negative *Aufhebung*) into the cosmos.
Sophocles did not rest easy with this understanding. Nor has
human thought been able to do so. It has searched out new
symbols in its attempt to free conscience from the cosmos.

II. Anthropocentric Cosmos

The "success" of this liberation may very well have surpassed
humanity's wildest imaginings. If the ancient cosmocentric world
compressed conscience into the cosmos, the modern age has con-
stricted the cosmos to conscience. Of this subsumption of cosmos
into conscience, Jean Paul Sartre and Jack Kerouac are prime
representatives. In their anthropocentric ontology the pre-given
material cosmos is not only not divine, it hardly is at all. The
human subject is no longer an object-part of the cosmos. It is
the cosmos.

The journey from the pure cosmocentric ontology of Sophocles
to a pure anthropocentric ontology has been long, but resolute.
Key movements were "the catastrophe of nominalism (which) robs
creation of all divine illumination rendering it pure night,"[21]
and its travelling companion, voluntarism, which robs creation of
its *logos*. Key figures were Giambattista Vico and Karl Marx, who
"share...the negative view that there is no human essence to be
found in individuals as such...,"[22] and Rene Descartes, who decisively de-cosmosized (de-natured, de-physisized) both human nature
and thought. In this modern Gnosis man no longer has a place in
the cosmos. Indeed, the cosmos as an orderly arrangement (*taxis*)
of being has ceased to exist. No longer is man either *Adamah*,
from the earth, or son of God, from heaven. Henceforth man is
from himself. At least he wants to be *causa sui*, blissfully unaware of the inherent contradiction involved in this project.

Nietzsche's super-man is not a mere Freudian parricide, he is
a truly Promethean theocide. However, Nietzsche is not unaware of

the sombre realities of this new anthropocentric cosmos, of which
he is priest and prophet.[23]

> What did we do when we loosened this earth from its sun?
> Whither goes it now? And whither we? Away from all
> suns? Do we not stumble constantly, lurching backwards,
> forwards, sidewards? Is there still an above and a
> below? Do we not wander through an endless nothing?
> Is not empty space breathing coldly down our necks?
> Is it not colder now? Doesn't night come on constantly
> ...constantly the night?

If Nietzsche sketched the ontological consequences of the
cosmos-less conscience, Fyodor Dostoievski quickly drew the practical consequences. Without the pre-given cosmos and its creator,
"What is the meaning of crime? All things are lawful then; they
can do what they like."[24] And once again there is a negative subsumption, this time of the cosmos into the conscience.

Sartre, denying both pre-given human and divine natures, is
consequent when he asserts that man is the desire to be God. Without counterbalancing cosmos or Creator, conscience automatically
becomes god, but a god with an extremely low case "g," as Sartre
himself reluctantly concedes. Such negatively defined freedom
can have as its *apeiron* only itself or nothing, which amounts to
the same thing.[25] For this Sartrean man-god is defined not by
communion with, but by separation from, the other. In contrast to
the Judeo-Christian God and God-man who is essentially for (ὑπέρ =
hyper) the other,[26] Sartre's man and man-god is essentially away
from and against the other: "L'Enfer--c'est l'autre."[27] However,
this other, whether cosmic, human or divine, refuses to go away.
Through it man's presumed absolute freedom becomes not heaven but
hell, at least hades. Precisely anthropocentric man is "condemned
to be free."[28] Human desire for divinity is slaked not by a bea-
tific vision but by the dimmed lights of the night of death.
Heidegger's description of human being as *Sein zum Tode* becomes
literal truth and fact, as does Sartre's proclamation that "l'homme
est une passion inutile."[29]

If Sophoclean conscience is incarcerated in the cosmos,
Sartrean conscience is equally incarcerated--only this time in itself. And this subjectivist solipsism of contemporary absolute
anthropocentrism may well be worse than the objectivist reduction-
ism of classical cosmocentrism. The ravages of ontological nominalism cannot be redeemed by the resolve of existential, psychological voluntarism. As Joseph Pieper has well noted, "absolute
affirmation of the universe cannot, strictly speaking, be based
upon a voluntary resolve."[30] Nor can human freedom, negatively

defined not only as absence of inhesion in the cosmos but also as
absence of symbolic relationships within the *anthropos* and to the
theos, be other than anguish and ultimately nothing.[31]

The same experience is shared by the Beat Generation of Jack
Kerouac, that prototypical modern man (How quickly they do come
and go!). Like latter-day Gnostics,[32] restless and wandering,
they are constantly *On the Road*, trying to experience everything
in every way. Their Sartrean pretensions to divinity are equally
Nietzschean and Gnostic, living as they do "for the sake of absolute freedom" in which they will be able to "experience the ragged
and ecstatic joy of pure being."[33] However, their ecstasy easily
became, as their own denominational designation denotes, "beat."
As all un- and anti-cosmic pilgrims must learn, negative freedom
is barren. Is there better testimony than the words of a genuine,
authentic, anthropocentric conscience, Jim Morrison of the hard-
rock group, The Doors: "The end product of liberation is
masturbation."[34]

Unfortunately, modern anthropocentric man has not escaped
from cosmocentric object-ism to the freedom of subject. He has
only exchanged his former prison for a new one. His *Road* has not
been the hoped-for royal road of the Gnostics, from alienation and
exile in the cosmos back to the external light and fire of heaven.
Purely anthropocentric man has trod, rather, a Hegelian "highway
of despair," on which the "unhappy consciousness"[35] has ended up
in the subjective solipsism of Sartre's *No Exit* cosmos. The fate
of Sartrean anthropocentric conscience is no less blinding and
exiling than that of Sophocles' cosmocentric conscience. And the
reason is similar too, an inadequate appreciation of the cosmos
rooted in an inadequate appreciation of the *apeiron* of the cosmos.

III. Anthropos: Conscience in Cosmos

Is there, then, only the dilemma of cosmos *or* conscience, in
which either conscience or cosmos is rendered null and void, being
subsumed into the other? Is the only option the cosmic incarcera-
tion of the conscience (the *soma-sema* metaphor taken to the nth
degree) or the self-incarceration of the conscience in subjecti-
vistic solipsism? Is the de-humanizing of man inevitable, the
option being only brute or demiurge?

There has been a Camelot moment which sustained the validity
of both cosmos and conscience, refusing to identify the one with
the other or either with the *apeiron* beyond both. It did not reduce the human subject to the status of cosmic object. Nor did it

reduce all being, cosmos and *apeiron*, to the status of the human subject. It did allow for the ec-stasy[36] of human being from both the cosmic being of this world and from the divine being of the *apeiron*. This moment provided for the existence of conscience in the strict and proper sense, namely the responsible exercise of one's freedom for the promotion, not demotion, of being.

Strangely, the proper understanding of conscience and cosmos has been mediated through St. Thomas Aquinas' doctrine that even the erroneous conscience must be followed.[37] Significantly, he was the first[38] to establish theologically this middle way between the extremes of pure cosmocentrism and absolute anthropocentrism. The conscience is truly the ultimate arbiter of human choice, but it is not the ultimate norm, not the ultimate source of reality. Indeed, it is clearly not the *apeiron*, not ultimate reality itself, for its decisions are made within the wider context of being other than itself. Anthropology is not purely and simply ontology. By virtue of its intellect, will, freedom, human conscience is not merely a homogeneous part of the pre-given material cosmos. Nevertheless it is also not simply beyond the cosmos. Human uniqueness and transcendence, precisely as free and finite, are always within a pre-given. And this pre-given includes not only the infinite *apeiron* of the uncreated God, but also the finite *apeiron* of the God-created cosmos. The human being is truly subject, truly spirit. But the human being is equally truly "Spirit *in* the World."[39] The soul is truly all things, but in a certain way (*quodammodo*)-- not purely and simply. The relationship is one of communion, not identity. Although the cosmos is not divine, it is divinely willed. Hence, it is not merely raw material for human *techne*. It is the context of the free choice of conscience. Likewise, the human being, although divinely willed, is also not divine. The Gnostic contention that *anthropos* is a secret, hidden name of God[40] is as unacceptable as, for example, Thales' numenized cosmos "teeming with gods." Within the order of the divinely created cosmos, divinely created human being is free, transcendent subject.

Not only St. Thomas' philosophical theology of the erroneous conscience illustrates this. So does Dante's poetic appropriation and transformation of the entire cosmos of classical antiquity into a completely Christian cosmos. Hans Urs von Balthasar explains: "This cosmos, thoroughly penetrated by divine powers, is interpreted and comprehended from a Christian point of view. The power and forcefulness of its esthetic expression is entirely taken up into the service and support of the Christian esthetic."[41]

Dante is able to save both cosmos and conscience because he
is able to accept human finitude and respect it as something positive.[42] For him human finitude is not that which is to be desperately fled, as in modern man's anthropocentric self-apotheosis.
Nor is it ancient man's cosmocentric capitulation to blind fate,
to be desperately endured. It is, rather, the only possible ontological state whereby that which is not God to begin with can be
godly at all. It is the transcendental condition of possibility
for the *theiosis* of humanity proclaimed by Peter (2 Pet 1:4) and
developed especially in the theology of Eastern Christianity.[43]
In human finitude Dante saw the possibility of communion with the
"First Cause...for what God wills we also will." Thus, the gods
do not overcome man, but man overcomes the "kingdom of heaven...
because it wills to be vanquished, and vanquished, vanquishes with
its own benignity."[44]

Has not Dante himself, unwittingly perhaps but nevertheless,
so humanized and indeed divinized (daimonized) the universe that
the image of man begins to eclipse the image of God? Has not
either cosmos or conscience or both been divinized once again?
And has not the dilemma been reinstated--certainly unwillingly
and unwittingly, but nonetheless--cosmos or conscience?[45] That
such has indeed happened in the West is undeniable. However, the
roots of this divinizing subjectivism and personalism are not in
Dante's sacramental cosmos but in the boundless "anthropocentric
optimism of thought"[46] of Descartes' philosophical system. Dante
is fully aware of human finitude's capacity, indeed, penchant for
failure. But he is not thereby compelled to the Freudian *Angst* of
the Oedipal conscience. Dante illustrates the true *Gelassenheit*[47]
which the sacramental consciousness of the cosmos and conscience
enables Christians to enjoy: "Gladly do I grant myself indulgence
for the occasion of my lot, and it does not trouble me....Yet here
we repent not, but smile; not for the fault, which does not return
to the memory, but for the power which ordained and saw."[48] Even
Rahab the harlot is at rest. This is especially important, since
Rahab is a classic figure of the simultaneously sinful and saintly
Church,[49] which is itself the sacrament of the salvation "of all
mankind."[50] Even real, not merely neurotic, guilt is able to receive therapy in Dante's Christian cosmos. The therapy is not
analysis, but forgiveness.

In Dante's poetic theology the question is not either cosmos
or conscience, but conscience in the cosmos. He is also clearly
conscious that conscientious human beings do truly and seriously

fail, as free responsible "Shepherds of Being." They are therefore really, not merely neurotically, guilty. But he is equally
aware that in the Christian cosmos, because of its gracious
apeiron, such failing is also a *felix culpa*, because "it has
merited such a great redeemer." W. H. Auden states so well, "For
Thy goodness even sin is valid as a sign."[51] Dante knows full
well that the human conscience must confess that it has failed.
However, he knows equally well that the last words belong not to
the sinner, but to the Abba Father who is the *apeiron* of both
cosmos and conscience. Speaking through his sacramental son on
the cross, this *apeiron* Father forgives even the most heinous
crime, the death of him who is simultaneously beloved son and innocent victim. The ultimate words of truth, even in a guilty
finite cosmos, are neither blinding nor exiling but envisioning
and home-welcoming: "Father, forgive them....Indeed, I promise
you today you will be with me in paradise" (Luke 23:34, 43).

     With these words both cosmos and conscience are freed from
the deflation and the inflation which robs them of their being and
identity. Not god, they are not godless either.[52] Each in its
own way contributes to the creation as the image and likeness of
the triune God. They are truly sacramental, for they both cause
and manifest the presence of the divine in the non-divine. Only
together are cosmos and conscience the image and likeness of God
(Gen 1:24-27), for only together do they represent both the un-
fathomable abyss of the pre-given "impersonal" being of the ontological *apeiron* as well as the "personal" logos of this *apeiron*
as the Abba Father of gracious creation and providence. Conscience
in the cosmos is the finite symbol of infinite logos-being. In
this way Dante saves finitude from vanity. Finite being, however
fragile and questionable, shares in the very meaning of the infinite being of which it is the symbol, for it is at all only in
communion with this infinite. Dante's redemption of guilt is not
otherwise. Within this conscience-cosmos symbol become sinful,
the divine Son and Spirit incarnate words not only of truth, but
also of forgiveness (John 20:22) of which the disciples themselves
are power-full witnesses and signs (Luke 24:47-49 with Acts 1:8;
2:33, 38). As ontological finitude is not for the sake of death
but for the sake of being (Wis 1:13-15) and the glory of God, so
hamartiological failure is not for the sake of damnation. It, too,
is for the sake of being and the even greater glory of God (Rom
5:12-21). This is all possible because of the God who created
this cosmos and the cosmos he did in fact create: in Dante's words,

because of "the power which ordained and foresaw" that even guilty
conscience in the finite cosmos should be symbol and sacrament of
the infinitely holy *apeiron* in whose image and likeness they have
been created.

Conclusion

Conscience describes the condition of the human being who is
in the cosmos but not of the cosmos. Jesus' words in John 17:14-17
have ontological as well as soteriological significance. This
Christic *anthropo*logical ontology is possible only because of the
*theo*logical ontology which is implied in the doctrines of Trinity,
Creation and Incarnation.[53] Since being is communion and symbol,
created being, both cosmos and conscience, is not "condemned to a
truth" which is both blinding and exiling, as are the consciences
of Kerouac and Nietzsche, Sartre and Sophocles. In the Judeo-
Christian sacramental universe the human subject is not only free
from but also free *to* and *for*.[54] The truth of this cosmos does
not encapsulate the conscience in either the cosmocentric prison
of objectivism or the anthropocentric prison of subjectivism, both
of which represent a finite cosmos of *No Exit*. The sacramental
cosmos represented by Dante is truly the house of God, the gate of
heaven. Like Jacob's ladder, it stretches beyond itself to the
"abundant Grace...Light Eternal...Infinite Goodness...where [is]
consummated the seeing" already truly begun by the conscience in
the cosmos. For "the Good which is the object of the will [read
conscience] is all collected in it [God as the infinite triune
apeiron of the finite cosmos], and outside of it that is defective
which is perfect there."[55] Defectively indeed, but truly present--
even in the cosmos not only finite but guilty.

That cosmos and conscience has always and everywhere been a
theme of the religious imagination is readily understandable. After all, the history of this theme is also the history of freedom,
which is also the history of humanity.[56] This history, recounted
in philosophy and poetry, myth and metaphor, drama and deed,[57]
discloses that human freedom can be fulfilled only in a Dantesque
sacramental universe, however little favor such a universe may
currently enjoy.[58] For only in such a universe are both cosmos
and conscience spared the burdens of being each other or divine.
Neither God nor Godless, conscience in cosmos is the sacrament-
symbol of divine communion with the non-divine, pointing to an
apeiron which is not blinding exile but envisioning homecoming.
Of this sacramental cosmos the innocent consciences of Oedipus and

Christ, both become guilty for us (2 Cor 5:21; Gal 3:13; Rom 8:3),
are ciphers and symbols,[59] the former negative, the latter positive, that we, although finite consciences and guilty too, might
understand ourselves as and be a fulfilled finitude, free and for-
given. For the *apeiron*, which has preoccupied philosopher and
poet from the very beginning and which surrounds the human being
from beginning to end, is not an empty, hollow, annihilating
(*néant*) into which mortal man falls at death, blinded and exiled.
Rather, the cosmos and conscience of Christ reveals that in death
"the Christian (and every human being) allows himself to fall into
the mystery we call God. He is convinced in faith and in hope
that in falling into the incomprehensible and nameless mystery of
God he is falling into a blessed and forgiving mystery which
divinizes."[60]

Conscience in cosmos is, then, the beginning of a fall not
from but into grace, not into the gaping maws of hell and hades,
but into the gracing mystery of heaven and home.[61]

NOTES

[1] See Werner Jaeger, *The Theology of the Early Greek Philosophers* (London: Oxford University, 1967) 24-37.

[2] Thomas Aquinas, *In XII Libros Metaphysicorum Aristotelis Expositio* (ed. M. R. Cathala and R. M. Spiazzi; Turin: Marietti, 1950) L.I., 1. 3(55).

[3] P. 165 in *Myth, Symbol, and Reality* (ed. Alan M. Olson; Notre Dame: University of Notre Dame, 1980).

[4] My translation from the original Greek in Hermann Diels, *Doxographi Graeci* (Berlin: Reimer, 1879, 1958) 476 (Anaximander, A9). On the difficulty of translating and interpreting this saying, as well as the importance of *taxis* in Greek thought, see Martin Heidegger, "Der Spruch des Anaximander," pp. 296-343 in *Holzwege* (Frankfort: Klostermann, 1963).

[5] *Apology*, 31-35.

[6] See Hans Jonas, *Philosophical Essays* (Englewood Cliffs: Prentice-Hall, 1974) 275-90.

[7] For "Oedipus Rex" and "Oedipus at Colonus," I have used the translation of David Grene and Richard Lattimore (*Greek Tragedies*, Vols. 1 and 3 [Chicago: University of Chicago, 1960]; here, "Oedipus Rex," 1, p. 176, line 1525.

[8] Line 1530.

[9] "Oedipus at Colonus," 3, p. 166, line 1224.

[10] Sigmund Freud, "The Interpretation of Dreams," p. 246 in *Freud: Great Books of the Western World* 54 (Chicago: Encyclopedia Britannica, 1952).

[11] Ibid., 247; see also his "General Introduction to Psycho-Analysis," in the same volume, p. 582.

[12] Ibid., 582.

[13] "Oedipus at Colonus," 3, p. 187, line 1779.

[14] "Interpretation," 247.

[15] Paul Ricoeur, *Freud and Philosophy* (New Haven: Yale University, 1970) 516.

[16] Ibid., 516-17.

[17] Paul Ricoeur, "The Atheism of Freudian Psychoanalysis," *Concilium* 6/2 (June 1966) 31, also 35.

[18] See Ricoeur ("The Atheism," 34), where he also indicates the serious methodological deficiencies of Freud's approach to religion and the history of religion.

[19] In this paper, cosmocentric and anthropocentric designate thought forms. A thought form is a mode or manner of thinking—in scholastic terms an *objectum formale quo*. It describes the

unthematic horizon, starting point, source, principle of all the
particular thoughts thought in a homogeneous set. Cosmocentric
starts from the cosmos--the material, space occupying, sensibly
perceptible. Whatever it thinks about, it thinks about in terms
of the cosmos. Anthropocentric thinks in terms of precisely the
anthropos--subjectivity, intellect, will, freedom. The inherent
tendency and danger of the anthropocentric thought form is Gnosticism or solipsistic subjectivism, in which precisely the cosmic
dimensions--corporal, material, sensible--of human being are ignored or denied. For elaboration of the nature and significance
of thought form, see Robert Kress, *A Rahner Handbook* (Atlanta:
John Knox, 1982) and John Baptist Metz, *Christliche Anthropozen-
trik* (Munich: Kosel, 1962).

[20] Freud, "Interpretation," 246-47.

[21] Hans Urs von Balthasar, *Rechenschaft 1965* (Einsiedeln:
Johannes, 1965) 31.

[22] Thomas G. Bergin and Max H. Fisch, Introduction, *The New
Science of Giambattista Vico* (Ithaca: Cornell University, 1970)
xlv. See also Isaiah Berlin, *Vico and Herder* (New York: Random
House, 1977) 120.

[23] My translation from Friedrich Nietzsche, *Die fröhliche
Wissenschaft*, *Werke* II (Munich: K. Schlechta, 1955) 127.

[24] *The Brothers Karamazov* (Chicago: Britannica, 1952) 165, 312.

[25] *Being and Nothingness* (New York: Philosophical Library,
1956) 89, 615, 626. Sartre emphasizes that "in anguish freedom
is anguished before itself inasmuch as it is instigated and bound
by nothing" (35).

[26] On this fundamental category of Judeo-Christian theology
and ontology, see Joseph Ratzinger, "Das Geschick Jesu und die
Urkirche," *Kirche heute: Theologische Brennpunkte* (Bergen-Enkheim:
G. Kaffke, 1965) 13-14; "Stellvertretung," pp. 566-75 in *Handbuch
theologischer Grundbegriffe* (ed. Heinrich Fries; Munich: Kosel,
1963); see also Karl Lehmann, *Auferweckt am dritten Tag nach der
Schrift* (Freiburg: Herder, 1968) 102-30, 247-57.

[27] Jean Paul Sartre, *No Exit* (New York: Vintage, 1955) 61.
See also Wilfrid Desan, *The Tragic Finale* (New York: Harper, 1960)
120-25.

[28] Jean Paul Sartre, *Existentialism* (New York: Philosophical
Library, 1947) 27. The same press saw fit to publish a collection
of Sartre's writings under the title *To Freedom Condemned*. See
also Marjorie Grene, *Dreadful Freedom* (Chicago: University of
Chicago, 1948) 76-79.

[29] J. P. Sartre, *L'Etre et le Néant* (Paris: Gallimard, 1943)
708, 721. His novel, *The Age of Reason* (New York: Alfred Knopf,
1947), ends similarly with "the failure of a life" (p. 397).

[30] Joseph Pieper, *Leisure: The Basis of Culture* (New York:
NAL Mentor, 1963) 62.

[31] Jean Paul Sartre's cosmos is such that "Anguish is the reflective apprehension of freedom by itself," for this is nothing
else for it to comprehend or be comprehended by (*Being and Nothingness*, 39).

[32]Compare the novels of J. Kerouac with the exposition of Gnosticism by Jacques Lacarriere,(*The Gnostics* (New York: Dutton, 1977).

[33]Jack Kerouac, *The Lonesome Traveller* (New York: Ballentine, 1960) 173; *On the Road* (New York: Viking, 1959) 195.

[34]Bernard Wolfe, "The Real Life Death of Jim Morrison," *Esquire* (June 1972) 182.

[35]See the "Introduction," G.W.F. Hegel, *The Phenomenology of Mind* (New York: Harper Torchbooks, 1967) 135.

[36]On human being (*Dasein*) and freedom as ec-static ek-sistence, see Martin Heidegger, *Vom Wesen der Wahrheit* (Frankfurt: Klostermann, 1943) 14-17.

[37]See *Summa Theologiae*, I-II, p. 10, a. 5, 6, but especially *De Veritate*, p. 17, a. 4 text. *Ille autem qui conscientiam erroneam habet credens eam esse rectam (alias non erraret), nec inhaeret conscientiae erroneae propter rectitudinem quam in ea credit esse: inhaeret quidem, per se loquendo, rectae conscientiae, sed erroneae quasi per accidens: in quantum hanc conscientiam, quam credit esse rectam, contingit esse erroneam.*

[38]See R. Hofmann, "Gewissen," p. 864 in *Lexikon für Theologie und Kirche* (ed. Josef Hofer and Karl Rahner; 2nd ed.; Freiburg: Herder, 1960): "Für die Anerkennung der Normgültigkeit des Gewissens (auch wenn es unüberwindlich irrt) bedeutete das stark objektiv gerichtete Denken der mittelalterlichen. Theologie eine grosse Schwierigkeit, die erst Thomas von Aquin grundsätzlich und mit Wirkung für die Folgezeit überwinden konnte."

[39]As Karl Rahner's anthropology would phrase it, *Spirit in the World* (Montreal: Palm, 1968), translates the title of his philosophical *Geist in Welt* (Munich: Kosel, 1957, the John Baptist Metz revision).

[40]See Hans Jonas, *Philosophical Essays*, 268-70.

[41]Hans Urs von Balthasar, *Herrlichkeit: Fächer der Stile 2* (Einsiedeln: Johannes, 1962) 422.

[42]*Convivio*, 3, 15; 4, 9; 4, 12. *Purgatory*, canto 3: 34-45; *Paradise*, canto 13: 88-130.

[43]See Robert Hotz, *Sakramente im Wechselspiel zwischen Ost und West* (Zurich: Benziger, 1979) passim, esp. 254-98.

[44]*Paradise*, canto 20: 136-38, 94-99.

[45]See E. Auerbach, *Mimesis* (Princeton: Princeton University, 1953) 202. Also, N. Scott, *The Wild Prayer of Longing* (New Haven: Yale University, 1971) 12.

[46]See Jacques Maritain, *Le songe de Descartes* (Paris: Correa, 1932) 261.

[47]Although associated with Martin Heidegger, this term and virtue go back to at least Meister Eckhart. See Reiner Schürmann, *Maître Eckhart ou la joie errante* (Paris: Planete-Denoël, 1972).

[48]*Paradise*, canto 9: 34, 103-5.

[49]See Hans Urs von Balthasar, "Casta Meretrix," *Sponsa Verbi* (Einsiedeln: Johannes, 1961) esp. 222-39.

[50]Vatican II, *Dogmatic Constitution on the Church*, 1, 48.

[51]W. H. Auden, *For the Time Being* (New York: Random House, 1944) 40.

[52]Thus, Judeo-Christianity treads a middle road between the divinized cosmos of the Greeks and the demonized cosmos of the Gnostics. See Hans Jonas, *The Gnostic Religion* (Boston: Beacon, 1963) 241-65.

[53]See Robert Kress, "The Church as Communio: Trinity and Incarnation as the Foundations of Ecclesiology," *The Jurist* 36: 1/2 (1976) 127-58.

[54]In regard to human freedom, Karl Rahner's succinct statement cannot be escaped: "Es kommt alles darauf an, wozu man frei ist" (*Schriften zur Theologie* 11 [Einsiedeln: Benziger, 1955] 98).

[55]Dante, *Paradise*, canto 23.

[56]See G.W.F. Hegel, *The Philosophy of History* (Chicago: Britannica, 1952) 369.

[57]Thus, Hans Urs von Balthasar, wishing to provide "at least a moderately well-rounded presentation of the uniqueness of Christianity for modern man" has proposed not only a "theologische Ästhetik, but also a theologische Dramatik and a theologische Logik." See his *Rechenschaft*(Einsiedeln: Johannes, 1965) 27-33, for an outline of his proposed undertaking.

[58]See Sallie Te Selle, *Literature and the Christian Life* (New Haven: Yale University, 1966) 34, 214.

[59]I do not, of course, intend in any way to equate Oedipus and Christ. One of the glories of the Catholic ontology, however, is that it cannot tolerate pure negativity. There can be no pure and simple evil. Hence, even in the errant cosmos of Sophocles and Sartre, of Nietzsche and Kerouac, the truth is able to be disclosed, although perhaps only negatively, insofar as their *dramatis personae* themselves reveal the inadequacy of the cosmos in which they dwell.

[60]Karl Rahner, *Grundkurs des Glaubens* (Freiburg: Herder, 1976) 413. Also *Schriften*, XII, pp. 290, 300, 308, 316, and *Everyday Faith* (New York: Herder and Herder, 1967) 186.

[61]How St. Thomas Aquinas and Karl Rahner concur in providing an ontological foundation for this understanding I have shown incipiently in "Karl Rahner and the Christian Philosophy of St. Thomas Aquinas" (pp. 94-101 in *Theology and Discovery* [ed. William Kelly; Milwaukee: Marquette University, 1980).

CONTRIBUTORS

JOHN BORELLI, Associate Professor and chairperson of Religious Studies at the College of Mount Saint Vincent, Riverdale, New York, completed his doctoral studies in the history of religions section of the Theology Department, Fordham University, in 1976. His articles on Vijñānabhikṣu, the sixteenth century Sāṅkhya-Yoga-Vedānta synthesizer, have appeared in *Philosophy East and West* and *Neoplatonism and Indian Thought*, a volume published for the International Society for Neoplatonic Studies by SUNY Press (1982). Borelli has also researched archetypal symbolism, especially in its Jungian context, and has published a number of articles on symbolism, Jungian psychology, and Yoga spirituality in such journals as *Thought* and *Jeevadhara*. He writes regularly for the Ecumenical Commission of the Archdiocese of New York in *Catholic New York* and other archdiocesan publications.

JOANN WOLSKI CONN is Associate Professor of Religious Studies at Neumann College, Aston, Pennsylvania. A former member of the spiritual direction staff of the Institute for Spirituality and Worship of the Jesuit School of Theology in Berkeley, her articles have appeared in such journals as *Spiritual Life, Horizons, Cross Currents*, and *Theology Today*.

WALTER E. CONN is Professor of Religious Studies at Villanova University. He is the author of *Conscience: Development and Self-Transcendence*, and editor of the collection of essays, *Conversion: Perspectives on Personal and Social Transformation*. His articles have appeared in *Theological Studies, Horizons*, and *Zygon*.

KEITH J. EGAN, Associate Professor of Historical Theology and Spirituality in the Theology Department of Marquette University, holds a doctoral degree from Cambridge University where he studied underthe direction of David Knowles, was Vice-President of the CTS, 1978-80, author of *What is Prayer?* (1974) and numerous articles in encyclopedias and such journals as *Horizons, American Benedictine Review, Review for Religious, Carmelus, Aylesford Review*, etc., and in various collections, including an essay on *The Interior Castle* of Teresa of Avila in the CTS annual volume of 1979. He was Co-Director of the Institute for Ecumenical Spirituality in America, 1970-80, and is currently preparing a volume to be entitled *The Medieval English Carmelites*.

ROBERTO S. GOIZUETA is a doctoral student in theology at Marquette University. He received a B.A. in political science from Yale University and an M.A. in theology from Marquette, and has studied at the Georgetown University Law School and the St. Meinrad School of Theology. He is a fellow of the Fund for Theological Education and will be a Marquette University Smith fellow during the coming academic year.

JOHN P. HOGAN, Assistant Grants Officer at the National Endowment for the Humanities, received the Ph.D. from Catholic University with a dissertation on Collingwood's contribution to hermeneutics. Formerly a member of the Loyola College of Baltimore Theology faculty, his articles have appeared in *American Ecclesiastical Review, Philosophy Today, Living Light*, and *Origins*. From 1979 until 1981 he served as Peace Corps director in Upper Volta, West Africa.

PAUL F. KNITTER holds a Licentiate in Theology from the Pontifical Gregorian University in Rome and a Th.D. from Marburg

207

University, West Germany. He is presently Professor of Theology
at Xavier University, Cincinnati. His publications, most of which
focus on the dialogue between Christianity and World Religions,
include: *Toward a Protestant Theology of the Religions* (1974), and
articles in *Concilium* (1980), *The Journal of Ecumenical Studies*
(1975, 1979), *Horizons* (1978, 1981), *Neue Zeitschrift für Systema-
tische Theologie und Religionsphilosophie* (1971, 1973). His most
recent publication is "Thomas Merton's Eastern Remedy for Christianity's 'Anonymous Dualism,'" *Cross Currents*, Fall, 1981.

ROBERT KRESS is currently Associate Professor of Systematic
Theology in the Department of Theology at The Catholic University
of America, Washington, D.C. With degrees in theology, philosophy
and education, his writings cover a wide range of topics numbering
over one hundred articles and reviews in scholarly and popular
publications and five books, of which *Whither Womankind?* received
the College Theology Society's Outstanding Book of the Year award.
His most recent book is *A Rahner Handbook*, published by John Knox
Press in 1982. Current projects include books on sacramental
theology and a critique of liberation theology.

ROBERT MASSON was appointed an Assistant Professor of Theology
at Marquette University in 1980. Formerly an Associate Professor
of Theology at Loyola College of Baltimore (1973-80), he received
his doctorate in theology from Fordham University. His articles
have been published in *The Thomist*, *Horizons*, *The Heythrop Journal*
and *Living Light*.

MARY AQUIN O'NEILL, RSM, received the Ph.D. in Religion from
Vanderbilt University in December, 1981. This article is drawn
from her dissertation, *Revealing Imagination: A Study of Paul
Ricoeur*. She has also published in *Theological Studies* and in
The New Catholic Encyclopedia.

WALTER J. ONG, S.J., *William E. Haren* Professor of English
and Professor of Humanities in Psychiatry at Saint Louis University, is known for his work in Renaissance literary and intellectual history and in contemporary culture, as well as for his more
wide-ranging studies in the evolution of consciousness. Among his
more recent books are: *Fighting for Life: Contest, Sexuality, and
Consciousness* (Ithaca/London: Cornell University, 1981); *Interfaces
of the Word* (Ithaca/London: Cornell University, 1977); *The Presence
of the Word* (New Haven/London: Yale University, 1967); *Rhetoric,
Romance, and Technology* (Ithaca/London: Cornell University, 1971);
In the Human Grain (New York: Macmillan, 1967); *The Barbarian
Within* (New York: Macmillan, 1962); and *Why Talk?* (San Francisco:
Chandler and Sharp, 1973). He has written and edited other works
and is the author also of numerous articles in literary and scholarly periodicals in the United States, Canada, and England as
well as in France, Germany, Italy, and Japan.

WILLIAM M. SHEA received his doctorate from Columbia University in philosophy of religion. He taught in the departments of
religion and theology at Catholic University from 1972 to 1980.
He was visiting scholar at Harvard Divinity School in 1976 and at
Yale Divinity School in 1980. His areas of special interest are
contemporary theologies, American evangelical religion, American
philosophy of religion, fundamental theology and Roman Catholic
thought, and he has published on these subjects in *The Heythrop
Journal*, *The Anglican Theological Review*, *The Thomist*, *The Journal
of Religion*, and *Horizons*. He is now Associate Professor and
director of graduate studies in religion at the University of
South Florida in Tampa.